# Modern Arab Journalism

# Modern Arab Journalism

## Problems and Prospects

### Noha Mellor

Edinburgh University Press

© Noha Mellor, 2007

Edinburgh University Press Ltd
22 George Square, Edinburgh

Typeset in 11/13 pt Stempel Garamond by
Servis Filmsetting Ltd, Manchester, and
printed and bound in Great Britain by
Cromwell Press, Trowbridge, Wilts

A CIP record for this book is available from the British Library

ISBN  978 0 7486 3410 1 (hardback)
ISBN  978 0 7486 3411 8 (paperback)

The right of Noha Mellor to be identified as author of this work
has been asserted in accordance with the Copyright, Designs and Patents Act 1988.

# Contents

# Contents

# Figures and Tables

*To Arab women . . . the real heroes*

# Introduction

If there is a book you really want to read but it hasn't been written yet, then you must write it.

Toni Morrison

If the buzzword for the past decade was "globalization", for this decade it is "Middle East", a region that has usually been associated with a fair amount of violence and turmoil since the independence of its states. Knowledge and research about this region, particularly the Arab States, has recently moved from a focus on politics and history into the field of media and popular culture. This shift has been made possible because of the increased interconnections brought about by globalization and the technological leap that has made access to information and news concerning this region fast and easy. The emergence of new Arab media outlets marking an Arab presence on the world communication scene has further stimulated the change. Recent research has moved beyond the thesis of the clash of civilizations into a new "clash of voices", wherein the Arab voice is constantly compared with Western voices, making the representations on Arab screens versus those seen in Western media the focal point of media research.

Despite the volume of publications about Arab media, our knowledge about this particular field is still limited in many aspects, and there are many questions that are still unanswered; alas, they have never even been posed. What is more, the issue of Arab journalism in particular has been sidestepped in Western scholarship, which tends to favor issues of representation, public diplomacy or media policies. This book diverges from the viewpoint adopted in the existing literature and offers a new outlook on studying Arab news media, exploring the road not taken in contemporary scholarship. In particular, this book focuses on Arab journalism, a rather under-represented research topic in Western scholarship.

The main aim of this book is twofold: provocation and stimulation. I aim to challenge current Western scholarship on Arab media, pointing out its limitations and the break with the tenets of Critical Theory. I also aim to utilize this provocation to stimulate new research directions, treading the deserted road in current Western scholarship on Arab media.

## Journalism and Critical Theory

Journalism and mass communication research has been the focus of social theory for decades. Zelizer[1] summarizes the trends in the sociological inquiry of journalism moving from administrative, behaviorist research into the critical research developed by European scholars. She divides the trends in sociological inquiry into three stages:

1.  The first stage of sociological inquiry tended to focus on journalists' interaction with each other and thereby it regarded journalism as "the practices of those with the power to determine the experience of others."[2]
2.  The second stage was concerned with the impact of organizational constraints on the journalists' practices and norms.[3]
3.  The third stage focused on the ideology and hegemony of these practices and norms. Journalistic output then was a manifestation of power as it is reflected in society, which prompted researchers to evaluate issues of representation and access to media in their analyses.

Zelizer also points to a fourth trend, namely the political economy approach. Here, the focus is on the dilemma of journalists caught between political powers on the one hand, and economic power – that is, news conglomerates – on the other.[4] Although this approach has provided new insights by linking the impact of political power with that of a market economy, it has not made clear the link between "the daily routines of journalism and the larger political economy of society."[5]

On the whole, social theory helped add journalism to the research agenda, seeing it as an independent social field wherein journalists act according to structural constraints "inside and beyond the news setting."[6] It is precisely here that Bourdieu's field theory may provide a fresh framework with which to analyze Arab journalism as a social field. Although *On Television*, Bourdieu's sole work that addressed journalism as a field, did not really provide such a precise outline, his research collaborators argued that Bourdieu's earlier works on cultural reproduction and the logic of practice have already provided the contours of such a framework. This book draws on field theory in as much as it focuses on the power struggle present on the Arab media scene and highlights the interplay between the journalists (agency) and structure (resources), which I believe has been ignored in recent Western scholarly works on Arab media. It highlights the distribution of power among actors engaging in the field of journalism, and shows how they constantly seek to reorganize their positions in the field, both regionally and globally. This is not to say that this theory, or any Western-developed theory for that matter, can be applied uncritically to the Arab context; rather, Western theories may indeed be put to test in the account "of the experience of countries outside the Anglo-American orbit."[7]

## Journalism as a social field

Field theory provides a useful framework for the analysis of differentiation, which is crucial to the late modernity research agenda, where the fragmentation of "spheres of action (e.g. the fields of politics, economics, religion, cultural production)" is the norm rather than the exception.[8] The advantage of field theory, as formulated by Bourdieu's research disciples, is that it values the role of active agency, not passive dupes, thereby parting company with previous theories such as hegemony, which would usually arrive at functionalist conclusions. In particular, field theory argues that agency does not automatically "reinforce the power status quo, but under certain conditions may actually transform power relations in other fields."[9] More importantly, Bourdieu sees journalism as a field that influences and is open to the influences of other fields in society; thus, "all fields of cultural production today are subject to structural pressure from the journalistic field [as a whole], and not from any one journalist or network executive, who are themselves subject to control by the field."[10]

Perhaps the most important advantage of field theory, and one that directly addresses the purpose of this volume, is that it allows a comparative approach.[11] Clearly, the study of the Arab journalism field is, in and of itself, important; but juxtaposing it with other external fields, such as the American journalism field, will prove a valuable research exercise if the purpose is to challenge existing (Western) theories or their applicability in non-Western contexts. Rodney Benson[12] provides an example of such a comparative analysis; he rightly points out that showing the differences cross-nationally does not necessarily have to relate to different cultural traditions, but perhaps more importantly relates to the position of journalism as occupying a social field vis-à-vis other fields nationally and vis-à-vis a global field of journalism.

Moreover, field theory can indeed provide a framework for the analysis of historical change on the media scene. For instance, the past decade has witnessed a huge development on the Arab media scene, and yet no sophisticated explanations have been given to account for this change. Central here is the role of journalists themselves in changing the news norms and practices. In other words, we need to inquire into the mechanisms that have shocked the field from within and have forced it to adapt in tandem with other political and cultural changes in the overall field of power.

## Western theories for non-Western practices

As I will point out in Chapter 7, Western theories developed to account for changes in Western societies cannot be used uncritically to analyze non-Western societies, a point raised by several Arab scholars. Although I base the following discussions on Bourdieu's insights, I am fully aware of their shortcomings and the implausibility of applying his views across-the-board to the Arab context. Rather, field theory is meant to serve as a first building block in a long research plan, which should help refine the theoretical contours to match those conditions that are unique to the Arab media.

There are, for instance, a number of points that should be taken into consideration when applying field theory to the Arab journalism field. First, it is hard to match Bourdieu's suggested homology between producers and consumers, "meaning simply that they constitute distinct but parallel social spaces, organized around the same basic divisions between economic and cultural capital."[13] This view suggests a match between the distribution of cultural capital on both the producer and consumer sides. However, despite their lack of cultural capital, for example, verbal skills or education, Arab audiences may still follow the news and current affairs programs communicated primarily via the elevated written variant of Arabic. So, for instance, a recent study found that viewers with a low level of education and a low income tend to watch channels such as al-Jazeera even more than do those with a higher educational level and income,[14] despite the fact that al-Jazeera and other pan-Arab news media tend to center on complex political issues communicated in an elevated style (see Chapters 3 and 4). This then poses a challenge to the homology theory in that there is a contradiction between the distribution of cultural capital, that is, education and verbal skills, and the economic capital.

Indeed, Arab journalistic practices can be distinguished from the Anglo-American journalistic culture, which has come to depend on simplified language. Indeed, the Arab news genre is the only media genre dependent on the written variety of Arabic, or Modern Standard Arabic (MSA). As mastering this language variant requires years of schooling, it inevitably constitutes a large part of the journalist's cultural capital. Yet, the rising number of new entrants to this profession, combined with the deterioration of MSA in the national curricula among younger generations, may result in drastic changes in Arab journalistic practices.

Second, Bourdieu seems to overestimate the power of the economic field. For instance, the changes on the French media scene, which Bourdieu indicates, may be caused not by commercialization per se but rather by the centralization of the French media, which allowed one channel (TF 1) to maintain a large share of the audience following its privatization.[15] On the other hand, Arab media, as will be discussed in more detail in the following chapters, are characterized by both decentralization and commercialization: so what would determine the distribution of audience share among the various outlets? Would these outlets compete to provide populist content to attract audiences, or would they draw on certain cultural elements that do not necessarily translate into economic profit? Moreover, while national news media outlets are centralized in terms of geographical locations (usually the capital and large cities) and ownership, the so-called pan-Arab media are dispersed across the region and Europe, particularly London. How, then, would de-centralization affect the journalistic culture in each country, and how would the movement of journalists from a national to a pan-Arab sphere reinvigorate or, conversely, weaken existing practices?

Third, as pointed out by Nina Eliasoph,[16] analysis of media producers should not replace analysis of the laity. She wonders if field theory, concerned with the study of institutions, can provide a proper framework to study the public, which "is not normally called 'an institution'." As she rightly wonders, should the struggle always be about "power and hierarchy" or is it about "making moral sense of the world"?[17] In light of Eliasoph's remarks, it is important to ask how the Arab media would consolidate or exclude a certain moral sense of the world.

Fourth, assuming that the ultimate goal of social theory is to point out how to "free" journalism from the shackles of politics or economics,[18] how would Arab journalists, distinguished by their cultural capital, avoid isolating themselves in a self-centered world? Could they not simply serve as a new hegemonic force imposed on the less privileged laity, rather than as a force to involve the laity in joint debates and discussion (see Chapters 3 and 4)?

Events such as 9/11 and 7/7 pushed the Arab media towards the top of research plans inquiring into the role of the media in agitating or assuaging civic unrest. Yet, current attempts to study the Arab media tend to focus on issues of representation rather than on the unique role of Arab journalists in the perception of their role vis-à-vis their audiences and vis-à-vis political power. Crucial here is the way journalists perceive their role and how this perception would consolidate or weaken the media's effect on promoting diversity and hence tolerance for others.

Finally, field theory may indeed seem to favor production over consumption, focusing on the role of producers/journalists rather than on that of consumers/audience,[19] and a pitfall that should be avoided in future research is that of tightly binding together fieldworks among Arab audiences and those among journalists. Indeed, such fieldworks may help further develop and validate the above observations.

## The road not taken

This book addresses questions that have been left unanswered or have never even been posed. For example, how is Arab journalism different/similar to the journalism fields in other countries? What defines the tasks of journalists? Who has access to this field? How is power distributed inside the Arab journalism field? When were the media programs launched at Arab universities and what characterizes them? As the field of Arab journalism is vast, I confine my discussion to the pan-Arab media, although I provide some comparative examples between pan-Arab and national media in order to illuminate the concurrent division and interdependence among them.

This volume begins with a discussion about the impact of globalization on the Arab media, thus setting the context for the arguments of the following chapters. At issue here is the view that focuses on the contradictions in the Arab media scene, for example, the availability of conservative programming at religious channels versus scantily-dressed women on entertainment channels, and the availability of news channels highlighting the regional and global political issues versus the reality TV genres that have invaded several Arab variety channels. As I argue in Chapter 1, the rationale behind this seeming contradiction is based on the view that sees hybridity as being out of sync with native Arab culture. I show, however, that hybridity has always been deployed as one significant tool for Arab development projects, with Arab intellectuals as the ideal embodiment of this hybridity. I also discuss the means by which media can be used as a bridge to connect social classes, serving as a new source available to the lay majority in their struggle to reallocate power in the overall social scene.

Central to this book are Arab journalistic practices and how they may influence and be influenced by the internal struggle among media professionals in local and pan-Arab media outlets. Chapter 2 sets the theoretical framework of the analysis of pan-Arab media based on Bourdieu's field theory, in as much as it addresses the struggle for power on the Arab media scene. It is the struggle among news media outlets over the status of the agenda-setter, a struggle between the news sector and the entertainment sector wherein the former attempts to consolidate a pan-Arab identity while the latter pulls towards diversity and plurality. Central to this discussion is the means by which actors (agents) accumulate cultural capital in their profession and how this capital can be transferred to other fields, for example, politics. I resume this discussion in Chapters 5 and 6 with a focus on journalism as a global field, and the position of Arab journalists (at least as they see it) vis-à-vis Western journalists. Central to this discussion is the issue of identity and how it has been sidestepped in recent works on the global public sphere. By identity, I mean the professional identity of journalists in East and West and that identity's relation to the distribution of power or capital among them. This discussion will be supported by a qualitative case study of news texts from pan-Arab newspapers. More specifically, I show how Western reporters served as an example of authentic eyewitnesses, whose testimonies were revered among pan-Arab newspapers. I also show the boundaries drawn between Western and Arab journalists and how some Western journalists, although acknowledging an imagined professional community encompassing all journalists worldwide, tend to position their media as the role model for Arab media outlets to follow.

Recent research on Arab news media highlights the role of these media in fostering a healthy pubic debate and forming a so-called Arab public sphere. I discuss the contours of this public sphere in Chapters 3 and 4, shedding new light on the kind of conditions or institutions needed to establish firmly the debate culture as well as the parameters of such a debate. Chapter 4 focuses on the content of news and debate. It shows how a sharp distinction between private and public spheres has resulted in a split between pan-Arab news media on the one hand and the national/local media on the other, with the former focusing on the abstract/general and the latter on the concrete/local. I argue that the theorization of the public sphere seems to sidestep a more interesting theorization of what constitutes the "private sphere." I argue that the private sphere can embrace several layers, depending on the interpretation of what is "domestic and intimate."

Chapter 7 presents a much-needed discussion on the role of Arab media scholars as both educators and researchers. I first present the problems in the education and research milieu in Arab universities; then I present an innovative and unprecedented discussion of the epistemological roots of Arab media research, that is, its overt reliance on quantitative methodologies. The second part of the chapter discusses the role of Western Arab media scholarship and whether it really contributes to the field of media studies in general and Middle East media studies specifically.

Rather than providing neat typologies or models of Arab journalism, this volume presents the questions that are under-represented and under-researched in Western scholarship regarding Arab media. Thus, it aims to open up a new research agenda and challenge concepts that are taken for granted, such as the pan-Arab identity.

Finally, I hope that this volume will serve as a guide on an inspirational journey through the intricate pathways of Arab journalism as a field of power.

# Chapter 1

# Media: The Bridge to Globalization

Do globalization and Arab culture represent an oxymoron? Judging by the typical image of a sheikh carrying a cell phone, or the contradictory images of a belly dancer vis-à-vis a religious fundamentalist, it may be argued that Arab societies need to undergo a renewed search for identity, exemplified by a general inability to hybridize a Western signifier with a native signified in a meaningful way.

Hybridity, then, can pose a threat to traditional values, particularly with the sweeping trends of consumerism, which turned the veil, for one, into a fashion business. Thus, several shopping centers have been established in Cairo, for instance, catering for the new "liberal veiled women," much to the irritation of traditional Muslim preachers.[1]

Western signifiers have also penetrated the Islamists' world, as we see more and more of them adopting a modern high-tech lifestyle, as, for instance, in Turkey:

> As can be observed in the Turkish context, not only are Islamists using the latest model of Macintosh computers, writing best-selling books, becoming part of the political and cultural elite, winning elections, and establish private universities, but they are also carving out new public space, affirming new public visibilities, and inventing new Muslim lifestyles and subjectivities.[2]

Thus, the oxymoron lies precisely in the inability to hybridize, or rather in the oddity of hybridizing a traditional core with a foreign periphery in an age characterized by increasing globalization or interconnectivity. Although globalization has been discussed in various Arab scholarly works, there is little knowledge among Western scholars of these Arab views. The aim of this chapter is to discuss the rival narratives of globalization and its impact as communicated in the works of Western and Arab scholars alike. Rather than seeing globalization and Arab culture as an oxymoron, I argue that hybridity was indeed part and parcel of the development plans of the Arab States following their independence in the second half of the last century.

Hybridity has been part of the national plans to modernize and beautify the national and even regional image, and central to these plans are two institutions, namely education and the media: the former to sustain the notion of an imagined community and hence national belonging, and the latter to help to sustain a sense of cultural togetherness and harmony. The above oxymoron of hybridity, however, underestimates the ability of individuals to manipulate resources in order to increase the amount of power available to them, and hence the subsequent social change. Indeed, this view can be rejected for its essentialism, that is, seeing native identity and foreign features as blocks that can be mixed and matched without changing the very basis of each block or changing the overall "rules of the game."

I begin my discussion by reviewing some Arab scholarly works on globalization that exhibit this essentialist view of hybridity. As a theoretical basis of my argument, Giddens' theory of structuration combined with Bourdieu's field theory are chosen for their equilibrium between agency and structure. I shall illustrate this dialectic relation between structure and agency in subsequent sections, discussing the process of hybridity as articulated by the elites in the post-colonial Arab States. The period following the independence of the Arab States was indeed a period of "searching for identity," a period that, in my view, serves as a point of departure for the discussion of the impact of globalization on Arab culture and media.

## Globalization as hybridity

Robertson[3] sees globalization not as a new phenomenon, but as a process that has been taking place for decades. However, the current interest in it is basically due to the consciousness of this phenomenon as manifested in the emergence of global issues debated across world regions, for example, human rights. The view of globalization as a process that intensifies global consciousness is echoed in Waters' definition of globalization as a "social process in which the constraints of geography on economic, political, social and cultural arrangements recede, in which people become increasingly aware that they are receding and in which people act accordingly."[4]

In the Arab region, globalization is one of the concepts that have caused what Georges Tarabishi[5] calls "ideological inflation." Several publications and special issues of cultural magazines have been dedicated to the discussion of this phenomenon. Globalization here is seen as a celebration of capitalistic values.[6] It is regarded as a chaotic phenomenon that does not have any historic roots in any cultural identity and cannot even offer individuals a new sense of identity.[7] Among the reasons claimed to lie behind the fear of the effects of globalization on local culture are the spread of consumerism and similar lifestyles sponsored by multinational corporations (the "Coca-Cola-ization" or "McDonaldization" phenomenon) and the fact that American cultural products have invaded different regions where they promote American values and lifestyle. Although globalization entails the exchange of goods and ideas at political, economic, and cultural levels, the cultural exchange (or the symbolic exchange) is argued to have a stronger effect.[8]

Several researchers, both Western and Arab,[9] agree on the nature of globalization, particularly in its independence from time and space. Globalization has been attributed to four different concepts: internationalization, liberalization, universalization, and Westernization (for which read: Americanization).[10] The latter concept has probably been the most widely used among Arab researchers when debating the impact of globalization.

For instance, al-Kahtani[11] conducted a media analysis of four Arab and four US daily newspapers. He searched the newspapers for instances of globalization and Americanization: in the Arabic data, he found examples of globalization dominant in culture news (45 percent), less dominant in economic news (31 percent) and even less in the political sections. In contrast, American newspapers contained most instances in the economic sections (36 percent), and almost equally in both cultural and politics sections, with 19 percent and 17 percent respectively.[12] The conclusion is that globalization has a larger impact on Arab cultural heritage than on the political and economic processes in the region. Mona Abaza confirmed this when she wrote that globalization "has become interchangeable with Americanization."[13]

For Awatef Abdel Rahman,[14] the consequence of globalization will be rather the accentuation of the gap between the North (developed world) and the South (developing world), and hence the dependence of the latter on the former. The cultural products of the developed world (meaning the West and particularly the USA) may be used by the people of Third World countries as a means of escapism rather than as a means of encouragement to participate in public debates. The Egyptian writer Saad Edeen Wahba once wrote that the presence of McDonald's restaurants in Cairo was an American conspiracy to corrupt Egyptian youth.[15] Another Arab writer wrote in *Al Hayat* that 500 satellite channels accessed by Arabs belonged to the West and thus were aimed at disseminating Western values and norms.[16]

Al-Yasin,[17] another Arab scholar, sees cultural globalization as a major challenge for Arabs. Negative effects lie probably in the exchange of cultural and media products, as it is generally assumed that the center (the West) will be the main exporter, that the periphery (the East) will be the main receiver, and that messages coming from the center may contain values deemed to be threatening for local cultures. Al-Jabri[18] explains the Arab attitude to the West as being dual in nature: on the one hand, Arabs associate the West with colonization and hegemony, but on the other hand it is also associated with freedom, modernity and science. Western (American) cultural products are flowing into the Arab region and with the emergence of satellite channels, Arab governments can no longer control the content offered by these channels.[19]

In a later publication, Al-Jabri[20] traces the root of the word "globalization," linking it to the USA, meaning the process of "generalization" and expansion. He deduces that the term implies the dissemination of a certain lifestyle, that is, the "American model."[21] The direct outcome of this expansion is the gap between the wealth accumulated by the rich countries and the deprivation of the poor countries, a gap that is even evident among people belonging to the same society, that is, the gap in salaries among workers sharing the same qualifications. Globalization, al-Jabri adds,[22] is an ideology that aims primarily at erasing the national memory and national belonging or, as he puts it,

> the globalization world is a world without a nation-state, or without a nation and without a state. It is a world of corporations and networks; a world of subjects or "doers", those in control, and objects of consumptions imposed on them, be it the consumption of food, drinks, canned products, images, data, movements and even silence. Cyberspace has become the new nation . . . it is the space which is made by the communication networks to encompass economics, politics, and culture.[23]

Western and Arab scholars share the view that globalization means the "commodification of culture" and hence the loss or damage of the authentic fabric, which may be an indirect reason for the rise of fundamentalism in an attempt to protect and maintain "tradition."[24] This view is illustrated on the cover of Benjamin Barber's book *Jihad vs. McWorld* (1995), which features a veiled woman, with only her eyes exposed, holding a can of Pepsi in her hand. This was supposed to be a sign of the paradoxical situation of globalization, wherein traditionalists might attack Americanization (and consumerism) and yet keep on consuming American products. However, there are at least two reasons why Arab consumption of Western, or particularly American, products cannot necessarily be interpreted as contradictory to the sense of tradition.

First, while it is true that Islamic fundamentalism is on the rise, there has scarcely been any analysis of the deep structure that lies beyond the mechanism of this movement. Stuart Hall[25] has identified two reaction strategies to globalization: 1) translation and 2) tradition. The former entails strategies to develop new signifiers and introduce them to the original culture, while the latter is a means of looking back to the original heritage and history rather than looking at the situation in the present. Local cultures do not necessarily reject global identities and/or brands. The challenge, as seen for instance by Arabs, cannot be reduced to being merely a choice between adopting foreign texture into the traditional fabric or rejecting it totally and indulging in a search for a past identity instead. Foreign brands, such as Coca-Cola, have been localized.[26] Even Barbie dolls have been made in an Arabic version.[27] The same applies to media in connection with the emergence of new (Western) genres in the news and entertainment industry. Furthermore, Wheeler[28] showed that the Kuwaiti feeling of national identity was not negatively affected by the presence of foreign media or the Internet. In fact, Kuwaitis regard it as an important element of their national identity to be open to global links and new technologies.

Besides, fear of Americanization was marked not only among Arabs but among Europeans as well. Four hundred European intellectuals inserted a petition in six European newspapers demanding the exclusion of cultural works from the GATT agreement in order to protect their European cultural products against the "supremacy of Hollywood."[29]

Second, the claim that Arabs fear globalization is indeed a new phenomenon. For instance, Mona Abaza[30] argues that Egypt experienced this hybridity centuries ago, long before the proliferation of the concept of globalization. An Arab scholar pointed to the fact that globalization was not at all a fearful concept to Arabs during the peak of Islamic civilization, and indeed one of them wrote of the attitudes of Muslims at that time:

> Secure with their own identity and self-definitions, Muslims were never loath to take for their own use, and build on, the scholarship of others. They were not, for example, threatened by exploring Greek philosophy. As a vibrant, cultivated people, they in fact translated it into Arabic (and, as it turned out, ended up preserving it for posterity by doing so). They not only mouthed, but actually lived the Arabic proverb: "Seek knowledge though it may be located as far away as China."[31]

Thus, rather than accepting the simplified account of globalization as a process of recent intense exposure to Western media products, it is important to recall that the process of exposure to these products has been ongoing for decades and is indeed happening at present. For instance, Rachty and Sabat[32] showed that during the period from 1965 to 1969, Egypt alone imported 80 to 90 percent of its films, mostly from the USA. The importation of these cultural products was reinforced by the advent of television (in the 1960s) and the increasing importation of foreign material to fill the empty programming slots.

One main characteristic of the accounts of the above views of Arab culture in the globalization age is their essentialism. In other words, these views see globalization as a sweeping process imposed upon rather "passive," not to mention powerless, recipients rather than acknowledging the recipients' power in "decoding" the incoming messages. Such views presume the stability of an "Arab" identity as a fixed notion, whose mingling with foreign elements may result in the agents' confusion and the deterioration of their sense of belonging. This, again, is an underestimation of the agents' awareness of their position in an overall "field of power" and their continuous struggle to redefine this position.

In sum, hybridity is not, as some may argue, the oxymoron of Arab culture; rather, globalization can be seen a process of transformation, particularly at the cultural level. The transformation can be seen as a catalyst for development as a result of a complex process of diffusion and hybridity affecting culture at various levels.

The dilemma for Arab citizens, including the media professionals who are at the center of this book, is not how to reconcile the modern with the traditional; it is instead how to keep on adhering to the rules of the game while manipulating the game itself for the interest of individuals and/or the community. The following section fleshes out this dilemma, drawing mainly on Bourdieu's and Giddens' works, in order to argue for the need for agents to enter into a continuous struggle over the allocation of resources as well as the imposition of norms.

## Struggle over power

Central to the following discussion are the notions of reflexivity and visibility. I draw on Bourdieu's theory of practice as well as Giddens' structuration theory as a basis for the analysis of these notions in an Arab context. The choice of these two theories, in particular, is grounded in their capacity to combine theory and practice, or abstract assumptions with empirical data. In other words, both views seem to reconcile the difficulties associated with previous social theories that failed to account for the role of active agency operating within objectified structures or resources.

One of Bourdieu's legacies was practice theory, which stresses the social agents' practical dispositions or habitus constrained by the rules of the field in which they are situated. Fields, then,

> engender and require certain responses, "hailing" the individual to respond to themselves and their surroundings in specific ways to the point of habituation. "Habitus" is the collective term for this array of dispositions. Thus, the field instantiates us as subjects and reproduces social distinctions via the enactment of habitus.[33]

Yet, agency is still bound rather than enabled by the habitus, and thus it may be constituted as an agency incapable of reflecting.[34]

Giddens[35] sees structure and agency as working in a dialectic relationship, in as much as the acts of agency reproduce the structure. Agents here are knowledgeable and have the ability to discard, replace, or indeed alter, structure including institutions, traditions, and norms. This is what Giddens refers to as the duality of structure. Agency and structure are then closely related, with the latter reproduced via the repetitive actions of the former. Structure includes means of signification (for example, media), legitimization (for example, moral codes), and domination (power).

Sewell[36] elaborates on the structuration theory and offers a more detailed account of structure. The aim here is to account for social change, and show how structure can generate transformation. Structures, Sewell argues, refer to rules or schemas as opposed to resources, which are the effect of structure.[37] According to Giddens, structures and agents' practices operate in a dualistic relationship, shaping and reproducing one another. In this sense, they "far from being opposed, in fact *presuppose* each other."[38] The knowledgeability of agency stems from the agents' ability to use the structures and resources available in a creative way. Sewell replaces Giddens' term "rules" with the term "schemas" in order to encompass rules, norms and procedures that can be transposed to other fields and situations in which they have not been conventionally applied. Thus, structures depend on the intersubjectivity among agents to act upon the available rules and resources.

Sewell divides resources into two types: human and non-human. The first refers to knowledge and affection and the latter to animate or inanimate objects. They are both

> media of power and are unevenly distributed. But however unequal resources may be distributed, some measure of both human and non-human resources are controlled by all members of society, no matter how destitute and oppressed. Indeed, part of what it means to conceive of human beings as *agents* is to conceive of them as *empowered* by access to resources of one kind or another.[39]

He then proposes five maxims through which social change can be analyzed. The first maxim is the multiplicity of structures, which refers to the agents' ability to apply different and even incompatible schemas, as well as access diverse forms of resources. The second maxim is the transposability of schemas, which, given the agents' knowledgeability, refers to the agents' capability of extending and creatively transposing schemas into new contexts. Given that the consequences of transposition are never predictable, the third maxim then refers to the unpredictability of resource accumulation. This could be related to the "unintended consequences" of action, in Giddens' terms. One may add here that this unpredictability is an inherent element of any social field, for every action, no matter how mundane or sophisticated it is, may result in unpredictable consequences. In this sense, unpredictability differs from "risk", which, in Giddens' and Beck's terms, is one characteristic of late modernity.

The fourth maxim refers to the "polysemy of resources" or the various meanings attached to resources in the agents' minds, which then determine their interaction. The fifth maxim is the "intersection of structures": structures enable as well as constrain agents, whose actions may then end up reproducing the social order. For instance, the discourse of modernity resting on the mix between a modern format and indigenous content, as I argue below, has at once made possible the establishment of skyscrapers and the parallel expansion of unlawful housing. Another example is the notion of pan-Arabism, enforced by the newly formed Arab States with the aim of disseminating the feeling of unity among laypeople while simultaneously accentuating the differences among Arab peoples as defined by the legislative order.

Combining Bourdieu's theory of practice with Giddens' structuration theory, Sewell suggests the hybridization of Giddens' reflexivity and Bourdieu's habitus. Seen in this light, agents, although free to innovate and navigate across fields, are still contained by overall field rules and norms, defined a priori as part of the game. Thus, those with the strongest capital have access to more resources, which enables them to define and, if necessary, re-define the rules of the game in order to maintain their power. Adopting Bourdieu's theory of practice makes it easier to see every social field as a separate empirical unit with its own rules, without losing sight of the fact that all fields are still contained in the same social space. For instance, the analysis of the Arab social space is not confined to the analysis of the apparent tensions between modernity versus tradition in media formats; rather, what counts is the kind of appropriations that have been brought about by this struggle for power in each field and how it interacts with other fields, that is, what kind of journalists have come to dominate the journalistic field. In sum, mixing the notion of reflexivity with the notion of habitus accounts for the agents' ability to realize opportunities and to re-shape their role in the game.

According to Giddens,[40] late modernity is characterized by the interconnection between extensionality (or global impact) and intentionality (or the personal position). Agents reflect continuously over their future by drawing on their experiences and comparing them with their present situation. Reflexivity is one of the three elements identified by Giddens[41] that explain the dynamic process of modernity: separation of time and space, disembedding of social institutions, and reflexivity or the continuous monitoring of social activities in the light of newly acquired knowledge. Furthermore, Giddens points out that "the reflexivity of modernity extends into the core of the self. Put in another way, in the context of a post-traditional order, the self becomes a *reflexive project*."[42]

Reflexivity is entrenched in the resources/structure or even a structure in itself, in as much as the agents' aim of monitoring is closely related to the overall aims and ambitions legitimatised by the structure (doxa). Hence, it is the rules within each field that define the ultimate goal, for example, the goal of visibility or acknowledgement.

Viewed against this backdrop, it is necessary to see structure and agency not as operating according to a push–pull relationship; rather, it is a dialectic relation wherein the structure and resources have even unintentionally resulted in the opening up of new possibilities for agents. Moreover, agents are knowledgeable and capable of mixing creatively the capital and borrowing from others to function in the overall game.

Figure 1.1, based on Giddens, [43] illustrates this dialectic relationship.

The agents are motivated by the basic goal or aim of recognition and esteem. This goal is discursively rationalized and communicated within the overall field, for example, the discourse of modernization. The dominant discourse here may lead to unintended, unpredictable, or undesired consequences which force the agents with the largest share of power to re-define and re-rationalize their action. The power of reflexive monitoring lies in its being an intuitive act directed at reaching the maximum benefit for the agents despite the restraints imposed by them.

The resources (for example, nation-state, education, urbanization, open market) are based on and defined by the social interaction among agents. The development of global, electronic, and new media has accelerated changes in social life, as agents now are "likely to acquire

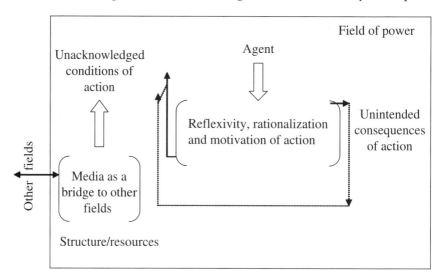

**Figure 1.1** dialectic relationship between structure and agents in an overall field of power (based on Giddens, 1984)

information and symbolic content from sources other than the persons with whom they interact directly in their day-to-day lives."[44] This web of interconnected sources of information has indeed added to the "unpredictability" of interactions among agents connected across different spatial contexts.

The media then have come to form a new resource that facilitates the agents' movement to and from other fields while serving as a communicative platform to disseminate the norms and rules that restrain these movements. The media serve as a bridge to other fields of power; they comprise a new form of interaction and discursive reflexivity. Using the media, agents are able to change their position within the field even temporarily. Metaphorically, the media serve as a theater stage on which the agents rehearse the rules of other fields, and become acquainted with different rules of the game. In sum, the media can be seen as a set of intersected resources, enabling and constraining at the same time: the media connect people and accentuate their belonging to one unified imagined community while enabling their movement across diverse and unrelated fields, which threatens the foundation of this community (see, for example, Chapter 3 on language). For instance, journalists can use the resources available to them within the field of media to navigate across and become acquainted with the rules in the field of politics. They can later use this accumulated knowledge to transform their position within the overall social field of power by transacting their professional capital to the field of politics (see Chapter 2).

Another example is the use of the media as a resource through which laypeople become acquainted with other lifestyles, not necessarily to imitate them later but to be able to live them even temporarily, such as the way ordinary people from humble backgrounds participating in reality TV programs on pan-Arab TV channels have managed to transcend their habitus and act as stars even for a short time span. The increasing reflexivity then allows this transcendence from contrasting habitus, although the overall rules of the field may not allow this transcendence to be sustained for a long time.

The real power lies in the agents' ability to manipulate the dominant norms and discourses enforced within the field in order to justify their acts against these very norms and discourses. I elaborate on this power below, using the veil as one example of a norm/rule that may be imposed by an overall structure, but which can be used by women as a means to act against patriarchal dominance within their social field.

Having the above model in mind, I argue below that the transformation of social life in Arab societies through the media as a resource has been fueled by this increasing reflexivity among agents who now see their lives as "reflexive projects." This reflexivity does not refer to the "luxury" or freedom of choice; rather, it refers to the increasing awareness of one's position within the field combined with and intensified by increasing knowledge of other fields. This knowledge is communicated by the media as one modern resource, as well as by other forms of interaction with, for example, tourists from immediate and/or distant geographical spaces, or through migration to these spaces.

Crucial to my discussion below are two terms: visibility and reflexivity. Visibility refers to the motivation of the agents to gain more power via recognition; this, as I argue below, has been the motivation behind post-colonial Arab governments' decisions to hybridize the local and the foreign in order to form a new modern image of their nations. The main aim is to build a bridge linking East and West, rather than to copy the Western model slavishly or to indulge in a romanticized admiration of one's heritage. Education and media are the key building blocks for this bridge: the former to spread a sense of national/regional identity and the latter to consolidate the vision of progress as envisaged by the governing elites. The problem, though, is that this vision is based on an essentialist view of identity as a static unit, easy to mould without changing its core element. It also discards the consequences of reflexivity, or the continuous process of reflection, the ability to monitor one's actions, to weigh up consequences, and to be aware of the impediments as well as the potential resources available. Indeed, as I argue below, a losing strategy in this process is to yield to, or accept, the essentialist classification of identity (that is, native versus foreign), while a winning strategy is to keep pushing this classification to its limits.

## Hybridity as a national project

Several Western scholars see the process of globalization as "a complex mixture of homogenization and heterogenization."[45] Globalization, in this view, does not entail the triumph of one meta-discourse or the meta-narrative of one civilization or culture,[46] as it is also accompanied by the process of localization[47] because recipients in different societies may interpret one particular media message in a variety of ways according to their cultural background. Communication, for instance, undergoes a process of localization, where the content is localized in order to be incorporated into the local (receiving) cultural context. The localization process is perhaps the strongest suggestion offered by Arab intellectuals to join this new "juggernaut world" successfully. Here, it is essential for Arab societies to adapt and indeed enhance a mosaic and hybrid cultural fabric by localizing and nationalizing imported content.

This hybridity was propagated by the Arab nation-state during the 1950s and 1960s, following the independence of several Arab States, namely, Egypt, Tunisia and Iraq in the 1950s and Algeria, Syria, Sudan and Libya in the 1960s. The first task for the newly formed nation-states was to gain legitimacy and sustain a sense of shared (imagined) identity among their citizens in order to mobilize all efforts towards the modernization project. To reach these goals, special attention was given to new forms of institutions, such as education,[48] as well as the media; both institutions play a decisive role in enforcing a sense of national belonging to a unified political community, rather than stressing apparent diversity in terms of ethnicity, gender, and class. The attention given to mass education has resulted in a remarkable expansion in the number of primary and secondary school pupils during the 1950s and 1960s, for example, in Egypt, Morocco, and Oman.[49]

Plans to spread education to all citizens were seen to counteract directly the colonial powers' previous attempts to hinder the establishment of higher educational institutions, thus maintaining the colonists' intellectual superiority. In fact, the socialist movements that swept the region during the first half of the last century had relied on education as the only path out of the backwardness that was, by and large, associated with the previous regimes. For instance, Lord Cromer (who ruled Egypt from 1883 to 1907) "tried unsuccessfully to deflect demands for more education into interest in simple elementary schooling for the masses" rather than sponsoring the establishment of a university,[50] which pushed a group of educated citizens to establish the university as a private institution, thus adopting Cromer's discourse of "private initiative" to counteract his attempt to put off the project. It was for this reason, perhaps, that some Arab scholars were suspicious of the hybridity with Western culture, and even cast doubts on the motivations of Orientalists or the Western scholars who taught at the Egyptian University (currently Cairo University) following its founding in 1908.[51]

Education was also deployed as a means by which the state secured a constant supply of public servants and spread the ideals of the socialist system. For instance, employment in the public sector soared in the newly formed states: in Egypt, there were 250,000 employees in 1952 but this number reached up to 1,200,000 in 1970, and in Sudan it went

from more than 176,000 in 1955 and 1956 to well over 400,000 in
1977.[52] In Algeria, the former president Hourai Boumedienne's reign
was known as the "bureaucratic dictatorship" for applying politics
similar to those of Nasser in Egypt.[53]

It was difficult for the new states, however, to unify the education
system, with the inheritance of "a variety of schools: some public,
some private, some modern, some traditionally Islamic; some teaching
through the medium of Arabic others through that of a European language, usually English or French."[54] Despite attempts to unify the
system, the language schools continued to attract the middle- and
upper-middle classes, producing a new type of elite – that is, the
Anglo- or Franco-Arabs – who feel at ease in an Arab as well as a
Western milieu, or as Hourani put it:

> An elite which tended to perpetuate itself lived, not – as it had done in
> an earlier generation – in an English or American or French cultural
> milieu, but in an Anglo-Arab or Franco-Arab one, knowing two or
> three languages well, at home in Arabic but acquiring its high culture and
> knowledge of the world through English or French (and increasingly
> through English, except in the Maghrib).[55]

The tension, then, was not between modernity projects as articulated from below (laity) and executed from above (politicians); the
tension was between the heritage of colonial times being rejected by
some intellectuals while admired and cherished by the middle classes.
For instance, elite jobs in the Algerian public sector required the
French language, which heightened the tension between arabophones
and francophones in Algeria.[56]

Thus, the educational field kept serving as a stage for a struggle for
power and the allocation of resources between, on the one hand,
those who embraced Western culture as a role model and, on the
other, those who held on to religious education, hailing it as the
emblem of the native self. It is important to stress that the struggle
was for power rather than being merely a manifestation of the tension
between the opposite views of modernity and tradition. Supporters
of the new educational institutions wanted a counterpart to, for
example, al-Azhar, which was regarded as "outdated", and even Dar
al-Ulum, an educational institution that mixed Western educational
curricula with a religious curriculum, was regarded as second best.
Students of the newly established Egyptian University, for instance,
prided themselves on their knowledge of cutting-edge research,

thereby dwarfing the curricula taught at Dar al-Ulum and al-Azhar. The famous Egyptian writer and former dean of the Faculty of Arts, Cairo University, Taha Hussayn, recalled his scorn of Dar al-Ulum's curricula when talking to his cousin, himself a student of the latter institute:

> I had not forgotten a day when I was arguing with my cousin, then a student at *Dar al-'Ulum*, and he, the *Dar al-'Ulumi*, had said to me, the Azharite: "What do you know about knowledge, anyway? You're just an ignoramus, versed in mere grammar and *fiqh*. You've never had a single lesson in the history of the Pharaohs. Have you ever heard the names of Rameses and Akhenaton?"... But now, here I was in a university class-room listening to Professor Ahmad Kamal... talking about ancient Egyptian civilization... Here he was making his point by reference to words from ancient Egyptian which he related to Arabic, Hebrew and Syriac, as the evidence required ... No sooner had I accosted my cousin than I drew myself up in proud scorn of him and that *Dar al-'Ulum* about which he had been preening himself. "Do you learn Semitic languages at *Dar al-'Ulum*?" I queried. My cousin replied in the negative. Whereupon I proudly explained hieroglyphics to him and how the ancient Egyptians wrote, also alluding to Hebrew and Syriac.[57]

The knowledge of one's historical background is one of the invaluable gifts of education, a gift that should be combined with knowledge of other cultures/languages as well. In a column in *al-Ahram* in 1933, the Egyptian encyclopaediaist Ahmed Attiyatallah had expressed his admiration of the Westerners' knowledge of ancient Egyptian history and his embarrassment at his own lack of this knowledge. He recalled his visit to a Birmingham school in England, which coincided with a lesson on the history of the Pharaohs. The English teacher, excited to have a guest from the land of the Pharaohs, offered Attiyatallah the opportunity to continue the lesson, an offer that he politely declined, as he felt embarrassed to admit his lack of knowledge of his country's history.[58]

Thus, progress and modernization via education necessitated the successful hybridity of Western intellectual progress and native historical and ethical backgrounds. That was also the reason why foreign languages have always been regarded as an important element in achieving progress. The Egyptian academic Ahmed Amin (who joined the Egyptian University in 1926) recalled the advice passed on by his professors, who saw the mastery of another language as a prerequisite for widening one's intellectual horizons:

> These professors used to tell us always that he who was limited to Arabic saw the world with one eye only, but when he learnt another language he saw the world with two eyes.[59]

Education, then, was regarded as the fastest path to knowledge, and hence power. In fact, I argue that education is an important cultural capital in Arab societies, more important than class or wealth. Lamont and Lareau[60] discuss the methodological problem related to Bourdieu's concept of cultural capital. In order to operationalize the concept of cultural capital, the researcher must see the relevance of this capital in the person's particular environment, and see whether it is used as a means of exclusion and hence an exercise of power. Lamont and Lareau see Bourdieu's framework as implying "that lower class standards are not autonomous, and that dominated groups have been eliminated from the competition for the definition of the legitimate culture."[61] The power of cultural capital, as they see it, is the power to exclude people through symbolic imposition. Thus, exclusion is the main dimension of cultural capital, and it is manifested through self-elimination or the adjustment of one's aspirations; or by assigning those with less cultural capital to the "less desirable positions."[62]

Thus, cultural capital is one of the resources available to the agents to use, intentionally or unintentionally, or even manipulate to enhance their chances of success. Contrasting the cultural capital as analyzed in French studies versus that in American ones, Lamont and Lareau show that knowledge is an important cultural capital valued in the French setting, but not particularly in the American one, where "purchasable signals" have more value than the "culturally acquired ones."[63] Likewise, this can be seen in the way education is portrayed in Arab popular culture genres such as TV serials, where "characters' desires for money and luxury lead them to compromise their principles and to go astray, only for them to be found out and confronted, if not condemned, in the end."[64] Thus, education rather than wealth constitutes a significant cultural capital in the Arab context.

In order to succeed in their modernization project, the new regimes sought to fight the old signifiers of primitivism. For instance, despite the socialist rhetoric adopted by Nasser's regime (1952–70), the Egyptian government of the time saw part of its mission as being the need to replace the rather primitive image of Egyptians with a new modern one, for instance, by encouraging use of the "popular suit" to replace the robe usually associated with peasants.[65] The peasants and marginalized, once portrayed as the "true sons" of the nation and the bearers of authentic values, are used to being portrayed as the center of backwardness that can only be lifted up by joining the educated elite in the capital, Cairo.[66] The plan to modernize the image of Cairo was carried further by Nasser's successor, Anwar Sadat, who worked hard on rebuilding Cairo to resemble Western (particularly American) cities. His plan invoked criticism and resentment, particularly among Islamists, which paved the way for religious discourse to proliferate as an alternative discourse of morality opposing the state privatization and capitalist projects.[67] Sadat's response, ironically, was to deploy the same discourse by immediately implementing the *Infitah* (Open Door) economic policy while stressing his role as the "believing leader."[68]

Western European cultures were also the yardstick by which the newly formed Arab States measured their cultural success in hybridizing the native fabric with exotic patterns. This was shown, for instance, in the attention given to folkloric art and the call to modernize it by incorporating into it Western elements. Following independence, the Egyptian government, for one, expressed interest in folk arts as well as in progressive arts such as ballet, and in 1957 the Center for Folk Arts was established under the Ministry of Cultural and National Guidance.[69] One leading dance troupe at that time was the Reda Troupe, whose members came from well-off middle-class families. The troupe's main dancer, Farida Fahmy, was half British and half Egyptian, and, despite her affluent background, has since come to symbolize the authentic *bint a-balad* (or native citizen).[70] The troupe members managed to show this successful hybridity between East and West in films such as *Love in Karnak*, where they appear as fully capable of communicating in foreign languages, and wearing modern clothes.[71] Their performances were supposed to present the authentic folkloric Egyptian dances, although the dances were in fact altered forms of native dances.

Hybridity was also evident in other arts, such as music. Arab musicians, particularly in Cairo, which led the music and film industry during the first half of the twentieth century, depended on *tatwiir* or the evolution of the music as a process of modernizing the local music. This process "has strong connotations of Westernization. It implies bringing the music closer to the rank of . . . 'international music', the ultimate exemplar of which is European art music."[72] Thus, composers could mix Western music with the native tones "without necessarily becoming less Egyptian or less Arab."[73]

Education has been the cornerstone of the progress project, as well as being synonymous with knowledge, and hence with power. Even in the most conservative Arab societies, such as Saudi Arabia, education was seen as the means to mobilize the nation and to regenerate a new image of the kingdom. The Saudi government has undertaken the task of building new schools and offering scholarships to Saudi students to study overseas. This process is still ongoing, with the kingdom's plans to build some 2,600 new schools as well as other technical colleges and training institutes by 2012, besides offering 10,000 Saudi students full scholarships abroad, mostly to the USA.[74]

However, the opening up of new resources, and the unpredictability of these resources, has unintended consequences as well: education, as well as the media, as the new form of interaction, provided the agents with new powers as well as new constraints. The new sources, as well as the new *Infitah* (Open Door) policies, which replaced the socialist policies in the 1970s and 1980s, and the new oil boom in the Gulf countries, have unintentionally exacerbated this tension between agents and resources.[75] Education encouraged people to doubt and to raise questions, while the media facilitated the meeting with foreign cultures and foreign lifestyles. The newly educated elite in the conservative Gulf countries rival the power of the religious *Ulama*, who used to enjoy a great position in society in their capacity to offer guidance and consultancy on how to live, behave, raise children, and work according to God's laws. In Oman, Islam was taught at school, which made it a "subject that must be 'explained' and 'understood'."[76] Young Omani in particular tend to interpret and justify their belief rather than taking it for granted, as opposed to the old generation who may "pray and sacrifice, but they do not know why."[77]

## Visibility: the motif for action

By hybridizing the native with the foreign, the Arab States have made it clear that they did not really desire insulation or isolation, but rather the visibility and ability to have an impact on other cultures. Visibility, as I argue here, is a crucial element in building the authentic national (Egyptian, Lebanese, Syrian, and so on) as well as regional (Arab, Islamic) identity in an age characterized by increased globalization and interdependence. Indeed, Arab countries have been competing to be the perfect East–West hybrid: Egypt has profiled itself as the

Hollywood of the East, Lebanon as the Paris of the East,[78] Dubai as the modern commercial cosmopolitan country (or Dubai Inc.) and Qatar as the host of freedom embodied in the Emir's project, al-Jazeera Satellite Channel, as well as the Doha debates, which are advertised as "a public forum for dialogue and freedom of speech in Qatar." The debates are hosted by the former BBC presenter Tim Sebastian.[79]

Dubai, for one, launched several international events to gain more visibility on the world scene, for example, the Dubai World Cup horse race, with the aim of "putting Dubai on the map", as argued by the executive chairman of Dubai Holding, which oversees most of the Emirates' investments.[80] Several Arab governments have established free media zones to host foreign and regional media institutions, granting them full operating freedom and total exemption from taxes and fees. Dubai Media City (DMC), for instance, serves 550 media organizations, among them CNN, Reuters, Sony, McGraw Hill Publishing and the Arab satellite channel, MBC.[81] The vision behind DMC is "to make Dubai a media and technology hub for the region,"[82] or as Saeed al-Muntafiq, the chief executive of DMC, put it: "Our vision is not to be a regional base for broadcasters, but to be one of four or five global bases for broadcasting as we move forward over the next few years."[83] In the same vein, the Jordanian government established a free media zone serving the Jordanian Media City Company,[84] while the Egyptian government decided to draw on Egypt's cultural capital in the region by investing in Media Production City, "envisioned as a 'Hollywood of the East,'" as well as a Media Free Zone.[85]

In order to accelerate the modernization project, Arab governments encouraged the establishment of super-malls, such as the French hypermarket Carrefour, built in Cairo, where "around eleven million people are living in unplanned housing; slums without sewerage and running water."[86] Consumerism, then, serves as the embodiment of the Western lifestyle (for example, shopping malls) and is an essential component of the modernity project, which connects for instance the Saudi city Jeddah to American cities such as Sacramento rather than to the old Jeddah.[87] The Cairo World Trade Center, a huge shopping mall, was built "through the cleaning up or pushing away of the popular quarter and getting rid of the 'ashwaiyyat [or stigmatized housing] surrounding it."[88] These 'ashwaiyyat are usually depicted as the land of disorder and deformity.[89] The Egyptian elites condemn "the spread of decadent culture," which results in an increase in "ugly brick houses with inadequate water supplies and sewerage and taxis . . . in the countryside."[90] Although the government would punish several of those poor citizens who built these 'ashwaiyyat by destroying these stigma-tized houses, some of the citizens realized that unlicensed extensions to their houses could be saved if they invested in making chic annexes, adding thereby to the new modern face of the city.[91]

Moreover, the elites maintain the exclusion of the less privileged groups by legitimizing the differences due to academic capabilities rather than by specific social habitus ingrained in the person's social milieu. For instance, the present Minster of Education in Egypt, Gamaleddin Moussa, expressed this view when he was asked about the government's plan to reduce illiteracy:

> There are 12 million people in Egypt who are illiterate – they are mostly in the rural areas and the majority are women. The main problem is that these people do not have *the will to learn*, with customs and traditions being the main obstacles (emphasis added).[92]

Lila Abu-Lughod[93] provides another example of an Egyptian TV program called *100 percent*, aimed at encouraging 100 percent literacy in Egypt. In one episode about child labor, the TV presenter inter-viewed children who were thrown into the labor market despite their young age, blaming them, rather than their families or the social care system, for their not pursuing school education in order to be able to get better jobs and hence higher incomes.

Exclusion is also evident on the cultural scene, where popular music genres such as *shaabi* or *rai* and rap music have been looked down upon by the well-established "cultured" artists.[94] Songs in these genres express resistance to "middle-class respectability,"[95] and have proved very popular despite being censored by the state media. Following their success in Europe, the North African (particularly Algerian and Moroccan) rap and *rai* singers, however, have managed to ally them-selves with some of the "cultured" Arab singers in popular duets, while *shaabi* singers such as the Egyptian signer Shaaban Abdel Rahim are still regarded as the epitome of vulgar culture. Yet, because of Abdel Rahim's popularity in Egypt, the fast-food giant McDonalds attempted to turn to him for product campaigning,[96] thereby adding an authentic indigenous color to its American-rooted product. The *shaabi* singer has also deliberately sought recognition by meddling in politics, the essence of the public sphere, with his anti-Israel songs, which secured him "instant stardom."[97]

In this modernity project, the new educated elite have become the undisputed experts who shape the modern face of the national/regional culture and promote it in global/cosmopolitan mainstream culture. It is these intellectuals who act as the gatekeepers of indigenous culture, sieving and weighing up incoming trends before accepting or rejecting them. Their main aim is to create modern collective visibility in a global world market, while concealing primitive past images. This modernity project served as a door, to borrow Simmel's metaphor:[98] it is a door to enter into a foreign place and become familiarized with the Other while retaining the freedom of exiting through that door at any time, and hence controlling the impact of the foreign resources. In this sense, it also requires essentialist categories and identities, which enable the agents to move smoothly between East and West (and across fields of power) without losing track of their internal mission to bring the best of the two worlds together and, above all, without losing the sense of their native roots. The main motivation of the elite was to reallocate resources and gain recognition in the global field of power.

However, the Western idea of a nation-state individualizes the citizens, who are now freed from their immediate communities. Slavish application of the same notion ignores the fact that peoples in the Arab States "are deeply embedded in communities in families, in ethnic, racial or other social grouping."[99] This has resulted in a new tension: the marginalized population, excluded from this elite's modernity project, entered into a continuous struggle not to attain "autonomy", but rather to attain visibility, as Bayat[100] argues. These are the same groups that are left out of the elite, as well as scholarly, accounts.[101] These are also the same groups that serve a double function in Arab societies: they serve as the epitome of the authentic cultures, while representing the raw material that needs be lifted up from the slums and refined to match the new modern face of Arab States.[102]

One important ingredient of the new modernity project has been urbanization; newly formed governments have poured financial and political resources into Arab cities, in an attempt to create new metropolitans to serve as centers of progress. However, increased urbanization has led to increasing migration from rural regions to the cities, thereby introducing rural citizens to city life, with its new opportunities:

> The increasing size of the population, the migration from the countryside into the city and the growing numbers and power of the national bourgeoisie – landowners, merchants, owners and managers of factories, civil servants and army officers – affected the nature of urban life in many ways. With the coming of independence, the indigenous middle class moved into quarters that formerly had been inhabited mainly by

Europeans, and the rural migrants moved into the quarters they had vacated, or into new ones. In each case, there was a change in customs and ways of life: the middle class took to living in a way that formerly had been typical of the foreign residents, and the rural migrants adopted the ways of the urban poor.[103]

Thus, cities were an important part of urbanization and modernization projects, with the construction of "public monuments to legitimize the young state"; consequently, the numbers in Arab urban settings have skyrocketed, constituting more than half of the population, who now compete over scarce state services.[104]

The growth of slums was noted even in wealthy Arab States, such as Saudi Arabia. One Saudi artist expressed this idea in his painting of Jeddah, the second-largest city in Saudi Arabia. The artist Abdullah Idrees shows in his painting "Untitled" the low standard of buildings accommodating the low-income foreign labor force and the city paralyzed by pollution; he even used rough paper to help reinforce this idea.[105]

Thus, although the rationale behind the urbanization project was to "beautify" the cities as the new "faces" of the new Arab States, the project unintentionally resulted in the creation of the so-called 'ash-waiyyat (or stigmatized) housing driven mainly by the rural population's desire to "survive and live a dignified life."[106] The phenomenon is still proliferating; for instance, Cairo has more than a hundred spontaneous communities housing more than seven million people who claimed "cemeteries, roof tops and the state/public land on the outskirts of the city, creating largely autonomous communities."[107]

Even the shopping malls, proudly built as a sign of modernity, have been used by Arab youth as a place to form new relationships and as a Western-style luxurious shelter from a polluted, overcrowded, and traditional space surrounding the malls.[108] The new malls provided a more "democratic" space to break up borders among classes and gender. The new social space provides new possibilities to negotiate the project of the self and mould it according to the surroundings.

According to Bayat, the very notion of a "civil society" discards such communities, which are quiet and dispersed but can be mobilized in collective action, despite their lack of leadership or clear ideology. This collectivity, however, can be "more extensive and effective than conventional institutions outside the state."[109] Hadj-Moussa[110] provides an example of such informal networks in Algeria. By the end of the 1990s, when ownership of satellite dishes was a collective act, neighborhoods of about 100 to 200 families each would come together and divide the cost of a collective satellite dish among them. A caretaker would be elected to oversee the installation, and another would keep the amount. The result was a gradual change of allocation of resources, as Bayat states, "by initiating gradual 'molecular' changes, the poor in the long run 'progressively modify the pre-existing composition of forces and hence become the matrix of new changes.' "[111]

## Reflexivity: the fuel of change

Far from being a straightforward process, however, this modernity project has been fueled by the increasing reflexivity not only among the new elite but also among laypeople. Success and acknowledgement was the motivation shared by the powerful as well as less powerful agents; each party played the game of hybridity and learned how to manipulate the resources available to serve their goal of attaining recognition.

The continuous rise of education opportunities among the masses, as well as their familiarity with foreign cultures via the media and via migration has constituted a challenge, not only to elite developmental projects but also to well-established traditions and values. Reflexivity here serves as a catalyst in facilitating a change fuelled by the countries' exposure to extensional lifestyles and norms. Thompson sums this up by saying,

> The development of the media also deepens and accentuates the reflexive organization of the self in the sense that, with the expansion of symbolic resources available for the process of self-formation, individuals are continuously confronted with new possibilities, their horizons are continuously shifting, their symbolic points of reference are continuously changing.[112]

In a particular reference to Lull's study[113] among Chinese viewers, Thompson reminds us that viewing other cultural forms can be a means by which the audience "get a sense of how people live in other parts of the world, a sense which could give them a point of comparison to reflect critically on their own condition of life."[114]

It is important, however, to recall that, although the media played and still play a crucial role as one main resource, their power lies in being a new form of interaction added to the interpersonal interaction accelerated after independence, particularly given the increasing migration of Arab citizens as an imported labor force either to the Gulf markets or to Western societies, not to mention increasing interpersonal interaction with foreign tourists.

Elite projects to modernize the national and regional images by, for instance, importing new program content did not take into account the unintentional use of this new content on the lives of the laity. Another illustration of this point is how the Internet, which the Arab intellectual elites consider a means for further development,[115] has been deployed by the Arab youth population as a dating forum.[116] This can be regarded as a paradoxical process of the "relaxation of norms," as Abaza[117] calls it, with specific reference to the increasing percentage of *urfi* (or informal) marriages as a legitimate means of sexuality. *Urfi* marriage, in particular, has become a prevalent phenomenon among Egyptians, particularly young people, and the number of those preferring this kind of marriage to traditional marriages is estimated to be more than 30,000.[118] The contracts are drawn up not only among Egyptian men and women, but also among the Egyptian youth and Arab nationals from the region. For instance, young women from humble quarters such as Imbaba in Cairo, best known for hosting militant Islamists, enter into informal marriage contracts, *urfi* marriages, with Gulf tourists, with the contracts lasting up to the end of the tourists' holidays.[119] Egyptian intellectuals and men of religion, however, regard this kind of marriage a form of concubinage because young people usually marry in secrecy without the knowledge of their families, not to mention that the law (at least until recently) does not automatically accept the legitimacy of children from this kind of marriage unless the case is brought before the court.[120]

The opportunities provided for women in connection with the new discourse of education and progress have made women more aware of their rights, pushing them to challenge the status quo even in small steps. Fargues,[121] for instance, argues that despite official reports that confirm the low empowerment of Arab women, the continuing decline in the birth rate among generations attested to the opposite. Thus, the following of Islam did not prevent the decline in births. He argues that education and women's entry into the labor market has had an impact on this, with more and more women never marrying. The scarcity of resources available has also indirectly helped reduce the phenomenon of polygamy due to the financial problems in affording a suitable martial residence.[122]

Moreover, Mona Abaza[123] offers an illustrative anecdote about the tendency of several Egyptian saleswomen and cashiers working in the new Western-style malls in Cairo to remove their headscarves upon arriving in the malls and to replace them at the end of the working day, thus re-negotiating a religious identity that may seem unfitting in this new hybrid space. These women, then, possess a vast knowledge of moving across social spaces and fields (of work, home) with ease. Conversely, those who adhere to the veil may also do this as a defense mechanism, as Abu Odeh[124] argues. In this case, the veil is a means of avoiding harassment in the street or workplace, using Islam as a discourse to declare chastity and to fight harassment as a signifier of male dominance.

Moreover, young Saudi women have protested against the increasing unemployment rate among female graduates in the country, a frustrating trend given that the number of women graduates is escalating.[125] In addition, Saudi women, despite living in a conservative society, rebelled after watching televised images of American and Kuwaiti women driving cars across the Saudi border (while the Saudi state denies Saudi women the right to drive). Saudi women demonstrated, using Islam as their main argument, defying the men of religion to find a Koranic reference that speaks explicitly against women's right to drive cars.[126] The rebellious women drew on the official discourse of religion as a means of justifying their resistance, thus casting doubt on the official exegesis of the holy script.[127] Saudi women used to organize collective demonstrations demanding the right to drive.[128] Likewise, some Qatari women, who were granted the right to drive only a decade or less ago, tended to challenge the rather unjustifiable law long before they were granted that right. The Qatari psychotherapist Mouza el-Maliki, the first Qatari woman to stand for local elections in Qatar, recalled her challenging the laws in the 1980s, when it was forbidden for women to drive. The laws did not stop her from driving her car, with the result that she was caught several times, yet she always had a challenging answer to the policemen:

> I just tell them [the police] OK . . . what you are going to do, take me to jail, thank you very much, because I want to go to jail to write papers about the prisoners there. You want to give me a ticket, I'll pay it; you want my license, I don't have one.[129]

With the increase in their educational and career chances, women now feel more independent, which may be seen as a threat to tradition, for "society's morals are endangered as the entire fabric of virginity, honour, and chastity is worn away from within."[130] This was also the case when 15-year-old Saudi schoolgirls were left to burn because they were not wearing their headscarves and the correct dress, *abaya*. The kingdom's religious police stopped the girls from leaving the blazing building, which resulted in a wave of criticism in the Saudi media against the kingdom's powerful *mutaween* (or religious police).[131] In general, as Yamani[132] argues, young Saudi men and women are skeptical about the government and its policies because of decreasing economic standards and resources available to their generation compared to those that their fathers' generation enjoyed.

To recap, education has been the path taken by the new nation-state to keep up with the Western modernization project. Education, rather than wealth or class, has become the main attribute of the new Arab elites. Therefore, Arabs are more likely to accept an expert opinion, as long as it is attributed to a well-educated source. For instance, Arab students "have learned that somebody who is more qualified, more educated, and more expert than they are in matters of education should be responsible for decisions relating to their education."[133] Thus, education is one important cultural capital that rises above even wealth in class distinction. That was illustrated when fifteen well-educated Egyptian young women carried a law suit against the Minister of Culture and officials in the censor's office, as well as the police, for preventing them from getting permission to work as belly dancers in the night clubs. The young women graduates, including one working on her doctoral thesis, refused to work in their fields, attracted by dreams of quick profits in the belly dancing profession.[134] Distinguished by their education as their cultural capital, these women openly declared their aspiration to wealth to complete their accumulated social capital, even if it meant a challenge to the rigid structure. Their cultural capital armed them with the confidence to seek a profession commonly seen as a form of prostitution, thereby re-defining the profession of belly dancing while working openly to re-distribute the economic capital by cutting across the social stereotypes that relate dancing with ignorance and education with chastity.

## Media as a bridge

In September 2005, after more than two decades of life under authoritarian rule, Egyptians could vote in the first presidential election in which poll was open to more than one candidate. Despite the fact that the 77-year-old President Mubarak secured himself a fifth term, observers praised the role of the media in "managing" the elections. In fact, the Egyptian cabinet had announced that the state media should play a new role in that historic election by allocating equal time to all ten presidential candidates, including the President. Although the state television channels allocated 30 minutes' coverage for each candidate, some commentators considered that the core message was still the same and nothing fundamental had changed.[135]

This debate, however, points to a new role claimed by the Arab news media, which serves as a window onto other worlds, practices and lifestyles as well as acting as a mirror that reflects a new, hybrid image of the self. This indeed is in line with the visions of the nineteenth-century cultural entrepreneurs, dominantly Lebanese and Syrian Christian immigrants, who sought to transmit Western culture to Arab societies as a sign of progress and development.[136]

The media embodied this hybridity project, and were seen as a main tool in the hands of Arab governments following independence. Arab governments then realized the potential of deploying the communications sector as one means of spreading their mission to "educate their audiences" (for example, in Saudi Arabia).[137] For instance, Lila Abu-Lughod[138] argues that the former Egyptian president Gamal Abdel Nasser had a mission "to educate and inform", and that he used television as an integral tool in this mission; thus, "a major part of programming included shows with developmental and educational themes." This is what Abu-Lughod terms development realism, insofar as it "idealizes education, progress and modernity within the nation."[139]

Moreover, the last decade has also witnessed an explosion in the number of satellite channels, particularly those committed to entertainment, financed by Saudi and other Gulf business tycoons. Arab television officials tend to see their main task as providing entertainment and hence "relief" to their audience, rather than burdening them with serious discussions.[140] In fact, entertainment programming has thus been seen as harmless and can hardly "incite people to speak up about their problems or make their demands in demonstrations."[141] Satellite channels are now seen to be a ticket to the West, bringing Western-style television journalism, entertainment programs, and Western lifestyles to Arab living rooms, to compensate for the inability of the majority of poor Arabs to access Western countries for tourism, study, and so on. As for those who can afford this access, they feel they "no longer need to travel abroad."[142]

Yet, for media-owners and policy-makers, the media were seen as a means to prove the success of hybridization through the incorporation of a foreign format with indigenous content. One Egyptian intellectual expressed this view when he said that the true Egyptian identity lies "in the ability to Egyptianize 'the other'."[143] Moreover, Chaker[144] gives further support to the same idea by confirming the possibility of maintaining indigenous cultural heritage while opening up to an economically interdependent world. He offers Dubai Media City as one successful illustration that "is surely likely to be in the business of generating wealth" while conforming to "the socio-cultural values of the Arab world."

News and current affairs programs are also hailed as the source of knowledge and education, with one Algerian viewer justifying his consumption of news as being "for learning with the goal of education in mind."[145] This is perhaps why the recent bombings of al-Jazeera (a news channel), which were alleged to be deliberate attacks by the USA forces, further enforce this view of a Western Other that seeks to hinder the dissemination of information, hence knowledge (power), to the native citizens. News in particular is usually associated with a serious genre; this is due to the traditional roots of the genre, a product of intellectual elites.[146] The solemnity of the news genre is manifested in its linguistic code as well as the choice of topics usually deemed as serious (see Chapters 3 and 4).

However, the media serve as a source that facilitates the monitoring of one's image in the Other's eyes. For instance, one Algerian viewer protested about what was shown on French news broadcasts about Algeria:

> I am affected by it. I can't help it. On election day, why didn't they go see the intellectuals, the students, educated people? They went to see the people dressed in rags with holes in their shoes and who didn't know how to speak French. Why? [very loud] Europe, the French, has preconceptions. They believe we live that way![147]

In sum, the media are the virtual bridge to other social fields and through which agents reassess their position. As mentioned previously, the media, metaphorically speaking, are like a theatre for rehearsing other roles. For instance, Lila Abu-Lughod[148] recounts an example of an Egyptian village woman who would decide what to wear in her trip to the city based on what she saw in a TV series about urban life; thus, she would replace her head clothes with a modern *hijab*, thereby "erasing her village identity." In other words, she would utilize the media as a means to know the rules of the game in the city.

Tourism has also been a form of interaction with the Other, and has offered a window onto different lifestyles. For instance, one young Saudi man expressed his confusion on seeing differences among cultures in Arab states, saying,

> In the open, in tea and coffee houses, we saw Egyptians openly discussing and debating political issues. It had never occurred to me before that ordinary people need to discuss such issues among themselves. I mean, if they are not the ones who are ruling the country, why should they bother themselves with such issues? What impact would they have? I was horrified to hear them express their negative opinions of their leaders. In Saudi Arabia, we never do this. I am still not sure what I think about it all, but such provocative behaviour (*fitna*) could lead to chaos.[149]

In addition, Ouis[150] showed the result of the high exposure of Gulfies, citizens of the Gulf countries, to Western culture and lifestyles. Her informants proclaimed their puzzlement with the claim that a modern Western lifestyle should contradict their indigenous culture, as expressed by a young woman from the UAE: "But we take the best from both, why do we have to choose?"[151] Another young man expressed a similar view exemplifying the compatibility of Eastern and Western elements by referring to his own Western outfit:

> I am writing to you now and I'm wearing shorts, a T-shirt and a cap and at the same time I'm smoking a light Marlboro cigarette with a can of Pepsi next to me, does this make me Westernized? No, I'm not, I still feel as a normal UAE national.[152]

For him, then, what matters are the social relations as the sine qua non of the formation of identity rather than mere appearances. This can be documented in Middle East societies where gender relations, for instance, have been subject to this power of reflexivity, as Yaquobi[153] illustrates, using reality TV as an example. *Hawa Sawa* was a reality program produced by the Lebanese company, Breeze, featuring eight women living alone, cooking, shopping, and showing their skills as future wives. The program targets young men who will watch and call up to meet the girls. According to a recent study on the impact of this program on youth values, a good percentage of young Egyptian women confirmed their willingness to participate in such a program in order to get a husband. As for young men, the majority seemed to entertain the idea of using such a program as a convenient means to find a life-partner.[154] Moreover, the majority of young interviewees involved in this study confirmed that reality TV programs have indicated to them the paramount role of physical appearance as a means to success and happiness. In fact, another study[155] pointed to a new trend in Arab societies of resorting to plastic surgery as a means of enhancing one's appearance. Among the Arab States, Lebanon is now the beauty center in the region, with 60 percent of patients in plastic surgeries being non-Lebanese.[156]

Thus, youth take advantage of media and technological advances to reorganize their roles, even if they challenge traditional customs. For instance, youth find in the new technology of SMS a means of communication, and even dating, which has paved the way for the rise of tens of music/SMS channels broadcasting music videos while having an SMS scroll bar moving across the screen with messages exchanged between men and women. Some of the messages are overtly sexual, carrying even "marriage proposals." And although some of the channels, such as Amuzicana, attempted to oversee the SMS traffic by using special software to remove phone numbers and e-mail addresses from the messages, the youth keep on finding "ingenious" ways of communicating; for example, messages may include poetry asking readers to count the letters of every word, which add up to the phone number of the sender.[157]

## Challenging tradition

A study among young Egyptians[158] showed that young people are in need of role models in their lives, not so much because they want to imitate them but rather to consult them. Asked to rank their role models in life, the prophet Mohammed, perhaps unpredictably, was not even ranked among the top five; rather, the late Egyptian religious preacher Mohamed M. Shaarawi, best known for his use of everyday parables in his exegesis televised talks, topped the list. He was followed by Dr. Mustafa Mahmoud, famous for his televised program *Science and Faith*.[159] Furthermore, intellectuals themselves have redefined the status of religious institutions by continuously questioning their legitimacy. For instance, Abdel Wahab al-Effendi[160] scorns al-Azhar for issuing what he calls "on demand *fatwas*," as a direct response to al-Azhar's *fatwa* calling for Muslims in France to abide by French (secular) laws and regulations. The *fatwa* came in the wake of a heated debate following the ban by the French authorities of the wearing of *hijab* in public schools.

It is no surprise, amidst this fervor to identify with contemporary problems and roles, that a young preacher like the Egyptian Amr Khaled achieves stardom as the new "tele-evangelist" of the Arabs. Khaled touches on the youths' desire to control their life project; his preaching appeals mostly to the middle- and upper-middle classes, but it is claimed that his popularity is spreading among the vast lower classes as well. His preaching, available on his multi-lingual website, calls for youth to define their "target in life" and reach it, calling them "life makers."[161] Moreover, Muslim women have also claimed a share in this stardom, so medical doctors such as Heba Qotb are frequent guests in Arab media outlets, commenting and giving advice on intimate sexual problems among spouses, using the mixed discourse of science and religion.[162]

Khaled's call for self-development is not, however, confined to the religious programs; rather, a new wave of personal development programs have come to dominate the Arab media scene, for instance, Smarts Way, a new TV satellite channel that "aims to affect its Arab viewers by impacting on the self development of their souls, thoughts, behaviors and career choices."[163] The experts hosting the main programs include human resources and self-help gurus such as Dr. Saleh al-Rashed and Dr. Ibrahim al-Faqih, as well as the tele-evangelists Amr Khaled and the Kuwaiti Tarek Suwaidan, with the latter known for his books on strategic management.[164] The rationalization of establishing such a channel is anchored in Islamic discourse, referring particularly to the Koranic verse, "Verily never will Allah change the condition of a people until they change it themselves (with their own souls)" – The Thunder *Surah*, verse 11.

So, individualist discourse encourages the realization of the life project fueled by continuous reflexivity. Agents then seek to transform social reality within the constraints of the hegemonic discourses. This reflexivity was shown in a study conducted amongst Arabs in several Arab countries[165] about their concerns, be they political, social, or economic. The study was an update of an earlier survey among Arab nationals conducted in the 1980s, which showed that the main issues that preoccupied Arabs then were the Arab divide, the Palestinian–Israeli conflict, social and economic backwardness, and dependency on the First World. Moreover, democracy occupied the last place on the list of the six main concerns. The survey of the 1990s, however, showed that new issues came to the fore, for example, economic/technological challenges, environmental and demographic issues, social problems. Democracy, however, ranked as low again, albeit with a higher percentage than in the earlier survey.

The researcher who conducted this survey, Saad Eddin Ibrahim, lamented over this list, particularly the ranking of democracy, wondering if there is something deeply entrenched in the Arab culture that makes it anti-democratic. This survey (in both its earlier and updated versions) shows a developmental stride amongst Arabs, who are now more concerned about inward problems, for example, demographic, social and economic problems, or issues that touch their daily lives and work, rather than distant and complex issues. This, I argue, is a sign of the increasing reflexivity that triggers more concern about immediate issues, particularly those related to risk, therefore democracy might rank low because the risk associated with it is hard to calculate; in other words, if the gap between rich and poor is an important issue for Arab citizens, they might nevertheless find it difficult to relate this directly to the lack of democracy or free elections, tending instead to see it as having a causal relationship with purely social and/or economic factors. The role of tradition and cultural heritage then acquires a less significant role while individualization increases in importance, given the recent improvement of education and the standard of living.[166]

## Conclusion

The modern Arab nation-state has brought about radical changes in Arab societies, offering new resources and opportunities to the laity, for example, mass education and the mass media, while opening the door to new kinds of risks that threaten the established hierarchy of power within those same societies. Thus, while hybridization has been one of the Arab governments' strategies to promote modernization, it has also been a source of fear over losing native heritage to "sweeping" Western values. In fact, it can be argued that this fear of hybridity in an Arab context resembles the Western (particularly European) fear of the "sweeping" influx of immigrants; in both cases, the openness to the Other's world, hybridization or immigration, although advocated in the public discourse, is feared for its unpredictable and unintended consequences. In other words, hybridity here is another resource available for the agency enabling the agents to work on shifting the power roles and the re-allocation of resources.

The process of hybridity – that is, Arabization – is used by Arab intellectuals (expert systems) to transform the face of their nations and thus gain visibility on the world scene. Less visible (and less powerful) groups, however, resort to their closed networks, fighting for recognition in local and regional spheres. Thus, there is a continuous struggle to legitimize the demands of each group by objectifying certain cultural practices: established artists snub *shaabi* art, journalists in mainstream media snub the tabloid press, and so on.

As I argue above, the laity is an active agency that has managed to move across fields and feel empowered. This reflexivity has indeed been the most vital factor in recent changes in the Arab region. The process of globalization can then be seen to take place in different layers and at a different pace across the Middle East. The process involves the flow of culture from outside the region, thereby forming pressure on existing traditions, a pressure that entails threats as well as opportunities for the lay citizens and for their interaction among each other.

In sum, what the Arab elites want is to build and keep a "bridge" that separates them from the West while giving them the chance to return when they want. Moreover, the elites see the laity as inevitably vulnerable to foreign impulses, while the laity, although acknowledging their lack of sufficient cultural capital to sieve the incoming impulses, strive to get their share of recognition using the available discourses, for example, religion or development. For the lay majority, however, the bridge serves as a door that connects them to the world out there, a world that they cannot access in practice, but can access through the media, and rehearse living in, albeit temporarily. This kind of bridge is like Abul Ella bridge in Cairo, separating and yet connecting two starkly different areas: one called Zamalek, an area inhabited by the rich and the celebrities, and the other called Bulaq, inhabited by poor and humble people. Young Bulaqis used to claim that they were from the rich area, Zamalek, "because only 'a bridge separates' the two neighborhoods. Although the Nile and a huge socioeconomic gap separates Bulaq from al-Zamalek, people focus more on the bridge that connects the two areas."[167]

# Chapter 2

# The Arab Journalistic Field*

Notwithstanding several recent publications about Arab (news) media,[1] there is still a knowledge vacuum about the Arab journalism field: for example, access to the field; reasons for its popularity; how Arab journalists, particularly in the so-called pan-Arab media, perceive their role and how can this be related to changes in Arab media. Most of the recent studies, on the other hand, have focused on what is seen as the "phenomenon" of Arab satellite channels (notably al-Jazeera), which are immediately considered to be a new communication challenge to American media hegemony,[2] and a modern anti-Western mouthpiece. Whilst attempts have been made to survey some of these changes,[3] they only presented a general (quantitative) overview of the educational and social background of samples of Arab journalists, merely analyzed the profession in terms of the degrees the journalists held. What was needed, however, was to unravel how journalists construct their occupation – for instance, an investigation of their habitus or the dispositions that give these journalists a "practical sense" of the field in which they work. Also needed is an analysis of how the proportion of the cultural capital possessed by a specific professional group of journalists can be transacted into other fields, for instance, politics.

Arab journalism is a rich research field, for it embraces a profession known for its contradictory images. This chapter aims to place Arab journalism in a contemporary context, in order to chart the questions that should inform future research on the Arab media scene. A secondary aim is to help unravel the hierarchical system within the Arab news media. As an analytical tool, Bourdieu's field theory is argued to provide a fresh framework in which to study Arab journalism as a social field congruent with other fields in society, such as the political and economic fields. Another aim of this chapter is to critically examine recent works on the Arab news media, showing their short-comings and their tendency to sidestep the analysis of power distribution, as well as highlighting the widespread tendency to frame Arab journalists as a uniform group of homogenous agents, rather than diverse participants in this field.

The aim of this discussion is to further a new research direction, one which is currently under-researched but nevertheless required as a basis for debates and studies on Arab media and their role in the contemporary polity. Rather than focusing on structure, for example, censorship and ownership,[4] I argue for the need to integrate the issue of active agency in future analyses. Otherwise, the role of the journalist in changing the Arab media scene will remain ambiguous, thus making the emergence of new ventures such as al-Jazeera merely a product of a rebellious and well-educated cadre of Arab journalists, rather than a dialectic of structure (ownership, technology, education) and agency (journalists as mediators of ideology and values). Thus, to understand journalism, as Bourdieu[5] suggests, is to understand journalism as a microcosm and "to understand the effects that the people engaged in this microcosm exert on one another."

Clearly, there is a lack of qualitative studies among Arab journalists; but what is worse is how little, if any, attention is given to the existing rich data such as journalists' autobiographies or ethical codes, which would provide significant information on the contextual background to then map the journalistic field. Such datasets provide a meta-discourse for journalists, by which they can negotiate their role within the field and society in general.[6] In addition, recent research[7] has also validated the practice of surveying both the Arabic and English (or other European language) literature side by side, rather than basing conclusions only on the studies in English. This has revealed valuable insights into the development of Arab media as analyzed by Arab researchers, and has also served as an eye-opener into the criticism launched by Arab scholars against some Western theories of Arab media.

Based on Bourdieu's theory of practice, this chapter seeks to draw the contour of future research into Arab journalism as an autonomous field with its own rules and capital. Bourdieu argues that in order to understand the logic of any field, the identification of the capital (social and symbolic) that operates within this specific field is required. Arab journalists, as active agents, do indeed possess a form of (symbolic and cultural) power,[8] which affects, and is affected by, current developments in the region as a whole.

The chapter unfolds as follows: first some useful concepts from Bourdieu's practice theory are highlighted and then suggested lists of practices, which merit attention, are presented. These include the internal struggle among pan-Arab media outlets over power in the media field, namely who is seen as the trendsetter and who as follower, and the hierarchy of players in the field. Moreover, certain Western news media have indeed served as a source of inspiration and training, and as such it can be argued that the internal hierarchy among Arab news media is closely tied to the practices adopted from Western (Anglo-American) sources of inspiration. The role of Western media in shaping the identity of modern Arab journalist will be further explored in Chapter 6.

## Bourdieu's contours of a field

Barbie Zelizer[9] sees journalists as a community with shared definitions of their practice. The reporters' community can be seen in parallel to the metaphor of the community of memory, as defined by Bellah et al.:[10] "one that does not forget its past. In order not to forget that past, a community is involved in retelling its story, its constitutive narrative, and in so doing, it offers examples of the men and women who have embodied and exemplified the meaning of the community." Thus journalists, as a community, are socially interdependent and share certain practices that define and delimit their community. At issue here is a history or past, which is crucial to the definition of a community. For instance, journalists' presence at the heart of events is one example of the metaphors that contribute to upholding this commentary or, as Zelizer puts it: "In producing metaphors like 'eye-witnessing', 'watch-dogs', 'being there', practices of discovery or 'being on the spot', reporters establish markers that not only set up their presence but also uphold its ideological importance."[11] In other words, being an eyewitness to distant events, while anchoring them in different temporality (past, present and future), allows a reporter to contribute to the upholding of the professional authority of this community and its position in society.

This view is similar to Bourdieu's[12] view of journalism as a field of practice within which forces engage in power struggles. By seeing journalism as a field, Bourdieu rightly points out that the "journalistic practice is not reducible to the choices and idiosyncrasies of individual photographers and journalists,"[13] and thus, the practices within the field are determined by the power relations and the positioning of each reporter.

As a tool to unravel the "rules of the game" inside this community, Bourdieu's[14] field theory offers a framework for studying journalism as a social field in line with other fields in society. One of the focal issues in Bourdieu's theory is the analysis of the distribution of power in a particular field. For instance, the Arab news media can be presented as a hierarchical system composed of the so-called serious versus yellow press, magazines versus newspapers, pan-Arab versus national/local outlets, and so on. The elements within the system are separated only by symbolic barriers created by the amount of "capital" assigned to each element. A hierarchical system also exists among journalists, reflecting their professional, editorial, academic and symbolic power, values, and reflexivity. In this sense, Bourdieu's field theory can be used to combine macro-societal and micro-organizational factors in the analysis of journalism. Its strength is that it does not rely on only one variable, for example, ownership or the role of technology.[15] Studying the process of the selection of news, for instance, is to see the convergence of habitus and structural position within the journalistic field.[16] Habitus is "an *open system of dispositions* that is constantly subjected to experiences, and therefore constantly affected by them in a way that either reinforces or modifies its structures."[17]

One example of the application of field theory concerns French television, where an analysis showed that it "no longer always bows to the news judgments of the serious print press."[18] A second example is given by Hovden,[19] who showed that within the Norwegian journalistic field, a distinction is made between weekly and daily press; a distinction that is further identified as one that separates "worthy" from "unworthy" participants in the field. Moreover, the notion of objectivity in journalism is related to the standard of respectability, with broadsheet journalists tending to cling to high standards of objectivity and impartiality to separate themselves from the tabloid journalists.[20]

At issue here is the proportion of the economic and cultural capital associated with this professional group of journalists, and how this capital can be transacted into other fields, for example, politics. For instance, several leading Arab journalists, such as Salah al-Qallab (Jordan) and Mohamed Heikal (Egypt), have abandoned the field of journalism to seek careers in politics. In fact, one Egyptian TV presenter once bemoaned the frequent appearance of politicians on her daily program because it made those politicians and the political analysts invited more famous by far than the TV presenters themselves.[21] Moreover, Benson[22] draws attention to the decreasing prestige associated with French academics writing feature articles in the press, which directly opposes the situation in the Arab world, where several academics, such as media researchers Awatef Abdel Rahman and Mamoun Fandy, regularly publish in the national and pan-Arab press.

Moreover, local/regional journalistic practices exert an influence on other local fields, be they literary, political, scientific or religious. For instance, the recent increase of religious newspaper sections or religious TV programs must be a direct result of this interrelation between journalism and the religious field; likewise, the the increase in popular science sections or literary comments in the pan-Arab press could be argued to be the impact of a similar intersection between journalism on the one hand and the science and literary fields on the other. Also, there is apparent competition among different media, electronic versus print. For example, one popular genre is the agony column, such as the one in the Egyptian daily *al-Ahram* Friday issue, which used to be edited by Abdel Wahab Moutaeh. This section proved so popular that it turned into a televised "agony program" on the Egyptian satellite channel (ESC) and has been copied by other Arab channels, which implies an internal struggle for winning a bigger audience share.

According to Bourdieu, every field operates according to its unique logic, which separates, connects and intersects with other fields. The participants in each field are defined by their unevenly distributed capital, whether economic, social or cultural. To account for social changes inside the field and society in general, Bourdieu acknowledges the internal struggle among field participants to re-define and rearrange the capital among them. Thus, participants endeavor to re-categorize and re-organize the relationships among fields, and among participants in the same field, in a continuous attempt to distinguish and render legitimacy to their capital. Against this backdrop, Arab journalistic practices are tied to the rules of an overall field, and this field both effects, and is affected by other social fields.

Journalists, as agents, enter into a dialectic relationship with their field of work, and they work according to their habitus, which relates to their specific social and cultural background, biases, values and stereotypes. Particularly in developing nations, journalists have gained increasing power with their multi-faceted roles of mobilizing as well as educating their public. As it is reasonable to assume that Arab journalists exert an important influence on opinion-making and development in the Middle East, it is essential to carry out analyses based on actual encounters with Arab journalists. There is a need to detail the Arab journalistic field, in order to shed new light on the journalists' social and cultural capital and to uncover their perception of their role with regard to the changes and challenges facing their profession; then, to determine whether this perception is enabling or constraining the media's contribution to the democratization of the region. Such an ambitious research agenda could also reveal gender differences inside the newsrooms in order to unravel the specific challenges facing women journalists.

The much-needed analysis of the Arab journalistic field could begin with the impact of pan-Arab news media upon the social transformation in the region; exploring issues surrounding the accountability and legitimacy of the pan-Arab news media. Certain pan-Arab media outlets, particularly al-Jazeera, are sometimes held up as being new democratic forums for Arab audiences, and hence postulated to have a significant real or potential impact upon the democratization of the region. However, little is known about the type of organizations these media represent with respect to:

- The basis of their legitimacy;
- How media professionals themselves account for their popularity vis-à-vis traditional media outlets and Western media;
- How close they are to other civil society institutions and their impact on such institutions;
- How power is distributed internally in pan-Arab media organizations and how representative this is in terms of, for example, gender and minorities;
- Whether their agenda is compatible with the needs of their audiences, particularly the poor and the marginalized.

I have previously[23] discussed how attempts[24] to categorize the Arab news media have not taken account of new developments in the region. For instance, the role of journalists as judged by news professionals themselves may be that of a mobilizer, educator, or informer, or indeed a combination of all of these. Subsequently, it is important to analyze this role in light of its unique cultural context.

The following sections aim to provide pointers to the understanding of the logic of the Arab journalistic field, both among the Arab main players and in relation to global players such as CNN and BBC. Before embarking on this process, however, it is imperative to sketch out the political and socio-cultural context of Arab journalism as a field, that is, the means of competition and power accumulation, hierarchy within the field, and content as a means of differentiation. The first level of this analysis is to map out the contour of the field, and

I shall, in the following section, confine this exercise to the so-called 'pan-Arab' media. It is important to stress, though, that the study of pan-Arab media *must* be integrated with the analysis of local media and the relation between the two, a task that seems rather daunting for current Western scholarship (see Chapters 3, 4 and 7).

## Pan-Arabism

When discussing the emergence of the Arab press as a forum for rational and political discourse, it is hard to talk in general terms about "Arab" press. Rather, each Arab country has developed its press and media systems and discourses at a different pace to that of other neighboring countries. For instance, whilst Egypt launched its first newspaper in 1800,[25] the first publication in Kuwait appeared in 1928, and in Bahrain in 1939.[26] Also, illiteracy rates (still) vary from one Arab country to another, which, together with the difficulty, at least in the past, of forming a media outlet with a regional rather than national audience in mind, have contributed to enforcing this distinction among Arab States. However, one common characteristic is the way in which national media was used as a means of enforcing a rather "imagined community" among diverse groups of people. The Saudi government, for example, appeared to establish television broadcasting in order to distract citizens from foreign programs, providing them with a sense of community despite the citizens' different tribal relations.[27]

Indeed, the sheer fact that the "Middle East" itself as a term was forced upon Western empires in the nineteenth century[28] is compelling evidence of how the new (imagined) geographical boundaries have prompted several Arab states to form a pan-Arab identity and deploy media as one means of achieving this goal. Therefore, the task of disentangling the local from the regional embraced in the overall "pan-Arab" concept has proved a difficult task, given its penetration in a plethora of discourses ranging from the politically- and media-based, to popular culture and everyday discourse. The field of news media has embraced a number of institutions targeting not a local but a regional audience, a tendency not born with the eminent satellite channels but traceable back to the nineteenth century and the emergence of the so-called émigré press,[29] which formed a transnational community of writers/journalists and audience alike. The pan-Arab news media have gained a paramount position on the present and future research agenda because of their success in implementing the challenging political project called "pan-Arabism" into the cultural domain. Pan-Arab media have therefore claimed increasing research attention for the following reasons:

1. They have a large audience share across Arab countries rather than being confined to only one country;
2. They can be regarded as trendsetters among other national and regional media institutions because they embrace a young, high-caliber generation of media professionals;[30]
3. The past few years have shown us that Arab investors tend to establish regional rather than national media institutions, thereby targeting as wide an audience as possible, not only in the Middle East but also Western countries;
4. These pan-Arab media also serve as a Diaspora media for Arab immigrants in Europe, USA and other Western countries.

This pan-Arabism, as one of al-Jazeera's top hosts, Faisal al-Kasim, argues, has "pulled the rug from underneath local, terrestrial stations, which in itself is some kind of Arabization and thus unification."[31] Thus, pan-Arab news media have managed to accomplish a political mission that was previously doomed to failure.

The concept of a pan-Arab identity was a movement that began in the eighteenth century[32] and flourished in the Arab States, particularly during the 1950s. In fact, it was the former Egyptian president Gamal Abdel Nasser who actively promoted pan-Arabism, which became known as Nasserism, and formed the union between Egypt and Syria in 1958 (United Arab Republic, UAR).[33] The idea of pan-Arabism was then met with some skepticism among Egyptians as Nasser himself admitted that "the Arab nationalist idea was new to them."[34] The objectives of the union were claimed to be democracy, achieving social equality and maintaining solidarity.[35]

The call for Arab unity took a "populist" character,[36] which regarded Arab citizens to be part of a larger collective (*Umma*, or roughly "nation") until the 1967 war (between Israel and Egypt, Jordan, and Syria, which ended with Israel seizing the Gaza Strip, the Sinai Peninsula, the West Bank, and the Golan Heights). Defeat in this war was regarded as a serious blow to pan-Arab ideology.[37]

The media were deployed in the 1967 war as a means of mobilizing a feeling of pan-Arabism among the Arab masses. The Voice of Arabs (or *Sawt al-Arab*) radio, for example, broadcast a false account of how the Arab forces defeated the Israelis, but the audiences found out about the defeat from foreign media such as the BBC.[38] The revelation of the truth about the course of the war resulted in heated debates within the traditional media as "a safety valve to release public pressures and suppressions and a way to absorb the inherent conflicts."[39] Journalists then acquired a new role as a mouthpiece for the existing political regimes, and the most prominent editorial writers did indeed belong to the influential elite. For instance, Ahmed Said, who managed *Sawt al-Arab* radio, was said to be close to Nasser,[40] and the Egyptian journalist Mohamed H. Heikal, the former editor-in-chief of the Egyptian *al-Ahram*, also had good relations with Nasser, who even consulted Heikal on various political matters. The good ties between them helped him to get away with openly criticizing the government in his editorials, a privilege that was not shared with many other media professionals.[41]

However, pan-Arabism as a national ideology did eventually continue, but more as a rhetoric than an action. As Bassam Tibi put it, "in the rhetoric of Arab politics every statesman paid the obligatory lip-service to Arab unity for which the Arab League was considered to be the right instrument; in reality, however, most Arab politicians undermined every action aimed at achieving this goal."[42]

One serious blow to this Arab unity come when Egypt signed a peace treaty with Israel (Camp David Accord) in 1979, which resulted in great tension between Egypt and several other Arab countries who opposed peace with Israel. For this action, Egypt was suspended from the Arab League but was re-admitted in 1989, when the headquarters returned to Cairo after being temporarily housed in Tunisia. Egypt was also excluded from the new satellite system, Arabsat, during the 1980s,[43] which later drove Egypt to launch its own satellite channel – Egyptian Satellite Channel (ESC). However, the role of the media as a mobilization tool continued and in fact the ESC channel was used during the 1991 Gulf War in order to provide Egyptian soldiers stationed in the Gulf with an alternative news diet than the one offered by the Iraqi media.[44]

## From scarcity to abundance

Scholars[45] agree that the 1991 Gulf War was the catalyst needed to initiate media reforms in the Arab region. The war was indeed a mark of the so-called CNN effect: Arab audiences with access to CNN followed the course of the war as it unfolded, despite the attempts by Arab traditional media to conceal the reality of this war, not to mention discussion of its real causes. Instead, the war was seen as a moral turmoil, particularly as the former American president George Bush used the metaphor of "Kuwait being raped"[46] to justify it. Arab artists, for example, the Kuwaiti singer Abdullah Roywashid, also used metaphors to pin down the fatal destiny behind the attack of one brother (Iraq) against another brother (Kuwait), affirming fraternal relationships among the Arab States.

Following the war, the Arab media scene witnessed an explosion in the number of satellite channels competing amongst themselves in offering new genres, such as debates and live news reports, similar to those offered by CNN.[47] Naturally, these new channels have had an impact on the development of the national and pan-Arab press. In terms of content, more specialized newspapers and magazines were launched. For example, the Egyptian Akbar el-Youm Publishing House issues a newspaper dedicated to crime news, another to celebrity news, and yet another to literature. The size of newspapers has also increased tremendously: the average number of pages in a daily newspaper increased from four to six pages during the 1940s to eight and ten pages during the 1980s,[48] doubling in the 1990s to reach twenty and twenty-two pages. The amount of soft news in the Arab press has also been on the increase, albeit much later than its initiation in Western news media. There is an increasing importance given to human-interest news in the so-called pan-Arab newspapers *al-Hayat* and *al-Sharq al-Awsat*. The Lebanese–Saudi *al-Hayat* has regular weekly supplements directed at different reader segments – young people, business, travel – and this type of news is also integrated in the daily paper.

The Arab press is now regarded as the catalyst for raising public awareness of global issues. This has indeed contributed to the reflexivity of Arab journalists over their own profession and output. For instance, prominent press journalists are regularly invited onto diverse talk shows on Arab satellite television, similar to the old print journalist practice of inviting media professionals from television and radio.[49] This has, in fact, reinforced the new role of prominent journalists in the political sphere, that is, as political experts. Moreover, there is now a tendency among Arab news channels to reflect upon their own journalistic practices, inviting news journalists to comment on their work and the difficulties facing them.[50]

There are several factors that have contributed towards the acceleration of changes on the Arab media scene during the past decade.[51] One of these factors is the emergence of a new generation of Arab journalists, who have either received a large part of their education and training in Western media institutions or have been educated in Western-oriented schools and colleges in their home countries. This new generation of Western-oriented and trained journalists is deemed an important catalyst to the introduction of new genres, such as political debates and talk shows, and more sophisticated interview techniques previously unpracticed by the Arab media.[52]

Another factor is the external competition that currently faces the Arab media. Drawing on its popularity during the 1991 Gulf War, CNN launched a website in Arabic, and several other media outlets have followed suit. CNBC Arabiya, for instance, was inaugurated on 27 July 2003.[53] Audience analyses conducted among Arab listeners during the 1980s showed a clear preference for foreign radio stations,[54] and, needless to say, the same stations were again the main source of news during the 1991 Gulf War. This competition may take an even broader dimension when the BBC launches its Arabic channel by the end of 2007. At the social level, there have been significant changes; chief among them is the importance of the English language in the Arab labor market. With increasing numbers of foreign corporations establishing a presence in several Arab countries, English has gained an important role as a new lingua franca within Arab labor markets. One natural outcome of this is that larger and larger segments of the population can follow the news media in English, albeit with some difficulty. Nevertheless, they become familiar in this way not only with the news genres but also with the debate traditions of the foreign media.

Thus, one can argue that large segments of Arab media outlets have, by and large, experienced a stable relationship between the political elites and the public until the disruption of the 1991 Gulf War. The increased access to transnational media (for example, CNN and BBC) since then has not only resulted in a more varied news diet being offered, it has also led to a change in professional practices. Thus, an opposition party press has appeared in Egypt, challenging the existing regime's ideology. The disruption caused by military operations in Iraq has further enforced distinctions among various religious and ethnic groups, with each claiming an ideological stance different from the other, for example, the multiplication of newspapers since the beginning of the war,[55] despite the claim that they all belong to one national fabric.

If increased commercialization, as Habermas[56] as well as other scholars claim,[57] has turned the media into a liaison between advertisers and customers rather than between politicians and citizens, it has in the Arab context resulted in a transformation of content, with a slight increase in soft news as well as rival political news presentation, for example, party press in Egypt. Despite the difference in ethnic, religious, class and gender aspects, some regional media outlets, such as the so-called pan-Arab press and satellite news channels, attempt to address as wide an audience base as possible, as an "imagined community". It has thus renewed its ideological weight among Arab journalists, who now propagate it as part of their role.[58] Hence, pan-Arabism has become a "unique selling point," a marketing strategy that aims at benefiting from increased market share.[59]

One characteristic of this pan-Arabism is, as al-Jazeera presenter Ghassan Ben Jeddou argues,[60] the number of Arab nationalities working together in these channels rather than confining their staff to the Mashreq area (or the countries lying to the east of Egypt, that is, Lebanon, Jordan, Syria, Palestine, and usually including Egypt and Iraq as well). However, those presenters who have managed to create a high profile for themselves on satellite channels still come predominately from the Mashreq area, argue a number of Moroccan female presenters. For instance, Fatima Baroudi, a Moroccan TV presenter, says that Moroccans constitute a minority in these channels, dominated mainly by Egyptian and Lebanese presenters. This, she argues, is due to the role of "personal contacts" as one main way to access this competitive field.[61] Another Moroccan presenter, Fatima Annawal, attributes the limited number of Moroccan presenters on pan-Arab channels to the fact that most of these channels are located in Lebanon, the Emirates and Egypt.[62] Moreover, language plays an important role in facilitating or delaying this access, as the Moroccan dialect is seen as distinctively different from the Mashreq area and hence mutually unintelligible compared to the Lebanese and Egyptian vernaculars. In addition, a recent study of the relationship between language (vernacular) and identity among Moroccan women in the UAE[63] points to the stereotype of Moroccan women as easy targets and "men stealers," referring in particular to the tendency during the 1980s and 1990s to bring Moroccan women to the country as second wives or even mistresses.

To recapitulate, the new(s) satellite channels, as well as the pan-Arab press, have provided a new era of "plenty",[64] performing a new function compared to the former era where the "plenty" was usually foreign and imported. The aim is to unite a multitude of audiences, within and outside the Middle East, connecting and yet keeping them apart. Thus, the new era can be argued to "provide a voluntary point of social cohesion, of being-together while being-apart."[65] A recent poll among a sample of Arab citizens[66] has shown that a large percentage of the respondents, thanks to the proliferation of pan-Arab media, particularly satellite channels, sympathize with general Arab issues; yet up to 40 percent of the respondents acknowledged the increasing differences among Arabs. This, argues Marc Lynch,[67] "follows from an exceptionally important change in the way this new public conceives of Arab identity," referring in particular to the consensus that takes for granted that certain causes are inherently Arab, for example, Palestine or Iraq, while differences arise as to how to deal with these issues.

However, I argue that the reason for this ambivalence is not necessarily to be found in politics or any media coverage of it; rather, one should look at the change in the Arab media scene as a whole in order to see the intersection between serious genres (such as news and political debates) and entertainment genres (such as popular talk shows, series and films). In particular, I refer to the fact that news coverage, in pan-Arab and local media alike, tends to focus on foreign politics and hence on "shared" issues of concern, such as the Israeli–Palestinian conflict. Yet, it is important to recall that news occupies only a minor part of the airtime on several of these channels, and even the news channels such as al-Jazeera have to compete with a vast and growing number of variety channels broadcasting TV series produced in different Arab States, in the vernacular associated with each state. Thus, if the news is about "shared" causes and is produced in the predominant written language (MSA), the variety programs by contrast deploy the diverse Arab vernacular and draw on local themes and concerns. In other words, the ambivalent relationship to the "pan-Arab identity" lies precisely in the audiences' tendency to wander between the universal (causes and language that are said to bind them together) and the particular (local issues in different dialects), fostering at once a sharing of regional togetherness and distinct nationalist identity.

This ambivalent stance towards pan-Arabism was further manifested in the attitudes of Arab audiences and participants in the pan-Arab Games.[68] The games were established in 1953 as a symbol of Arab cultural unity, although recent contests such as that in Jordan in 1999 staged parades of nationalist feelings among audiences and participants alike. The games, then, along with similar ideological projects, add to the tension between nationalism and regional solidarity.[69] Kraidy[70] provides a further illustration of this tension in his analysis of reality TV programs on pan-Arab channels, where the elimination of a Lebanese contestant in the reality program *Super Star* resulted in riots throughout Beirut in suspicion that Syria was behind the elimination in order to support their semi-finalist. The huge popularity of such programs and their impact on fueling feelings of nationalism among Arab audiences has even pushed political activists such as Hamas to dissuade Palestinians from following these programs, calling for "real heroes" and fighters rather than "singers and corruption mongers."[71]

## Internal hierarchy

Previous studies[72] seem to take the pan-Arab value for granted without questioning this ambivalent attitude to shared identity. This also over-looks an important debate concerning language and identity, which has been ongoing for centuries. Suleiman[73] succinctly points to the sym-bolic role of language in forming a national identity in the Middle East. His analysis provides evidence for the awakening of such links over the past two centuries. For example, Qandil[74] dedicates a whole book to his argument that the Egyptian identity and language is markedly dis-tinct and cannot therefore be subsumed under the all-encompassing label "Arab", which, according to him, refers to the identity imposed by former colonial powers and has no historical or cultural validity. The subtle relationship between language and identity should not be underestimated within the media context, for it can prove to be very fruitful in empirical analyses of textual representations as well as in fieldwork among Arab audiences and/or journalists, for example, the impact of deploying the formal written variant of Arabic (MSA) in news and current affairs programs versus the various dialects in pro-ducing variety programs, and the consequence this has on enforcing versus enfeebling a shared Arab identity (see also the discussion in Chapter 3 on the role of MSA).

Arab leaders have realized the political implication of enforcing this pan-Arab identity: it could add political weight to the region by aiding the formation of a single political actor rather than diverse nations, each with limited power. However, an internal struggle to gain political power exists among Arab States, for example, in the Arab League, which has resulted in difficulty in drawing up a unified communications policy.[75] This struggle has been intensified in the cultural arena of the media, in as much as pan-Arab news media outlets enter into an internal struggle to obtain and retain the posi-tion of credible agenda-setter. In so doing, the media defines, and perhaps re-defines, the concept of Arabism for example, what issues ought to be discussed as inherently pan-Arab, or the representation of Arabs, not only as a "group in itself" but also as a "group for itself."[76] This is to suggest an internal–external dialect of definition: on the one hand, the identity of belonging to a certain group (a group *for* itself) and on the other hand the external identification by others (a group *in* itself).

A possible starting point from which to research the pan-Arab journalistic field is to pin down the main indicators of this pan-identity in terms of internal hierarchy (among internal players in the regional scene) as well as external hierarchy (how the pan-Arab actors see themselves vis-à-vis global media players such as CNN). Given the nature of pan-Arab media outlets as addressing primarily regional (and even global) audiences from within the region or in Diaspora communities, it is interesting to analyze this hierarchy in light of the fact that Arab media outlets are decentralized, with some of them in the newly established media cities (in Egypt, Jordan and the Emirates) while others are outside the region (in London).

Benson[77] argues for the need to map out the journalistic field not only at national level but also on a global scale. Indeed, journalists represent a cohort of cosmopolitans, as Hannerz shows us in the case of foreign correspondents who exhibit "an awareness and appreciation of diversity in modes of thought, ways of life, and human products and to the development of skills in handling such diversity."[78] Due to the nature of their work, news journalists are cosmopolitans par excellence engaged in the continuous process of interpretation and meaning-making across distance.[79]

Seeing the Arab journalistic field in the context of global news media means unraveling the weight that global media such as CNN and the BBC occupy in this domain, and whether such global media play the role model to follow. Would Arab journalists, for instance, see American political news as an important ingredient in the daily news diet, assuming thereby their audiences' interest in this type of news?[80] If this is the case, then the media consumption pattern among Arab journalists should reflect this, for example, regularly reading international newspapers such as the *New York Times*, or watching CNN. It would also show in the development of the news genre.[81]

Global media outlets such as CNN and BBC have exerted an influence on the news agenda in national news media around the world (see Chapter 6). They have also attracted a huge audience of Arab citizens, particularly from the 1950s until the mid-1990s, or before the advent of satellite news channels.[82] Moreover, besides serving as a source for other national and regional news media, such global media may also help revolutionize the media content on Arab channels. For instance, the Egyptian TV presenter Yasmin Abdallah (from the Egyptian Satellite Channel, ESC) once declared that female circumcision was debated on Egyptian channels only after CNN aired a program about it. It then became imperative for the Egyptian media (and government) to respond to the raised debate.[83]

Each player on the media scene enjoys a share of power, determined by the overall political and/or economic weight of the host country/ ownership. Being located outside the Middle East, the London-based pan-Arab newspapers have managed to profile themselves through press review programs in the Arab channels. For instance, BBC Arabic radio usually draws on the four pan-Arab newspapers (*al-Hayat, al-Sharq al-Awsat, al-Quds al-Arabi* and *al-Ahram*) in their daily review of the Arab press. Likewise, the increase in TV supplements in the pan-Arab press[84] indeed signals the weight of TV on the Arab media scene. Future analysis could indicate whether this relationship has resulted in the development of the news genre accordingly. For example, the TV news usually draws on the image as well as different "testimonials"[85] from laypeople and officials alike, which marks the difference between newspaper and TV genre characteristics. However, will the increasing interdependence amongst the media result in a blurring of these differences, for example, by increasing the number of images in newspapers, enforcing the role of newspaper correspondent as eyewitness, or by citing ordinary citizens as sources?

In sum, the political power assigned to each Arab State, which determines the internal hierarchy in the regional political field, seems to be reflected in the pan-Arab media scene. For instance, these satellite channels seem to adhere to a policy of not entering into details about the local affairs of Arab States,[86] particularly social taboos. However, political taboos, discussed on these channels, seem to be in proportion with the size (and political weight) of each Arab State, which is the reason some commentators use to justify al-Jazeera's tendency to move away from the problems in its host country, Qatar.[87] In fact, one presenter on such a satellite channel warns that this tendency may damage Arab unity as prejudice and stereotyping prevails among Arab nationals, for example, the stereotype of an Egyptian belly dancer; the figure of the rich Gulf man; the Lebanese merchant.[88] In this age of satellite channels, stereotyping has taken another direction, with the Lebanese channels being a magnet for some of the most attractive female TV presenters, who in turn attract the wealthy Gulf audience.[89] Some Arabs commonly make a pun of this by playing on words, replacing the acronym of the Lebanese satellite channel LBC with the Arab gender-inflected verb *Elbesi* (or "dress up"), referring to the female hosts' tiny dresses and music videos broadcast featuring women in flimsy clothes.[90]

## Popularity of the field

One columnist of the pan-Arab daily *al-Sharq al-Awsat* wondered about the situation of some novice journalists in the region.[91] She particularly referred to one journalist she met, who had just began his career. The journalist complained about chief-editors who rarely offer financial rewards, which, for him, was a misuse of his and other newcomers' talents. The columnist did not bring up this story out of sympathy for the journalist's situation. Rather, she used it to juxtapose the situation now with the situation when she began her career (obviously many years ago). She paid tribute to her former editors, who declined from paying her for her first articles. Her first financial reward, however, came years later when she compiled her articles and sold them in one volume.

But if working in print journalism as a field is not particularly rewarding, how can the press attract new trainees? The attraction to any profession probably correlates with the reputation associated with that profession. For instance, if the reputation of chemists becomes related to weaponry and bombs, it will be much less attractive for young people to join it. Arab journalists' reputation has fluctuated with the rise and fall of press freedom in each country. Subservience to colonial powers during the nineteenth and the first half of the twentieth centuries had in fact contributed to enhance the journalists' image. The newspapers issued then called for independence and unity, which attracted a wide readership. In the beginning of the 1940s, for example, several Lebanese journalists who called for the independence of the country from colonial power boosted their public image.[92] After independence, however, several Arab countries had to deal with other type of power, namely the military and dictatorship. In Egypt, for instance, the new government, consisting of army officers who led the revolution of 1952, put a stop to partisan press. Several journalists were detained for writing on issues or in a style that the government regarded as provocative. Among them was the Egyptian veteran journalist Moustafa Amin, who was detained in 1952 for publishing material the government regarded as damaging for its authority.[93]

Yet, the new independent Arab States regarded the news media as their representatives among the masses, thereby controlling the flow and the content of news media rather than seeing the media as a forum to foster the longed-for democracy. Consequently, journalists' integrity has been questioned by a readership that saw their national press turning into a mouthpiece for the government. Awatef Abdel Rahman[94] pointed at this as one of the serious challenges facing journalists and the journalism profession in the region. In Algeria, Kirat[95] argues, the profession of journalism has lost respect and consideration from both its practitioners and the audience. The journalist is not very well-regarded and welcomed in offices and administrations; the audience does not trust him/her, and the people do not want to hear or deal with journalism or journalists. Because of the difficult conditions in which they operate, journalists have not been able to gain the sympathy of the readers.

Algerian print journalists, particularly women, expressed similar frustration with regard to the impact of the status of their work on their private lives. Some of them recalled the difficulty in getting married, as men equate journalism with late working hours, meeting men, facing dangers, and so on, or, as one Algerian female journalist put it, "The Algerian society still looks at the female journalist as a woman who smokes and mixes and indulges in relationships with men."[96]

And yet, journalism is currently one of the most popular subjects for female Arab students at Arab universities. In Lebanon alone, women students in journalism and communication constitute around 85 percent of the total number of students, which is higher than the numbers in several European schools.[97] This is not surprising if we take into account that female as well as male Arab journalists, particularly in satellite channels, have become stars known for their bravery in reporting from the heart of violence, for example, the Iraq War or the Palestinian *Intifada*. They have become the new "heroes" who endure harassment, murder, and arrest in pursuit of their truth-seeking mission.[98] The power of the Fourth Estate has become very much related to its reporters' stamina, and their solidarity with one another in confirming the credence of their profession. Arab TV presenters, particularly in the satellite channels, have become glamorous celebrities too, admired by thousands of fans. The attractive female presenters in variety programs, particularly the Lebanese, have become "dream women" for millions of young Arab men,[99] whereas the "brave" female and male presenters in the more "serious" news channels, hosting hot political debates, can now claim to "outshine" pop stars in popularity among the Arab youth.[100]

It is not only TV presenters who have become stars on the screen and frequent guests in the audience's favorite programs; print journalists have claimed their own share of fame as well. Prominent press journalists also host their own TV programs, for example, the Egyptian Hamdy Qandil has his own program on Egyptian television called *Ra'is al-Tahrir* (or *Editor-in-Chief*), and the former *al-Ahram* editor Mohamed H. Heikal has his own program slot in al-Jazeera (*Ma' Heikal*, or *With Heikal*). This has, as mentioned before, reinforced the new role of prominent journalists as political experts. Likewise, in Lebanon, several journalists sought to enter the parliamentary elections in 2000. One of them was the head of the *Voice of People* radio, and he defended the tendency among journalists to seek political careers by affirming that the journalist is closer to understanding political work than is, for example, the medical doctor or engineer. For him, "the relation between the journalism and politics is solid."[101]

However, the seriousness of the politics in, for example, hard news and current affairs programs is now scorned by a rising breed of journalists specializing in "soft" and light talk shows. For instance, in a special episode of al-Jazeera's program *From Washington*, about the place of the USA in Egyptian popular talk-shows, one of the guests, a famous Egyptian "light" talk-show host, began by sarcastically reprimanding al-Jazeera host, Hafez al-Merazi, for dumping the smiley face and adopting a grumpy one once the camera had turned on, in order to look "serious."[102] I shall come back to the tension between political and light talk shows in Chapter 4.

## Gendered newsrooms

Wu & Weaver[103] remark upon the increase of female students in journalism schools in less developed countries such as China, and wonder whether this could serve as an indication of a new trend of "feminizing" journalism. Could we extend this argument to the Arab region, arguing that the presence of female Arab journalists will inevitably lead to a change within the field and perhaps in the distribution of capital?

In Saudi Arabia, Wright[104] found that the women reporters, at least those he met, were much more educated by far than men journalists, despite the fact that women constituted only 6 percent of the workforce in journalism. In Kuwait, more than 70 percent of graduates in mass communications department are female. Most of them abandon the field and find work in other fields, either due to family concerns or because of people's misconception of the profession.[105] Another study that dealt with the working situation of women journalists in Lebanese TV stations[106] showed that typical women journalists, although they held higher degrees than their men colleagues, expressed more insecurity about maintaining their jobs compared to their men colleagues. They were also less likely to be promoted to higher positions, although they worked as hard as their male colleagues. In fact, women journalists identified double standards among men as the main reason for men promoting other men, and even those women who managed to get professional recognition did not receive much acknowledgement among their women colleagues, who regarded the promotion as a reward for these journalists' involvement in personal relationships with their bosses. The hierarchical gap between male and female journalists was also reflected in their financial rewards: while men received educational subsidies for their children, insurance, and other benefits, women journalists typically received subsidies for make-up, hairdressing, and the like. This played a role in the journalists' view of the success criteria in the profession: male journalists defined experience as the most significant criterion, while their female colleagues saw that appearance and youth were the most crucial criteria. Also, the way each group viewed their role differed: men typically related their task to educating the public, while women journalists saw that entertaining the public as their primary responsibility.[107]

A previous study by UNESCO[108] found that women journalists in several Arab States are still in the minority compared to men journalists (particularly in print media). Even when women reach senior positions, this seniority cannot be the sole marker of the "feminization" of content due to the presence of scores of prohibitions that control the broadcasting protocol, for example, taboo subjects that relate to religion, family, female circumcision, and so on, all of which make it difficult for women journalists, even those in senior positions, to change the status quo.[109]

In another study, Abdel Rahman[110] points to the segregation of content depending on its feminization. Thus, letters to the editor written by women were rarely published, especially if they dealt with women's issues. Even when the women's section sought to present a role model for women, they usually referred to an American woman, thereby ignoring other role models from the region. Moreover, women's sections seem to become the exile of those women journalists who are not wanted in other sections. Political sections are the number one prestigious section, followed by economics, society, and, at the bottom, women's sections.

According to Abel Rahman,[111] some women journalists have managed to reach senior positions in the Egyptian press, but only in women's or children's magazines. Yet, journalism education has been a magnet for hundreds of female students in the region, as mentioned above, although those students usually aspire to a career on screen rather than in the print media.[112] Working in the press is more demanding, as the Jordanian Rana Husseini (from the English-language daily, *Jordan Times*) proved. Husseini won her fame through a series of articles on honor killings in Jordan, a controversial issue that brought her great intimidation (although it was reported that she was backed by the Jordanian royal family). Husseini visited some hospitals and police stations to gather information about recent incidents of honor killings In her articles, she concealed any clear identifiers of the victims' identities.[113]

Women, however, have dominated the new and abundant variety channels, where their fame beats that of pop stars and even sex icons such as Marilyn Monroe,[114] leading the pan-Arab newspaper *al-Sharq al-Awsat* to question whether there would be an "expiry date" for female TV journalists. One of the TV presenters interviewed, the Lebanese Soad Qarout, acknowledged that the increasing number of young media graduates may have an impact on the jobs available to elderly female journalists. Nonetheless, she argues, the experienced and professional bulletin reader, embodied in an elderly female presenter, plays an important role in adding "credibility" to the news.

In addition to being deployed as "bait" to attract high viewership, female broadcasters have also marked themselves in the serious genres of news and debate. One example is the Jordanian Montaha al-Romhei, who was one of the stars at al-Jazeera and now at al-Arabiya. She talked proudly about her capabilities as a news anchor, being particularly able to hide her emotions with her firm look to the camera; she regards the combination of presenting news and debates as a plus, compared to her male colleagues who won their fame in debates only.[115] Another al-Jazeera star, the Algerian Khadija Ben Qana, warns against the inclination of some of those presenters to host diversity and light shows, which, in her opinion, "kills their image."[116]

In fact, Ben Qana won the hearts of a large segment of al-Jazeera's audiences when she appeared with the veil (*hijab*) during the French debates over the banning of the veil in French public schools. Ironically, Ben Qana herself fled her home country of Algeria when she was threatened with having to wear the *hijab*.[117] Likewise, the past three years have witnessed a number of protests from Egyptian TV presenters who have been suspended from appearing on the screen after wearing the *hijab*. Some of the presenters went to court and got permission to practice their "personal freedom". The court thus overruled the decision of the Minister of Information in suspending them.

Furthermore, women journalists have particularly proven their abilities as reporters, since being a woman could be an advantage in that women are usually regarded as less threatening.[118] For instance, TV journalists, particularly those working in the Palestinian territories, are often seen to epitomize bravery in practicing this "trouble-seeking profession". Abu Dhabi TV correspondent Laila Ouda, for instance, recalled her difficult "mission" in covering Palestinian affairs, including being shot in the foot once in Rafah, but said, "This did not stop me from resuming my media mission."[119] For al-Jazeera correspondent in the Palestinian territories, Sherine Abu Aqla, the Palestinian journalist in particular is a solider-figure: "The Palestinian journalist fights by the side of his Palestinian brother who fights with sword. . .we fight to reach the truth, nothing else." [120]

Female journalists usually have higher degrees, as shown for example in the empirical study reported on in al-Qadry & Harb.[121] This study, carried out among men and women journalists in Lebanese TV stations, documented the high educational level, that is, university degrees as well as mastery of one or more foreign languages, among television journalists, and yet points to the constant role of social and personal contacts in accessing the field. This, in sum, enforces the combined role of education and contacts as means to access this highly competitive field.

## Access to the field

There exist two Arabic words referring to the work of a journalist: one is *sahafi* and the other is *i'lamai*, usually designating the print journalist and the broadcast journalist, respectively. According to Ibrahim Helal, former editor of al-Jazeera, the word "*sahafi*" has an incorrect implication in Arabic compared to English, where the word "journalist" refers to reporters in either print or broadcasting.[122] This points to the blurring of the boundaries between working in broadcasting versus print media, particularly if we recall the status enjoyed by certain print journalists due to their appearance as "experts" on the newly emerged satellite channels. If the distinction between the two sub-fields is still effectual, this may have an implication on new entrants to the journalism field in terms of their education and training.

In order to provide a detailed account of the journalistic field, it is imperative to consider issues such as education, autonomy, and code of ethics in shaping the professional identity of Arab journalists. Previous studies[123] show that the majority of Arab journalists hold a college degree, although there is generally a lack of on-the-job training.[124] However, we know little of their reasons for entering this field, for example, whether it was out of an interest to exert an influence on another inaccessible field, as Weaver argues: "People who go into journalism are typically people with a strong attraction to politics, sports, business, or some other arena in organized society but people who stop short of actually becoming a politician or executive and choose to stand on the sidelines as an observer instead."[125]

Kirat's survey[126] among Algerian journalists shows that a large percentage of the respondents give their main reason for joining the field as the wish to help the country and their landsmen. Al-Rasheed's[127] survey among Kuwaiti journalists shows that most of the respondents would choose journalism again as a career, if they had a chance to start again, and would even recommend it to their sons (although not to their daughters!). This stems from a belief that journalism does exert an influence over public opinion.

Yet, according to al-Jammal,[128] access to jobs in print journalism is not open to all citizens in the Arab region. Six of the Arab countries (Egypt, Sudan, Saudi Arabia, Lebanon, Tunisia, and Morocco) do not enforce any conditions for people wanting to work in this field, while other countries (Kuwait, Bahrain, Qatar, Oman, Syria, Yemen, Libya, and Algeria) require that incoming journalists should obtain a license from the authorities. The same situation, however, does not apply to the electronic media, particularly the newly emerged satellite channels, which makes it imperative to inquire into the definition of a journalist and what distinguishes this profession from others, for example, talent, specific educational degrees, or contacts. As Turkestani[129] argues, one needs to have personal contacts to get the job with the minimum requirements, whereas advancing in the job hierarchy demands mastery of voice and editorial skills.

Some Arab scholars seem to value "innate" talent polished with the relevant educational degrees. For instance, Abdel Nabi[130] groups print journalists into four main categories, according to their skills and talent:

1. Those who had relevant education and talent;
2. Those who had relevant education but no talent;
3. Those who do not have relevant education but have talent;
4. Those who do not have talent or education (particularly those who worked in other fields, such as administration, before obtaining their college degree as a ticket to the journalistic field).

While there is an abundance of journalists from the second to fourth categories, there is a shortage of journalists of the first category (with education and talent), argues Abdel Nabi, thereby stressing the importance of talent, rather than training alone, as a prerequisite for the profession. Thus, "learning by doing" seems to be the main strategy in working in the television sector, which has experienced a huge expansion during the past decade. As one Lebanese station manager put it, "TV is a sea that we throw you in. Either you swim or you drown."[131]

Although relevant education is valued, news media institutions are accused of headhunting ready-trained professionals rather than investing in educational programs for novice talents. According to Amr Nassef (from the Hezbollah-supported channel, al-Manar TV), the news media, especially the satellite channels, would rather headhunt the best caliber of broadcasters in the field rather than train new talent.[132] However, this trend may be changing, as the recent decade has witnessed the inclination of certain media institutions to enhance their own training facilities. For instance, Akbar el-Youm Publishing House, located in the Media City in Cairo, launched its own academy inaugurated by the Egyptian president on 6 October 1998. The academy offers BSc degrees in Media Studies, equivalent to the degrees offered by national universities. It aims to develop journalistic practice in Egypt and provide a new caliber of journalists with a wide range of specialties. One of the aims was to apply an "open door" policy towards foreign media schools via special agreements. The rationale behind this academy was to provide for the constant need for advanced technical specialization and a highly trained workforce. Al-Jazeera has also launched its own academy, which offers short vocational courses and organizes seminars and workshops. The academy draws on the expertise of a British organization that offers instructors and curricula for these courses.[133]

Providing highly-specialized training for press as well as broadcast journalism is one means of distinguishing journalism as a "profession," especially in the current era where the Internet has served as a platform to a large number of new, alternative media. Central here is the formation of professional associations with shared codes by which journalists abide. The following section briefly touches upon the importance of such associations in fostering a collective identity shared by the new entrants as well as established journalists, with particular regard to the Arab context in which several pan-Arab media outlets are dispersed within and outside the Middle East region.

## Institutional identity

Al-Jammal[134] argues that, in the Middle East, the organization of journalists and communication professionals is subject to the internal policy of each country. Arab governments control the communication profession with laws and rules, despite the fact that constitutions in the same countries have not included such rules.[135] The authorities justify this interference by their wish to maintain political and social stability within civil society. The establishment of journalist syndicates in the Arab region began in the 1940s and '50s, lagging behind those in other countries. The labor force was allowed the right to be organized into syndicates according to their professions, so printing workers were organized in an syndicate independent from journalists. In Lebanon, for instance, there exist two syndicates: one for newspaper-owners and another for journalists. Such organizations seek to ensure journalists' rights in protecting their sources as well as defending their rights to write without facing the risk of judicial penalty or pressure of any kind.

Likewise, the Yemeni Journalists Syndicate is one of two press organizations in Yemen. It has the right to give or withdraw membership, and it usually takes the side of journalists in the struggle for increased freedom, but without making the syndicate an anti-government organization. Although the syndicate is not affiliated to any political party or organization, its rather pro-government stance pushed several journalists to form another union, the Committee for the Defense of Journalists, in 1999.[136]

As al-Jammal[137] sees it, these labor organizations can be classified into three types: the first belongs to those countries that prohibit any form of such organizations; the second type belongs to countries where journalists themselves are unaware of the significance of the work of such syndicates; and the third type refers to other cases in which journalism has not yet been maturely developed as a profession and thus there is no urgent need for such syndicates.

On the other hand, we should not neglect the impact of the re-distribution of journalists from those countries with a longer press history, such as Egypt and Lebanon, to those who developed a modern press culture in the twentieth century, such as several Gulf countries.[138] For instance, in Kuwait, a large number of press journalists are non-Kuwaiti, which in turn plays a role in the degree of attachment to professional unions and organizations. Al-Rasheed's survey[139] shows that most of the Kuwaiti journalists were more active in the press association, compared to non-Kuwaitis, and particularly that the constitution of the association prerequisites Kuwaiti citizenship for an active membership or for taking part in the general assembly meetings.

Also, the waves of émigré press[140] have resulted in the dispersion of pan-Arab media outlets inside and outside the region. Given that the pan-Arab media outlets are decentralized, with some having their headquarters in European cities (particularly London) and others in Arab capitals such as Beirut and Cairo, it is important to consider the implications of this on the organization of journalists, now subjected to different legislative and cultural regulations. In the Arab countries, editors, rather than organizational regulations, exert a great power inside the newsroom. For instance, one prominent TV presenter (Mohamed Kreishan, al-Jazeera) pointed out that a change of editor may be accompanied by a change in the whole editorial policy, and hence inconsistency. What is needed, he argued, is the kind of "institutionalism" enjoyed by well-established media outlets such as the BBC, so that a managerial change would not cause any change to existing policies.[141] One important implication of this commentary is whether those pan-Arab outlets located in London, such as BBC Arabic or *al-Hayat*, do indeed adhere to different institutional constraints regarding their editorial policy, as well as to their organization into professional unions.

## Measuring success

The capital assigned to the participants in the field is convertible into prestige and status within and outside the same field. Thus, winning a prize or an award is an appreciation from one's peers, which indeed increases the "value" of reporters who obtain this prestige.[142] The past few years have seen a keen interest among Arab media forums and officials in organizing journalistic prizes and awards. For example, Dubai and Beirut have now become centers for journalism prizes: the Dubai Press Club has introduced the Arab Press Award (in 1999), under the auspices of the crown emir of Dubai, with the aim of promoting creativity in the field;[143] and Beirut has recently become the center of the Middle East Broadcasting Award (MEB), a 24-carat, gold-plated Mebby, manufactured by the same company that produces the Oscar and Emmy Awards.[144]

In addition, prestige may be gained in the profession via the ability of journalists to invite leading Western, as well as regional, figures to appear as sources/guests on a political show. This can create a snow-ball effect in TV journalism in particular. For example, when al-Arabiya News channel, in December 2005, aired a controversial interview with Abdul Halim Khaddam, the former Syrian vice president, other channels, newspapers and radio stations followed suit and competed for a statement from Khaddam, whose attack on the Syrian regime made sensational headlines. Sources then exert an influence on determining the amount of capital possessed by the media, and hence its power in the hierarchy.

Another means of converting capital into status lies in the commercial success of the journalists' output. Al-Jazeera's most famous TV presenter, Faisal al-Kasim, wrote proudly of how copies of his program were sold in video shops, and a copy of one particular episode was even sold in the black market for a hundred dollars. Clearly, commercial value is not sufficient, as it only reflects the popular capital gained among the public; however, as professionals, journalists are keen to gain more recognition amongst their peers and colleagues from inside the region and, perhaps more importantly, from foreign institutions. Al-Kasim, for instance, recalled the attention his program gained in Western countries, which drove scores of journalists from Europe and USA to visit his show and interview him, in order to produce articles or whole documentaries about the show.[145] In the same vein, Abdel Bari Atwan, the chief-editor of the pan-Arab newspaper *al-Quds al-Arabi*, based in London, relates the objectivity of his newspaper to the invitations he received from various Western news media to comment on important Arab events,[146] arguing that he would not have been invited if his newspaper was not known for its objectivity. The implication of this view, then, is that the yardstick of measuring objectivity is based on Western criteria, for example, the messages and guests for whom the Western news media provide space. It may also indicate an implicit hierarchy of media institutions in which the top places are occupied by the most global and international institutions, such as the BBC and CNN, whose credibility will also benefit those who appear in their news stories as sources. Chapter 6 discusses in more detail this role of Western media as yardstick.

## Analytical framework

Based on the above discussion of the various factors characterizing the
Arab journalism field, I provide the following grid as a more systematic framework for future empirical analyses of the hierarchy of power,
for example, in fieldwork among Arab journalists in diverse media
outlets in different countries (within and outside the Middle East).

This hierarchy is diagrammed in figure 2.1.
The grid is based on three factors:

1. The main target audience(s): this is an important factor in determining the impact of the media on public opinion as well as the intersection between the field of journalism and the fields of politics and
   economics.
2. Journalists' power (according to their cultural capital): this is crucial
   in understanding the particularity of the Arab journalistic culture
   and how it may differ locally as well as regionally.
3. Content: media outlets, whether regional or local, should be measured
   according to their content, for example, commercial/popularized or
   political/elitist. Central here is the style and language used in different

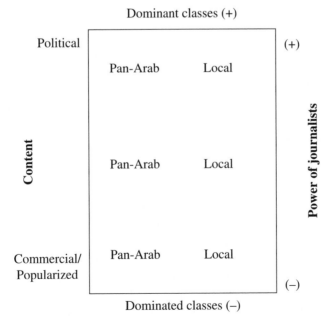

**Figure 2.1** The distribution of power among Arab news media

content and how this may affect the popularity of each media outlet (see Chapters 3 and 4 for a detailed discussion).

At the top of the grid $(++)$ are those media outlets that appeal to the elite classes and whose journalists enjoy a large portion of cultural capital, that is, education and knowledge of certain policies. These journalists also enjoy more fame than others in the same field, and they may even act as political commentators rather than only as journalists. Crucial to their cultural capital is also their mastery and use of the written variety of Arabic (MSA) (see Chapter 3).

At the bottom of the grid $(--)$ are those media outlets whose content primarily targets the dominated classes. Here, content is popular/commercial, thus serving the economic interests of these media organizations in as much as it appeals to as wide a segment of the audience as possible. Journalists in these outlets may not be as famous or influential in the field in general as those positioned at the top of the grid; yet, they enjoy a large share of recognition due to the popularity of their programs, not to mention that the style and language adopted in these programs tends to appeal to the laity rather than the elites, for example, using the vernaculars rather than MSA.

Each of these poles represents a cultural territory: one elitist and one popularized. In between these two poles, there are other outlets with content and practices that mixes the elitist with the non-elitist perspective.

The elitist content refers mostly to the hardcore political talk shows, particularly those concerned with foreign policy issues. The popularized genres can also include political shows but these may deal instead with local politics, which may be seen as a "soft" topic. Therefore, each pole or territory may embrace pan-Arab as well as local media outlets, because some pan-Arab outlets may indeed depend on "popularized" programs while others "specialize" in more elitist content.

The power of journalists influences the weight given to each medium and even their host country, while being influenced by the content. For instance, a channel such as al-Jazeera managed to profile its host country Qatar as a beacon for press freedom, thanks to its cadre of journalists and their practices rather than the Qatari press tradition.

Moreover, it is important to recall that the real power lies in the agents' ability to manipulate the dominant norms and discourses enforced within the field in order to justify their acts against these very norms and discourses. For instance, the outlets placed at the top of the grid may exhibit particular characteristics in their utilization of the resources made available to them, for example, technology, while those at the bottom of the grid may not enjoy the same resources. Also, journalists in the elitist outlets interact more with policy-makers than do those from the popularized outlets, making the former group more influential in setting the standards of the profession. Yet, the latter group also enters this struggle over resources and power in as much as they seek to promote themselves as "representatives" of the laity, thereby offering a challenging yardstick for success in this field.

In general, journalists working with certain political issues may enjoy more power than do those dealing with "softer" issues. The former group, as mentioned above, enjoys a large share of cultural capital, defined as a significant share of education (as a synonym of knowledge) and an elitist linguistic code, that is, MSA.

The above grid serves as an analytical tool to map out the Arab journalistic field based on interaction between structure and agency rather than on either one alone. It also goes beyond the idealization of certain media outlets as liberal or autonomous without accounting for their position vis-à-vis other media outlets and focuses on how journalistic practices there influence and are influenced by other media. The aim, then, is to analyze the complex relation between content and power; local and regional; content and audience; and between journalists' power and content.

## Conclusion

The aim of this chapter was to open the arena for stimulating future research on Arab journalism, focusing on both "agents" and "structure." My theoretical frame is Bourdieu's field theory, which takes into account the dialectical relation between agents (journalists) and structure (media institutions). The strength of Bourdieu's theory, according to Benson,[147] lies in its focus on the "mezzo-level" of practice rather than adopting an either/or view of research spearing macro-societal levels from micro-organizational approaches. It is also the theory of power, where participants engage in a continuous struggle to gain power through accumulation of capital, unevenly distributed among them.

I have, albeit briefly, provided some pointers which could inform future research. Chief among these is the definition of power and how it is practiced in the Arab journalistic field. By this I mean the distribution of power among the different media players, particularly the so-called pan-Arab news media such as al-Jazeera TV or *al-Hayat* newspaper. In order to be able to impose a certain set of beliefs, one needs to accumulate symbolic capital and hence power; but, to reach this aim, one has to "command credit" and be seen as a credible authority.[148]

In the next two chapters, I resume this discussion with particular focus on the content of the news in the prestigious news media outlets such as al-Jazeera or *al-Hayat* versus that in the so-called yellow press or tabloids. Central here is whether news media have managed to serve as a public sphere allowing for diverse voices in the debate and current affairs programs. My overall aim is to provide cursors for an unexplored research area that could offer a solid basis for current debate concerning Arab journalism and Arab news media.

# Chapter 3

# Journalism as a Beacon for Democracy

The recent development on the Arab media scene proves there has been a fundamental change to the formation of and participation in public debates. Earlier studies[1] argued that, prior to the 1990s, Arab media were controlled by governments with the sole aim of keeping laypeople uninformed, and hence unprepared to participate in a rational debate. Alterman[2] provides an optimistic vision of this development, arguing that certain media outlets, particularly al-Jazeera, have indeed served as modern "coffee houses," moving the traditional space of rational discussion from salons and public gatherings to the air. Other scholars[3] share this view, seeing in the new channels evidence of pluralism and diverse opinions, a rich basis for vigorous public debate.

Thus, the recent development in the Arab media landscape has urged new analyses of the relation between media and citizen deliberation, drawing in particular on Habermas's model of the public sphere, rather than examining the applicability of this very model to non-Western contexts.

The public sphere is first and foremost a space for exchanging information on common topics, which in turn form public opinion. However, the notion of the public sphere implies an idealized form of public participation; so, when the people show a willingness to participate in the political process, they are hailed as rational beings acting out of a utilitarian interest in their own progress and happiness. If, however, they deploy the democratic means available to them to support a reactionary movement, for example, rightist parties, they are then "portrayed by intellectuals as being duped by ideology, manipulated by the media, and seduced by politicians."[4] Central issues here are how to conceptualize the laity and the criteria needed to ensure their participation in rational debate about shared issues.

This chapter discusses this normative model of the public sphere and whether it is plausible to apply it to the Arab case. I first review previous critiques of the norm; then I discuss a recent attempt to apply this model to the Arab context by Marc Lynch.[5] This discussion will lead to a new definition of the criteria needed for a sound Arab public debate, locally and regionally, namely a functioning civil society, and media that are accessible to the laity, providing content in a style and language that are not exclusive.

## The Habermasian ideal

Habermas's normative ideal of the public sphere has been criticized by a number of scholars.[6] Fraser,[7] for instance, reminds us that the public sphere is based on discursive relations among specific groups of citizens; thus, other "non-bourgeois" groups such as workers and women have been excluded. Indeed, it is not only status that has been "bracketed" in this discursive network, but also the topic of discourse. Fraser provides the example of domestic violence as a theme that only recently entered the public debate, after being dismissed as part of the private (domestic) sphere. Feminists who brought forward this topic formed what she dubbed a "subaltern counter-public." Even when women take part in the debate, their participation may be confined to the discussion of private economic and domestic issues[8]. Benhabib[9] criticizes Habermas's public sphere ideal for being a patriarchal model, stressing the false dichotomy of private versus public, pointing to the interrelation between the private and the public and or, as Dahlgren puts it, how "the public spaces of politics are intertwined with the private spaces of the home and personal relationships."[10] Furthermore, Schudson[11] points to "participation" as a prerequisite for critical, rational debate, and questions the rather romanticized depiction of earlier assemblages that serve as ideal examples of such a debate. In sum, the normative model of the public sphere presupposes an idealized consensus among agents to fulfill the aim of reaching what is good for humanity.

Thus, any realistic appraisal of the public sphere as a democratic model rather than an unattainable normative archetype must take into account the role of the "counter-publics" and the popular, or the link between the political and the private/popular. Van Zoonen[12] defines the gap between politics and popular culture as a struggle between the "oral culture and folklore versus literacy and modernism" or a struggle between "ordinary people versus the power elites." Yet, it is this interdependence between formal genres such as news and popular entertainment genres that merits our attention. This is not to blur the boundaries between the private and the public altogether, but to point to the need to analyze the tacit relation between them.

In addition, Calhoun[13] points to the potential of the mass media to give rise to alternative publics such as civil society groups. Habermas himself admits the presence of alternative, albeit weaker, public spheres, acknowledging the "healthy" link between formal decision-making institutions and civil society institutions:

> The culture of the common people apparently was by no means only a backdrop . . . it was also the periodically recurring violent revolt of a counterproject to the hierarchal world of domination, with its official celebrations and everyday disciplines.[14]

Acknowledging the role of civil society institutions in the formation of public life, Eliasoph defines the public sphere as "the realm of institutions in which private citizens can carry on free and egalitarian conversation, often about issues of common concern, possibly welding themselves into a cohesive body and a potent political force."[15] She defines three characteristics of this public sphere, where "participation is optional, potentially open to all, and potentially egalitarian."[16]

The public sphere, then, is characterized by the publicity or visibility of a whole range of actors and topics, and these are the criteria that are at the center of the discussion in this chapter. Central to this is how pan-Arab news media constitute a public sphere for rational debates among concerned citizens. I begin by presenting the outcome of one recent academic endeavor to analyze the pan-Arab pubic sphere as illustrated in the TV debate programs and press editorials, namely Marc Lynch's *Voices of the New Arab Public* (2006). I present Lynch's definition of the public sphere, and discuss his portrayal of Arab citizens, a portrayal that is rather narrowly defined. This discussion will be the point of departure in deciding which of the above criteria are present and which are absent from the current "Arab public sphere." The discussion continues in the next chapter, where the focus will be on the content of the mainstream news media versus tabloids and partisan media.

## An idealized Arab public sphere

Lynch begins his account by offering a unique definition of the Arab public sphere, confining it to what is being "said" in the debate programs. He defines the public sphere as follows:

In contrast to public sphere conceptions that revolve around particular institutions (the coffeehouse, television, civil society) or public opinion (as measured by opinion surveys), I define the public sphere in terms of active arguments before an audience about issues of shared concern.[17]

His definition deliberately excludes related activities or debates occurring in the private sphere, as he later elaborates:

> private arguments, carried out behind closed doors, lack the critical dimension of publicity. What makes a public sphere is the existence of routine, ongoing, unscripted arguments before an audience about issues relevant to many.[18]

Nor does he equate the public sphere with civil society, or "the more institutionalized network of social and civic organizations outside the state,"[19] although Habermas himself acknowledged the role of civil society institutions (see above). Lynch's public sphere embraces only satellite TV programs dealing with "shared" pan-Arab content, addressing a pan-Arab audience. In so doing, Lynch discards almost completely the more interesting debates that occur in the civil society institutions (although, towards the end of the book, he mentions in passing one such institution, namely the *Kefaya* movement in Egypt, primarily as a consequence, rather than one of the causes, of the rise of such a public sphere).

He further specifies such a sphere as one that is confined to discussing the political:

> Only when al-Jazeera refocused the satellites away from entertainment and toward politics – more precisely, toward political argument about Arab issues defined by an Arab identity – did it become a public sphere. It is this emphasis on public argument about common issues, along with shared language and identity, that allows the new Arab public to transcend . . . [the] fear that transnational mass media are [unlikely] to be the foundations for a genuine transnational public sphere.[20]

In terms of content, then, Lynch's public sphere is confined to the debate output on TV and in the press, usually dealing with political issues, particularly those concerned with a shared pan-Arab identity. Excluded from this public sphere, however, are private arguments, media output other than debate programs and editorials, popular culture, and other topics related to the local rather than the regional political context. I come back later to the link between the political programs and popular culture, but first it is necessary to discuss the type of public that populates Lynch's public sphere.

Lynch's definition is based on a taken-for-granted definition of Arabs as one folk, speaking one language, sharing the same cultural background, the same interests and the same goals, with the suffering of some of them being regarded as the hardship of all. But if we resort to this definition, we completely wipe away any diversity in language,[21] interests, goals, history, alliances, social problems and concerns, as I show below (and as discussed in the previous chapter). Indeed, Arabs themselves acknowledge these differences among them. Furthermore, such a generalized view of the "Arab public" disregards the nuances and complexities brought about by the increased immigration of Arabs to the West and the enlargement of the Arab diasporic communities there. For instance, Lynch himself refers to the abundance of public involvement on the part of diasporic communities as illustrated in the number of letters to editors sent by such communities: "68 percent of the letters to the editor published in one [pan-Arab] newspaper in 2001 and 2002 came from Europe or the United States."[22] It was, then, imperative to take into account in his analysis the type of audience, the difference between diasporic and local audiences, and how both types relate to the news and debates about the region and for what purpose. Before discussing the diversity among the audiences, let me first juxtapose Lynch's public with the normative model of the ideal citizenry.

## An ideal citizen

The ideal informed citizen is a rational person who carefully weighs incoming information and arguments against each other in order to reach an independent balanced opinion, which they in turn express in their interaction with other equally informed citizens. Such citizenry distinguishes between "serious" topics that may enter the realm of public discussion versus other, "less serious" or even trivial topics that should be kept apart. Van Zoonen[23] explains this distinction between the serious and less serious:

> An informed citizenry which relies on information, facts and rational argumentation for its political sense-making, is considered a prerequisite for modern politics and democracy, and this can only come about by properly functioning news media, it is usually claimed. It is information

and not entertainment, "serious" journalism and definitely not popular journalism that is considered the cornerstone of modern democracies; UFOs, Elvis coming to life, people turning into animals and other high-lights of tabloid journalism . . . hardly seem to construct an appropriate context to understand the budget deficit or national health care.

Thus, one essential requirement of a deliberative democracy is that citizens should be receiving serious content, which makes it possible for the citizens to place this content in an overall context, enabling them to draw a link between their own local problems and a complex surrounding world. If they fail to do so, however, it is usually because the news media are not doing their job properly. If the media inform but the citizens act differently then it is because the citizens are not sufficiently shrewd, or perhaps because the education system has failed to produce a well-informed citizenry. In sum, the ideal citizen is responsible for their local community, duly performs their daily work, rejects corruption and other social vices, and remains attentive to the information provided by diverse media on local and global events, from the local school board election to the task of fighting insurgents in Iraq. These ideal citizens are also considerate to the feelings and sufferings of others, so, in their free time, they co-organize demonstrations against certain social policies that they think are unfair, or against a war launched in a foreign country, or help collect donations for the poor in foreign lands.

Graphically, such a citizenry can be illustrated as an entity simultaneously linked to local and global spaces, while remaining loyal to both spheres. The citizenry is regularly supplied with incoming information about local and global issues that are directly linked to the citizens' equally divided sphere of concerns, as shown in figure 3.1.

Needless to say, such citizenry is as normative an ideal as the notion of the public sphere itself. People may be merely repeating what columnists or TV hosts proclaim, for most of them "do not have the time, energy or knowledge to develop their own original arguments on most issues."[24] Crucial here is the fact that modern citizens are in constant movement between the local and the global, and across their self-, group and regional or perhaps global identities, hence they express "multiple loyalties" or, as Dahlgren puts it:

citizenship has traditionally been associated with the nation-state, but increasingly debates about citizenship refer to a variety of entities. The neighbourhood, the city, associations and organizations of civil society, the region, even global society, are invoked. Within diasporic communities many people experience multiple loyalties, multiple identities, and increasingly even insist on multiple citizenship.[25]

Yet, if such an ideal citizenry existed, then the Arab audiences would occupy this place par excellence as the epitome of the ideal citizens. Lynch provides evidence showing that the most discussed issues are Palestine and Iraq, not to mention the shows dedicated to covering elections in the Middle East, including Israel and Iran, as well as in the USA and France.[26] However, it is strange that he hardly wonders whether this should make the Arab audience exceptionally knowledgeable about regional affairs or political affairs in international arena. The Lebanese academic Nabil Dajani, for instance, recounted how his students did not believe him when he told them that famine had reached the USA's borders. In his view, the satellite channels do not cover American society and people; hence, Arab audiences tend to relate the USA with the US administration and foreign policies.[27]

Lynch's audience, however, is overwhelmed by a large number of news and current affairs programs on terrestrial and satellite channels, not to mention the pan-Arab press, which constantly introduce "serious" topics ranging from the war in Kosovo to aid to the developing world. Nevertheless, do the Arab audiences constitute a well-informed citizenry? How much do we really know about their preferences, which topics they really care about, and how they make sense of an overwhelming amount of information on international

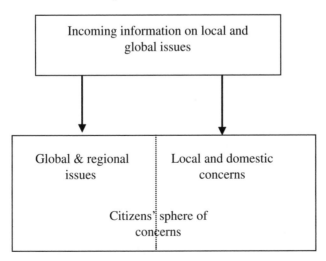

**Figure 3.1** The ideal citizenry

affairs? Studies of American audiences have, for instance, shown that American readers' knowledge of current events may not be in proportion to their consumption of news weeklies, while TV viewers may find it hard to retain information from news bulletins.[28]

Above all, do we know whether the pan-Arab news media have helped foster a sense of pan-Arab identity that prevails over multiple local loyalties? Do the Arab peoples possess a vast amount of knowledge about the history and political affairs in most Arab countries that may enable them to digest incoming updates on these news channels? In fact, there is evidence to the contrary. For instance, a recent study among a sample of the Egyptian youth audience shows that this segment of the audience refrains from watching the news, preferring to watch entertainment channels, the number of which has mushroomed during the past decade.[29] Likewise, Tunisian viewers seem to favor entertainment over news. Recent statistics show that 13 percent of the Tunisian audience watch the news, compared to 70 percent who prefer to watch French game shows and Tunisian dramas.[30]

Clearly, the news media may indeed play the role of educator, but how much would an ordinary citizen, burdened with her own troubles, pay heed to this? Why do we assume that this citizen should respond to the dilemmas faced by her "brothers and sisters" in other Arab States, when she herself lives in constant hardship with her own literal brothers and sisters? In my view, Lynch paints an unrealistic portrait of an Arab public who are strongly bound by a shared identity, faithfully occupied by shared political causes, and morally connected to one another in times of hardship.

## Arab solidarity

What unites Lynch's public is the *feeling with* one another; so, for instance, "arguments about the Iraqi sanctions allowed Arabs to rebuild the sense of sharing a community of fate, as Iraqi suffering under the sanctions became a potent symbol of the suffering of all Arabs."[31] What is implied here is that Arab audiences in Egypt, Saudi Arabia or Kuwait are primarily concerned about their "brothers and sisters" in other Arab States, for example, Iraq. However, perhaps the public concern about issues such as the Iraq War, for instance, is motivated by local concerns before regional solidarity, as illustrated in the slogans of the public demonstrations in Cairo prior to and during the war in 2003. Here, the public was chanting "Today they enter Iraq; tomorrow it will be Warraq" (a popular quarter in Greater Cairo).

Thus, the Egyptian public expressed their fear that Egypt would be the next target. What the slogans suggest is a conception of foreign policy as being concerned with imperialist power and acquisitions, rather than a shared public debate about mutual concerns.

Also, Lynch's definition rests on a moral assumption that links sympathy towards the Other with the ability to *feel with* the Other in their hardship. I discussed this topic elsewhere,[32] calling for cross-cultural audience studies that could unravel the audiences' sense of morality, as well as justice, as a basis for future debate on media ethics. I referred to work by other scholars[33] that highlights issues such as gender difference in the audience's response towards news about the Other's hardships.

Furthermore, the sense of pan-Arab identity, which may be reflected in the abundance of political news and views, is just one side of the coin, with the other side being the interpretation of this identity on an everyday basis. This comes to the fore in the way lay Arabs feel treated, or maltreated, by their "brothers and sisters" in other Arab States. For instance, Shiblak[34] shows examples of the difficulties facing Palestinian refugees in their host Arab States, which usually deny them naturalization, for various political reasons. At times, the rights of the Palestinians to remain or leave the host countries may be determined by the host countries' relation with the PLO, for example, in Libya and Kuwait. Lesch recounts how Palestinians in Kuwait were targeted following the liberation of Kuwait, thereby becoming "the scapegoats for the policies of the PLO and Arab governments that had tilted toward Iraq."[35] In general, Palestinian refugees have little or no access to "education, health, and social benefits," and even marriage to female natives is not a ground for naturalization.[36]

Moreover, according to the laws in most Arab States, men have the right to pass on their nationality to their non-national wives and children, while women married to foreign nationals, including other Arab nationals, do not exercise the same right. The Lebanese government is one of those that justify this with the claim that its intention was to preserve its demographic stability, an argument that hardly applied to men.[37] In Morocco, marriages of Moroccan women to non-nationalists outnumbered those of Moroccan men, with most of the husbands being French rather than men from other Arab countries.[38] A number of those women who had married men from other neighboring Arab States expressed their dismay at not being able to register their children in their own native country on the grounds that the fathers were "aliens." What is worse, the temporary union of some Arab countries, for example, Syria and Egypt in 1958, encouraged some women to consent to marriage with other Arabs in the belief that both spouses belonged to the same country,[39] only to face later the repercussion of depriving their own offspring of their basic rights of citizenship, to travel, to work, to own property and to access education. This drove several women to question their so-called constitutional rights; as one Moroccan woman says, "I do not understand why it is easier for the foreign wife of a Moroccan man to obtain the [Moroccan] nationality, than for the foreign husband of a Moroccan woman. I am also a citizen; I work, and I pay taxes."[40] These women then have become aware of the tensions in the official discourse of Arab unity versus the actual laws that enforce diversity, not to mention the apparent discrepancy between the official discourses of gender equality versus actual nationality laws that contradict this.

The continuous interaction among Arabs, particularly Arab laborers in the host Gulf countries, has further enforced the feeling of diversity and difference. For instance, the publication of the annual US State Department report on human trafficking, which highlighted the horrendous situation of human trafficking in the Gulf countries, particularly Saudi Arabia, has fuelled an intense debate among Arab citizens. One such debate on an interactive forum revealed the tension surrounding the sensitive issue of foreign labor, particularly the 'kafeel' system in the Gulf.[41] Saudi participants in the online discussion accused other Arab participants of conspiring against the Gulf countries due to the former countries' envy of the latter countries' wealth. One Saudi participant accused foreign laborers of coming to the Arab kingdom with the sole intention of stealing their kafeel's money. On the other hand, other nationals such as Egyptians and Sudanese expressed their dismay at the Saudi system of 'kafala'. One Egyptian equated the 'kafeel' system to human trafficking, recounting examples of security guards and street sweepers in the Gulf who work for twelve hours a day for modest salaries. Another Sudanese man told of his personal anguish in the Saudi kingdom, where he spent 23 years of "humiliation and contempt," not to mention the restriction of his movements to travel or even to take part in the pilgrimage inside the borders of the kingdom. On the other hand, citizens from the rich Gulf countries may also be the targets of ill treatment in these poor countries. For instance, one boutique in the Cairo World Trade Center carries the sign "We don't cooperate with Saudis," as a signal of some Egyptian merchants' protest against the bad treatment of Egyptian workers in Saudi Arabia.[42]

Aware of the cultural differences among them, Arabs have also succeeded in incorporating each other's particularities as a means to gain
acceptance. For instance, Khalaf and al-Kobaisi[43] showed how Arabs
(and other) laborers in the oil-rich countries in the Gulf tend to use
diverse strategies to gain acceptance and hence prolong their stay in
these countries: for example, Syrians tend to wear the national clothes
of Emirate natives, while Pakistani and Afghani laborers tend to
emphasize their religious affiliation as Muslims, and hence enforce
their belonging to an overall "imagined community" with the host
nationals.

My aim here is to point to the two present discourses of Arab identity: the official discourse, which declares a deep sense of pan-Arab
identity as shown in the political shows on al-Jazeera and other pan-
Arab media, and another, which is performed on an everyday basis.
Both discourses, however, should be carefully weighed against one
another during analysis of the manifestation of the pan-Arab identity
and solidarity as reflected ideally in the media and political discourse
and actively in everyday practices. Clearly, Arab journalists in the pan-
Arab media play a role in promoting this sense of togetherness but this
could be for various reasons, including the visibility of the region as a
whole rather than as individual states, or simply the desire to retain the
attention of Western media and other institutions interested in monitoring what the Arab media say.

Indeed, as I discuss in Chapter 7, Arab scholars themselves tend to
specialize in one or two Arab countries' affairs rather than cultivating
knowledge and expertise in the whole Arab region. The lay audience,
then, is no exception; they also prioritize their engagement and interest in other neighboring countries' affairs. Arab journalists, however,
prefer to stress their expertise in regional affairs, even if this
means situating themselves above their "ignorant" audience. I recall an
instance of a few Egyptian journalists from pan-Arab news institutions ridiculing some of the public comments expressed on the occa-
sion of the return of Michel Aoun to Lebanon in 2005.[44] As it has now
become "editorially correct" to incorporate the voices of "people in
the street" in the news and current affairs production, those journalists wanted to capture the laypeople's opinions on Aoun's return and
added these "vox pops" to the program. The journalists poked fun at
a number of lay Egyptians who were asked to express their feelings
concerning Aoun's return, and at how those people's comments
revealed their lack of knowledge about Aoun's role on the Lebanese
political scene or why he was forced into exile in the first place. One

citizen had even mispronounced Aoun's name, mixing it with his title (General),[45] which the journalists took as evidence of the people's ignorance.

## A rational debate out of the rational sphere

Dahlgren[46] refers to Wyatt, Katz and Kim's study, which shows that the home is "the site where most political conversation takes place, i.e. the most private space has become the most frequent site of the public sphere. The workplace is reported as the second most common site for citizen interaction."[47] Clearly, then, the Arab audiences are not merely "Arab", with "shared" goals or motifs, as there exist stark differences among local audiences living in an Arab State compared to an audience living (or even born) in a Western country, in terms of the motivation to watch political talk shows, the way they make sense of these shows and how they incorporate the political into their private sphere, for example, at their workplace, at family gatherings or charity projects.

For instance, Eliasoph's work[48] among American volunteers showed the volunteers cared about people rather than the grand political issues, therefore they concerned themselves with the issues about which they felt they could make a difference, namely in the "small, local and unpolitical" sphere.[49] Eliasoph shows how activists felt that politics was an issue to be avoided, preferring instead to talk about personal matters and local issues. Thus, she rightly points to the cultural context of citizen interaction, or, as Dahlgren puts it, "the unspoken 'rules' that define what kind of talk is appropriate (and not) in which kinds of situation."[50]

In my view, the strength of Eliasoph's work lies in her attentiveness to what is being said and done both front- and backstage, or the conversations that take place *behind* the public scene as well as what is said publicly. Contrary to this view, Lynch confines his analysis to the front-stage, defined narrowly as what is being expressed on political talk shows, rather than what lay people express, both on- and off-mic, in public meetings.

In addition, Lynch overlooks the issue of professionalism among Arab journalists and how they perceive their role. He mentions how the "Arab states often leveled accusations of a lack of professionalism on the part of al-Jazeera,"[51] but he does not delve into the definition of professionalism: for example, is it merely the journalists' compliance with the policy-makers? Furthermore, if al-Jazeera's professionalism

was under question, how could it manage to capitalize on its professional image in promoting al-Jazeera Academy (see Chapter 2)? He
also ignores completely the role of entertainment (although he mentions it, albeit very briefly, in the conclusion, perhaps to avoid future
criticism of ignoring it altogether!). However, a brief reference to
popular culture does not do justice to the significant role it plays in
connecting the private with the public. For instance, what is the contribution of entertainment, such as films, TV serials, or caricatures, in
revealing social malaise? How do people negotiate their identity and
see it reflected in popular culture versus political talk shows? Why
should political programs be the only arena for the public sphere and
hence gain publicity and visibility?

Finally, Lynch overlooks several nuances on the Arab media scene,
for example, the role of the tabloid press. He briefly states that the conventional Western distinction

> between elite and tabloid media, commonly employed in media analy-
> sis, does not hold in the Arab case; the Arab satellite stations, which
> stand accused of pandering to the masses though sensationalism, are also
> the premiere venue for elite political discourse.[52]

Thus, his definition of tabloids rests on the degree of "sensationalism"
alone; but there is more to the distinction between tabloid and non-
tabloid than just "pandering to the masses". For example, there are distinctions in terms of content, style, subjects of the news and debate, as
I discuss in more detail in the next chapter.[53]

Regretfully, a data-rich research project such as Lynch's, which was
based on "976 episodes of the five most important general interest talk
shows appearing on al-Jazeera,"[54] could have led to richer insights into
the role of pan-Arab media in the public sphere. For instance, it could
have been supplemented with audience analysis, or been based on a
comparison of a score of satellite TV political shows with those broadcast on local TV, or been based on a review of relevant Arab scholarly
works (see Chapter 7).

Dahlgren[55] points to the particular significance of "interaction
among citizens" in political theories of democracy. If interaction is the
core element of open and democratic communication, we must then
inquire into the style used in interaction and the range of topics and
voices included in the discussion. The following section deals with the
style (language), while the next chapter will elaborate on the range of
topics as well as voices in the "serious" versus "less serious" genres.

## The role of media in the public sphere

How could the media help invigorate rational public debate? In her critique of the public sphere as a normative model, Nancy Fraser defines the ideal public sphere as

> a theatre . . . in which political participation is enacted through the medium of talk. It is the space in which citizens deliberate about their common affairs . . . it is a site for the production and circulation of discourses that can in principle be critical to the state.[56]

Later, Fraser sees the public sphere as functioning only when it considers "which social groups most need access to what kinds of participation and what sorts of conditions or shifts in power are necessary to produce democratically viable solutions."[57]

In an Arab context, however, this ideal seems implausible, for the Arab region includes a number of states, each with its own interest, history and concerns. What kind of state, then, is represented in and by the pan-Arab media: an overall imagined nation (or *Umma*) represented by many presidents/kings? Would not such a nation conceal the power struggle among the states and state leaders to promote their own interests and agendas? In my view, a wholesale ideal of one pan-Arab public sphere dictates a wholesale solution for the democratization of the region, a task easier thought of than completed. It is therefore imperative to acknowledge that "some social locations hinder, or even prevent, certain participants from speaking in public, from full participation in citizen deliberation."[58]

The irony is that pan-Arab journalists seem to disapprove of a common pan-Arab media policy, while they tend to promote the pan-Arab identity by stressing the political and regional perspective of news and current affairs programs. For instance, al-Jazeera's top host, Faisal al-Kasim, refused the suggestion of establishing a pan-Arab news agency to counterbalance the Western monopoly of news gathering, saying that the suggestion of having a central Arab agency "only reminds us of the Arab unity projects which have gone rotten on the shelves at the Arab League."[59] Yet, his program (see Chapter 4) consolidates this sense of togetherness by focusing on the foreign policy issues of the Arab States.

Moreover, Fraser[60] warns against "unbracketing inequality," since vital public debate is a prerequisite to the openness necessary to highlight and discuss differences rather than concealing them. Thus, the news media "could become a means through which citizens understand not only that they have different, and perhaps conflicting, interests, but also that some interests may be more in need of protection and promotion."[61] Rather than seeing the "multiplicity of competing publics" as "a step away from, rather than toward, greater democracy," Fraser stresses the need for this multiplicity to continue, or else "members of subordinated groups would have no arenas for deliberation among themselves about their needs, objectives, and strategies. They would have no venues in which to undertake communicative processes that were not, as it were, under the supervision of dominant groups."[62]

Haas and Steiner[63] use Fraser's critique mentioned above to discuss the link between the public sphere as a theoretical concept and public journalism as a practical tool to invigorate public debate. They propose, among other things, to break the line between citizen and politician or expert so that the former is allowed to address and debate with the latter actors directly.[64] But how realistic is this suggestion, if it cuts across the journalists' cultural authority or the power to mediate and moderate? This is the power that journalists are unlikely to yield to lay citizens, preferring to serve as the filter in between citizens' concerns and political actors.

Splichal[65] sums up the essential criteria that define a managed public sphere, as follows:

1. access (who should speak);
2. content (what should be discussed);
3. style of speech (how it should be discussed) and the outcome of discussion.

I use these criteria as the point of departure in the following discussion about the role of the media in fostering public debates. I deal with the first and second criteria in the next chapter, while the third criterion, style and language, is discussed in the following section. I first define Arab news journalists as "a discourse community" sharing one linguistic code, namely the written variety of Arabic. Elsewhere,[66] I discuss in more detail the role of the written variety of Arabic or Modern Standard Arabic (MSA) in the news, and in the following section, I aim to show how the use of MSA is crucial in analyzing the Arab journalism field and the contribution of the news media in fostering a sense of a shared public sphere.

## A discourse community

The news genre can be characterized as the group of discursive features shared within a particular discourse community and which can be recognized by the members (and audience) of this community. Todorov defines genre in this sense, as follows:

> In a society, the recurrence of certain discursive prosperities is institutionalized, and individual texts are produced and perceived in relation to the norm constituted by that codification. A genre, literary or otherwise, is nothing but this codification of discursive properties.[67]

   Swales[68] analyzed genre in terms of the surrounding socio-rhetorical discourse community, where the linguistic behavior is determined functionally. A discourse community is primarily characterized as a "specific interest group" linked by training, profession or another qualification rather than class, birth or inherent characteristics. Thus, the genre dominant within a certain discourse community serves the goals of this community and the convention of the genre plays a role in distinguishing members of this discourse community.[69]

   I find Swales' concept of "discourse community" a powerful analytical tool, as the news genre has its own conventions and therefore journalists may be seen as forming their own discourse community. These genre conventions help define the community of journalism and its professional practices. Deviance from these conventions, however, is a sign of "outsiderness" from this community and its shared codes. A discourse community shares a certain way of reading and communicating its discourse/texts. For our purpose here, we need to specify the characteristics of the language and style of news and debate, in light of the fact that the Arab region hosts a variety of languages and ethnicities.

   As I argue elsewhere,[70] the idea that all Arabs share one language is rather a misconception. Although the written form (or Modern Standard Arabic, MSA) is a shared linguistic code, it is nonetheless *not* the mother tongue used in daily communication. The vernacular is the mother tongue, and it varies from one country to another in the forms of Egyptian Arabic, Palestinian Arabic, Moroccan Arabic, and so on, while the written variety is confined to formal writing and speeches. Thus, Modern Standard Arabic serves a transnationalistic function in the Arab region. Furthermore, Arab media officials stress the correct use of the classical language and wish to see it replace the vernaculars and take its place as the main tool of daily communication among Arabs. The code of journalistic ethics approved by the Council of Arab Information Ministries addressed this matter, calling for Arab journalists to act as guardians of the classical language and the literary heritage of the Arab nation.[71]

Previous analyses of the use of MSA in the news[72] found that the use of vernacular words in hard news is rather rare. Newspapers usually use the written form of language, reserving the vernacular for humorous or sarcastic commentaries and caricatures. The media's role, then, was to convert these vernacular phrases into classical Arabic when reporting on a speech. Thus, the language marks the difference in social hierarchy and authority in society and at the same time emphasizes the news media's role in upholding this difference and in guarding classical Arabic from the "impurity" of the vernacular.[73]

The use of MSA versus the vernacular has actually been the cause of some tension in the Arab World. While some scholars are pro-dialectist, such as the Egyptian writer Salama Mousa, who called for the use of the Egyptian dialect and the Roman alphabet as a step towards modernization,[74] others have defended the use of MSA as the only code that unifies the Arabs as one nation. For instance, the first media policy in Saudi Arabia was aimed at preserving the classical form of the Arabic language, making it the official language of broadcasting in order to increase the level of the audience's understanding of the classical form.[75] Thus, MSA has several functions as:

1. A tool for correct expression;
2. An instrument of religion;
3. A mediator of culture;
4. The basis of Arab nationalism;
5. A tool of communication in the news media;
6. A tool of mobilization.[76]

Habib's[77] survey amongst Saudi citizens showed that Saudis supported the use of the vernacular only in "folklore" programs. His content analysis of the programs on Saudi radio showed that classical Arabic was used exclusively in news, religious and public service announcements.[78] In contrast, a recent survey among the Lebanese audience showed that 83 percent see MSA as the language of print rather broadcasting media, while the proportion of those who preferred the use of MSA in broadcasting was at most 5 percent.[79] Likewise, a recent survey among Lebanese students showed that more than 68 percent of them wish to remove the study of Arabic from the school curricula, and that 79 percent prefer to study a foreign language rather than Arabic.[80]

This shows that there is tension among the public (that is, the audience) over the usability of MSA in the "serious" genres, a tension that reflects the audience's desire to use a linguistic code that represents them. If MSA, however, is used as the only code of the news and debate programs, it may then be considered as a field of power contestations, that is, with the laity watching the well-articulated hosts and guests talk about politics. Moreover, the risk is that a large segment of the public will be excluded from this "serious" circle and forced into the private sphere, where local concerns are discursively contested in local vernaculars.

In his account of discourse changes in Britain, Norman Fairclough[81] highlights the tendency to democratize discourse through informality, or what he calls conversational discourse. This means that public discourse in the media, politics, and even education is "taking on an increasingly conversational character," thus blurring the boundaries between private (informal) and public (formal) spheres.[82] He illustrates this by citing the increasing number of informalities in the written discourse of media, that is, the incorporation of informal slang into the formal written language of the media. This contemporary trend departs from the past view in which writing and formal discourse had precedence over informal (spoken) discourse. In the Middle Eastern context, one can argue that the two stages (of formalization and conversationalization) are experienced at once: whereas conversationalization has gained legitimacy in the media discourse particularly entertainment and popular politics, formalization still dominates serious genres of debates and news.

## Why does language matter?

The issue of language, strangely enough, seems to be sidestepped in Western media scholarship, as if it were non-existent or irrelevant to the analysis of media development in the Arab region. However, I strongly believe that language plays a crucial role in this analysis for several reasons. First, MSA is indeed a symbol of pan-Arabism, a political project that was doomed to failure but has recently been revived as a cultural, rather than political, project.

Secondly, MSA is considered the *only* code of the "serious" genres of news and debates, hence it constitutes an integral part of the journalists' cultural capital. Its significance is related partly to the power distribution among journalists in the "serious" versus the less serious programs, and partly to its role in excluding certain segments of the population who cannot converse in this code. This is a crucial issue in the analysis of the role of the media in the public sphere, particularly in terms of the potential access of all citizens to this sphere and the style of debating.

In analyzing Arab media, the role of the news language, or MSA, comes to the fore as part of the symbolic power assigned to each journalist.[83] For instance, the new Arab news media use MSA to consolidate the pan-Arab ideology, specifically by imposing MSA not only in the newscasts, as in the traditional media, but also in the debate programs. Since the illiteracy rate among adults in the region is 40 percent, it is doubtful how many Arab citizens would be encouraged to participate in call-in programs using the written language, since it requires years of school and university attendance to be able to speak it as fluently as do the TV hosts. For example, al-Jazeera's program *For Women Only* (which has now finished) used mainly MSA, which may have indeed cut off various segments of the female audience, although the program used to discuss domestic affairs. Furthermore, al-Jazeera has now launched a children's television channel that deploys only MSA. Thus, MSA has retained its position as the marker of pan-Arabism and indeed as part of the "cultural" capital of its user.

Third, the rivalry between MSA and vernaculars is a struggle that has extended to other fields such as literature and art, resulting in tension between what to use and for what purpose. Mahfouz, for example, sees the use of the vernacular as imperative on stage in order to close the distance between the audience and the actors; otherwise, artists risk "losing the link between the language of the actor with that of the audience."[84]

Fourth, the explosion of Arab satellite and private channels, not to mention the privately owned press, has thrown media outlets into harsh competition with one another, with the positive result that some private outlets tend to focus on local topics communicated in the local vernacular. Yet, this leaves us with a rather divided public who, on the one hand, follow certain grand issues in one code, and follow other more immediate and mundane issues in another code.

Finally, the sphere of vernaculars is not a "weak" sphere confined to local and domestic issues; rather, it is a sphere of struggle over power involving diverse actors, each promoting their own dialect. This is clearly manifested in the entertainment sector, where male and female

Arab singers have endeavored to promote certain dialects either for nationalistic reasons or for purely commercial interest in reaching certain markets. For instance, the Egyptian dialect used to be the culturally dominant dialect in the entertainment sector, yet several Lebanese stars seem to have abandoned this dialect and prefer to sing in Gulf dialects to gain access to the lucrative Gulf market. As the entertainment channels and production companies are usually owned by Gulf business tycoons, there is now an openly announced strategy of promoting Gulf dialects. For instance, Saad Shaalani from Rotana Gulf Channel, one of a variety of channels owned by the Gulf conglomerate Rotana, declared that, as the Egyptians and Lebanese managed to "market" their dialects across the Arab region, it was now the "time of the Gulf dialect as most of the Arab singers resorted to the Gulf dialect in their songs and now the task is on our shoulders as Gulfies to contribute to the spread of our dialect to all Arab countries."[85]

Apart from songs, there is a commonplace exchange of programs among Arab terrestrial and satellite channels to compensate for the reduced local production. For instance, the Tunisian channel produces 60 percent locally and imports 35 percent from other Arab countries. Likewise, Morocco TV imports 23.4 percent, while Algeria, Oman and Abu Dhabi each import approximately 25 percent of their broadcast programs.[86] The end result is a diversified public that is pushed by the serious genres to accept a unified identity and pulled by the entertainment genres to return to their local roots and accept their diversity.

## The heated debate around language

Arab scholars as well as media professionals seem divided concerning the "ideal" linguistic code for the media, both entertainment and news. A group of them favors the use of MSA in all genres, while another group sees MSA as an impediment to development, calling instead for the development of language before the development of media policies.

The first group criticizes the use of the vernacular in television in general, whether for news or entertainment, as several dialects are not intelligible across Arab States. For instance, Moustafa al-Mesnawi, a Moroccan academic, praised the Moroccan channels for adopting MSA, while criticizing the Egyptian and Lebanese channels for overwhelming Moroccan viewers with programs in the Egyptian and Lebanese dialects respectively (the latter in particular is not easily understood by Moroccans).[87] In so doing, the "ideal speaker" seems to "censor the actual performer."[88]

The Lebanese academic Nasim el-Khoury[89] sees the vernacular as an embodiment of the "coarse and vulgar" while seeing MSA as a sacred and sophisticated language. El-Khoury laments the fact that MSA has been abandoned by Lebanese journalists and broadcasters who would rather use the Lebanese vernacular as a symbol of their national roots. News bulletins therefore remain the only programs that use MSA, although the reporters' dispatches broadcast in the bulletins are usually in the vernacular. The Lebanese channel LBC, for example, was the first channel to use the vernacular in broadcasting, and it even thought of producing news bulletins in the vernacular as well "in order to reach all classes, the educated and non-educated."[90] According to el-Khoury, the media was "condescending to the style of the laity, and it has not managed to rise to a culture or language."[91]

Scholars, and a segment of the educated elite, tend to favor MSA and issue warnings against abandoning it that equate to abandoning one's roots, or even one's mother "because of her ragged clothes."[92] Some favor the intervention of the authorities in protecting MSA because, for them, living without MSA is like living "without a father or an authority to protect it or claim the responsibility for its future."[93]

Yet, other scholars and writers seem to favor parting company with MSA on the grounds that it "represses" the mother tongue, namely the vernacular, or, as the Palestinian writer Fawaz Turki puts it:

> I grew up in a society that in fact conditions the individual to fear any form of originality. We are conditioned to look upon the authority figure as someone to fear. This notion of conditioning is reflected in the way we speak our language. Arabic is a language that it not suitable for logical thinking. Arabic is probably the most degraded and dehumanized language in the entire world. It blocks us from being part of the global dialogue of culture. Why is that? Because language is culture. We come from a culture that is repressive; the language we speak is equally repressive. So, we have a problem on two levels: the problem is to liberate ourselves from occupation and on the other level to liberate ourselves, to have an Intifada, directed against our home.[94]

More importantly, ordinary Arabs refrain from using MSA and some even call for its destruction. For instance, el-Khoury's[95] survey among a sample of Lebanese audiences showed that a large percentage saw MSA as difficult, particularly women (49 percent versus 40 percent male), and most of the respondents saw grammar as the most difficult part of the language.

It is precisely because of the gap between users of MSA and ordinary people that popular talk shows adopt the vernacular as their only code. For instance, in an interview with al-Jazeera, Moutaz al-Demerdash, the host of a popular talk show on a private Egyptian TV channel, objected to al-Jazeera's host's pronunciation of the title of al-Demerdash's popular show. The al-Jazeera host pronounced it as it would be in MSA, but al-Demerdash said congenially, "We do not pronounce it this way here in Egypt . . . we choose to speak the vernacular so as to reach the public."[96]

There are also innovative attempts to mix the vernaculars, usually related to the private and domestic, with the serious genres of political talk shows. An example of this is the popular TV program *Bel Arabi* (literally, *In Arabic*, which is a phrase usually used in the vernacular as a request to use simplified language) on al-Arabiya (al-Jazeera's rival). Here, the presenter conducts an interview in her Lebanese vernacular with famous politicians, unlike other political debates and news that are communicated exclusively in MSA.

In fact, the vernaculars have always proven useful as a rhetorical device in the hands of politicians and religious men alike: the former Egyptian president Nasser (the father of the pan-Arabism movement) used to spice up his speeches with vernacular words, and immensely famous and popular religious men such as the late Sheikh Shaarawi and the young Amr Khaled have seen in vernaculars a fast path to reach the people's hearts.

Politicians also have seen the value of deploying the vernacular in this way. For instance, the 2005 Egyptian presidential elections marked a new era of political campaigning, with the incumbent president Hosni Mobarak competing against nine candidates (and yet he still won the majority of votes!). Mobarak was marketed using a new look: soft tone, a more relaxed style and a bilingual website on which voters/citizens could participate in polls regarding various issues.[97] According to al-Qassas,[98] the other candidates realized the inevitability of adding a "new look" and so presented their younger-looking photos to be printed in daily broadsheets, not to mention their use of a mixture of slang and formal words in their slogans, for example, al-Wafd Party's slogan "We suffocate" and the election watchdog entitled "We watch you."[99]

On the other hand, el-Khoury blames the deterioration in the use of MSA in some media outlets on the politicians who "do not learn

MSA in the military colleges, and hence feel encouraged to address the audience in the vernacular."[100] He gives an example of the former Lebanese president Bechair el-Gemayel, who, up to his assassination in 1982, gave "49 speeches" of which "five speeches were in French, one in English, 38 in the vernacular and five in simplified Arabic."[101] El-Khoury also refers to a survey among Lebanese parliamentarians that shows that the use of MSA has been decreasing since 1991 while the use of the vernacular has increased.[102]

In sum, scholars, as well as the laity, are divided among themselves about the role of MSA in the mass media. What complicates the issue is that those who endorse the use of MSA in all genres, not only news, tend to justify this through the discourse of Arab unity. The late Edward Said had joined this group, as illustrated in his personal account of his experience with MSA.[103] Here, Said lashed out at Laila Ahmed, herself a prominent "diasporic" Arab scholar, because Ahmed dared to attack the use of MSA at the expense of the vernaculars in Arab schools. However, Said seemed to romanticize the role of MSA in the everyday life of the Arab laity; for instance, he wrote that "educated Arabs actually use both demotic and classical Arabic, and that this totally common practice neither prohibits naturalness and beauty of expression nor in and of itself does it automatically encourage a stilted and didactic tone." He blamed Ahmed for not learning MSA, which was "an easy enough thing for her to have done." Yet, despite his life in Arab-speaking countries and the lessons he had with a retired Arab professor of Semitic languages, Said admitted that he found he had to try hard to deal with his inability to express himself eloquently in MSA. Thus, scholars like Said tend to see an innate ability to reach a certain degree of eloquence in MSA, thereby discarding an equally important tension created by the use of vernaculars; the tension, in Said's words, between "the language of intimacy" and MSA, which I call the language of solemnity.

There has still been no analysis of the importance of MSA skills in accessing the journalistic field (both in print and electronic media). For example, the increased commercial pressure on news media in the USA has driven editors and managers to hire journalists who can write for different sections of the newspapers rather than focusing on their language (and spelling) skills;[104] could this also be the situation in Arab news media, where the competition for a qualified workforce is fierce? Above all, how can Arab journalists manage to establish a rapport with their readers and viewers, if they do not use the popular vernacular? Would there be another means to achieve the same goal without sacrificing the use of MSA, for example, by depending on visual elements such as photos or other discourse-markers such as metaphors?

## Conclusion

In this chapter, I discussed the rather idealized picture of the Arab news media in fostering public debate and hence serving as a beacon for the democratization of the region. In particular, I have tried to suggest that the Arab news media may indeed play the role of educator but I wondered how the laity responded to this education, particularly if the incoming information does not directly relate to their daily problems.

In particular, I evaluated Marc Lynch's attempt to romanticize the role of news media as a forum for public debates, throwing into relief the criteria needed for such a functioning forum, namely accessible content and style, and the impact of these on participation in public debates.

Although Habermas's original theory accredited arts and literature as being the center of public discourse, scholars' concerns for the development of the public sphere rarely address the aesthetic embodiment of this public sphere, for example, in the use of language in news and debate genres. To my knowledge, no Western scholar has ever looked at the politics of language among Arab media outlets or posed questions on the role of language in a functioning public sphere. As I argue above, language politics constitute a crucial issue in the analysis of the role of the media in the public sphere, particularly in terms of the potential access of all citizens to this sphere and the style of debating therein.

Language is also an integral part of the "symbolic" power of Arab journalists, and thus its role cannot be overlooked in the analysis of contemporary Arab journalistic culture. I also discussed the impact of language politics on audiences torn between the universal and the particular, or between the language of intimacy and the language of solemnity.

The discussion on the role of Arab journalists and news media in fostering the public debate continues in Chapter 4, where the emphasis will be on content. I juxtapose the content of the formal pan-Arab news media with the lesser local tabloids, showing the stark differences in the laity's use of both kinds of media. In so doing, I draw once more on the Habermasian notion of the public sphere, throwing it into sharp relief with the private sphere, an important, yet under-theorized, notion in contemporary media scholarship.

# Chapter 4

# The Dichotomy of the Public/Private Sphere

This chapter resumes the discussion raised in Chapter 3 concerning the role of the pan-Arab media in the public sphere. As I argued in that previous chapter, language plays a significant role in the "symbolic" power of Arab journalists; likewise, I argue in this chapter that part of that symbolic power relates to what is deemed the "serious" content of the public debate. Central to the discussion in this chapter is the content of public debate as illustrated by random examples from formal pan-Arab news media versus local outlets. If the public I described in the previous chapter is torn between the language of intimacy and the language of solemnity, the public in this chapter is divided between the private and the public realms, although the majority of them navigate across both.

Nancy Fraser stresses that "what will count as a matter of common concern will be decided precisely through discursive contestation."[1] If this is true, then it is important to analyze the type of subjects that gain visibility in the public realm, juxtaposing them with those that are cocooned as domestic private matters and hence shielded from publicity. This is important in cross-cultural analyses of the role of the media, as "private" may indeed have different connotations across different cultural contexts. Poverty, for one, has always seemed a private/domestic issue in Arab societies, so, for instance, many Lebanese, despite their poverty, tend to deny their poor status on the grounds that "poverty is shameful" and to "evade social stigma."[2] In the following section, I argue that the local/private, long shielded from the pan-Arab media, has recently begun to claim a position on the media landscape thanks to the explosion of the number of private media outlets, whether print or broadcasting, during the past decade.

I first provide a brief overview of Arab scholars' critique of the urbanity of news in pan-Arab and local media; then I discuss the tension among Arab journalists themselves, between an elite audience and a humble laity. The following sections discuss the notion of the private sphere and how it embraces several "layers," with each layer acquiring a position in the private "hierarchy" depending on its position vis-à-vis the public domain. I conclude with a criticism of Western and Arab media alike for favoring the global over the local, with fatal results for audiences in both spheres.

## Urban news

Elsewhere,[3] I have pointed to the abundance of political news in the Arab news media compared to news on social issues. This type of news focuses mainly on inter-relational and foreign policy issues, and thus it can be argued that its effect will be limited to informing or influencing public opinion on these issues. If Arab journalists seem to focus more on "hard news" than on soft news, it is perhaps due to the prestige associated with the former. For instance, Hannerz[4] argues that a foreign correspondent usually aspires to be published on the front page, and this is why they will most likely prefer to report from a place characteristic of "hard news," such as Jerusalem, which makes hard news "more dominant."[5] For Michael Schudson,[6] the task of American journalists is regarded as focusing not only on objective reporting but also on helping the general public make sense of political acts, thus undermining the role of the public as active, not to mention rational interpreters by themselves. Journalists, then, are there to reveal and make public the "real" intentions of political actors, a task that has turned their job from that of being mere "stenographers" to being "interpreters" of politics.[7] As such, journalists enjoy a double role of interpreting what has been said (by politicians) as well as what has not been said.[8]

In an Arab context, Arab elite journalists are known to enjoy close ties with politicians and presidents. In fact, several Arab ministers have journalistic backgrounds: the Bahraini Minister of Information was the former chief-editor of the Bahraini daily *al-Ayam*; the Iraqi former chief-editor, al-Hadithi, was appointed minister during Saddam's former regime, and in fact Tarek Aziz, the former Iraqi foreign minister, had a career as a chief-editor; the Algerian Minster of Information was a journalist; and the Jordanian writer and journalist, Saleh al-Qallab, served for a short period as a Minster of Information in Jordan.[9]

In general, Arab communication can be characterized as urban, serving city inhabitants, particularly the elite, and ignoring the rural areas. One serious implication here is that, despite the modern format of the new pan-Arab media, outlets actually still adhere to the traditional hegemonic discourses of the elite and indeed ignore the immediate social problems in modern Arab societies. Several Arab media scholars warned against the press's preoccupation with privileged groups and journalists' ignoring the developmental problems that the region is facing,[10] making the rural press a non-existent phenomenon.[11]

For instance, both rural women and poor urban women are almost totally absent from the media, which seem more occupied with special groups of women, namely urban women who belong to the middle classes. One study showed that interest in the issues of women in rural areas comprised less than 3 percent of the total content. As for the weekly magazines, the focus was almost totally on women in the urbanized areas (97.5 percent), while a modest percentage (2.5 percent) was on the rural areas.[12] Another study of the situation of female journalists in Egypt showed that the journalists included in the study wished for *serious* social problems to be covered in the press, such as illiteracy among rural women, family planning, and health issues;[13] however, these were problems that they did not cover, although they agreed on the significance of these issues to public debates.

In fact, according to Jameel Matar (the Director of the Center for Future Development, Egypt), the negative impact of the satellite dish is that it has added to the alienation of the marginalized majority, for example, citizens from Upper Egypt. Thus, satellite channels represent an elite phenomenon, addressing only the cohort of peer colleagues of presenters and media professionals.[14] Furthermore, one of al-Manar's[15] presenters, Amr Nassef, says that satellite channels have become like Arab parties in as much as they get further away from their real audience and their real problems. So, there are channels that think they give the audience what they want in terms of variety and songs, while others prefer to give the audience what they need to know in terms of news and information.[16]

On the positive side, the rivalry among satellite and terrestrial channels, public and private alike, has resulted in the generation of new types of programs and talk shows based on purely local concerns. One example of these is *Ten P.M.*, broadcast on the private Egyptian channel Dream TV. The program host, Mona al-Shazli, once said that the program is concerned with the daily problems of average Egyptian citizens, whose concerns are transport, ensuring the education of their children, and ensuring the life of their family in the future.[17] Examples of problems dealt with in her program were the spread of cancer among children, and the death of 1,000 Egyptians following the sinking of a Red Sea ferry, which was said to have been caused by a fire breaking out below decks. The ferry was on a journey from Saudi Arabia to Egypt and most of the passengers were poor Egyptian workers coming back from Saudi Arabia. The accident was followed by a remarkable degree of public outrage because of the scarcity of information available on the rescue efforts and the identities of the survivors, not to mention that the owner of the ferry left the country even before investigations were completed.

Justifying the tendency among local shows to deal with local concerns rather than political issues, al-Shazli said, "We want to be close to the viewer . . . if he is sad and depressed because of something that happens in the street, home, town, he should feel that we share his mourning and we are consoling him; and if he wins the African Cup, we want to share his happiness, too . . . we want to be the neighbor, the relative or the person with whom we know we can share our happiness and hardship, and who can contribute to solve our problem."[18]

Her colleague, Moutaz al-Demerdash, a former newsreader-cum-talk-show host, defended the local angle of his popular talk show *Ninety Minutes*, broadcast on another private channel, saying that Egypt has 70 million people, each burdened with problems, which makes the priority of talk shows like his to deal with these problems (or "files", as he called them), rather than with foreign actors such as the USA or Israel.[19] He also affirmed that his program puts pressure on the local "executive authority."

For the Lebanese Diana Muqalled (Future TV), reading the headlines in the Arab newspapers or hearing the newest bulletins may dismay those who support endeavors to include other non-political issues. The irony, she adds, is that one Western training initiative after another teaches Arab journalists to focus on social, environmental, and human-interest stories, yet Arab journalists usually regard such issues as insignificant, which means they are usually non-existent in the news and current affairs coverage.[20] I personally recall the dismay of a native-Arab journalist who was involved in such a training initiative financed by a Western NGO. The journalist told me that he was astonished at the paradoxical attitude of his Arab trainees, who on the one hand embrace the Western news technical format but then decline from applying Western news values, which favor "soft" news. Thus, the trainees could not see any local story about the failure of their educational system, sewage work, and so on, as worth covering, particularly on the front pages.

One of al-Jazeera's top hosts, Faisal al-Kasim, whose program cen-tered on core politics, expressed a view similar to that of Muqalled. He told of his shock when he lived in Britain and watched the British news bulletin dealing with mundane incidents. Soon, however, he realized the need to "humanize the Arab media." He blamed the Arab mental-ity that "relegates human matters to a very secondary position, as if they were of no importance art all," adding that

> Arab totalitarian regimes forced media over the past five decades or so
> to focus mainly on so-called "big issues" and every thing else should go
> to hell, as if the issues themselves are much more important than the
> people.[21]

Yet, such issues hardly reach the media, and if they do, the focus is usually on the overall political context rather than on scrutinizing the social and individual repercussions of these issues. One prominent Lebanese journalist said once that if she could, she wished she could cover the situation of the Palestinian refugees in Lebanon, but such a program would never be permitted to be broadcast.[22]

Even covering human crises inside the Palestinian territories is subject to the same professional censorship. Take the recent crisis in which more than 160,000 public servants did not receive their salaries: the field reports among citizens rarely reflected the individual tragedies resulting from this situation. Instead, Palestinian journalists preferred to report on the situation from a purely political perspec-tive, rather than zooming in on human tragedies. Those stories that focused on individuals were taken directly from foreign agencies such as the AFP and Reuters.[23] Likewise, the Jordanian journalists' cover-age in the economic supplements in the Jordanian newspapers seemed to paint an unrealistic, but more favorable, picture of the Jordanian economy. Thus, the economic pages tend to focus on stock market activities, economic conferences, or news on new trade agreements with other countries, rather than on revealing the deteriorated situ-ation of the poor in Jordan, whose news is usually confined to the inside local sections of the newspapers.[24] Moreover, an Egyptian scholar[25] previously criticized Egyptian economic sections on the same grounds; for him, reading the economic and business sections would give the mistaken impression that Arabs live a luxurious life, because the media tend to focus on the life of urban, well-educated, upper-middle-class citizens rather than addressing the average citizen's problems.

The absence of social and human-interest stories is due to many factors. First, Arab journalists, as indicated above, do not see in such stories a "route to fame" in a profession where the real prestige lies in covering hardcore politics and interviewing famous politicians. Second, such issues are indeed difficult to cover, for they require extensive research and investigation, which drives journalists to prefer to cover available political issues, easily accessible in foreign sources. In fact, the Arab-American academic Mamoun Fandy sees the media's preoccupation with high politics as a means to distract the Arab audiences from their internal affairs by glorifying foreign policy issues, or else journalists may be accused of "political heresy."[26] By contrast, the local or economic sections are dull, for there are no specialized journalists to write well-researched articles about such issues. Third, Arab governments usually intervene to stop the production in their territories of programs about social issues, for example, prostitution or the status of foreign labor or refugees; among them are those countries that pride themselves on their "free" media zones. In sum, while "human-interest" stories serve as the backbone of the private realm, Arab media, unlike their Western counterparts, are reluctant to center on these stories.

In their analysis of the public sphere, Western scholars tend to focus on the "erosion" of the public by the private.[27] According to this view, the increasing commercialization of media genres has been accompanied by an increasing apathy among Western publics to engage in public life, eroding any form of commonality and solidarity. In other words, "it seems, the 'public' is being privatized, the private is becoming oversized, and this undermines democratic life."[28]

Sheller and Urry[29] summarize the different conceptions of the division between public and private: one perspective equates the "public" with the state, working for the public interest, while the "private" designates the market, individual interest. Another perspective distinguishes between the "public" versus "private" spheres, where the former serves as an area for rational debate and the latter for domestic matters. Other theorists see the distinction as being spatial in nature, with the public taking place in public spaces while the private occupies the domestic space. Finally, others see the distinction lying in the degree of visibility, or media "exposure," referring particularly to the popularity of bringing private matters into the public domain, thus violating the privacy of citizens. In addition, Sheller and Urry criticize these conceptions as static, stressing the dynamic dialect between both spheres and the increasing hybridity and fluidity between them.

Acknowledging this hybridity and the ability to "navigate" across them, moreover, should be the basis of social and political theories.

In my view, this hybridity and fluidity plays a crucial role in the analysis of private/public spheres in the Arab context. The Arab private sphere overlaps and yet secedes with the public domain in terms of visibility, language, interest, representative voice and distinctive capital, as shown in table 4.1.

This shows a public realm that is dominated by the "community" interest, based on reason rather than emotion, with elitist viewpoints and topics communicated in an aloof linguistic code. On the other hand, the private realm is dominated by the individual interest, based on emotion and a middle-class voice and topics communicated in a simpler language. The capital needed in the public realm is solely cultural, symbolized in the education and in verbal skills, while the social capital, that is, networking, is characteristic of the private realm. Also, both realms seem to be affiliated to different institutions, with the public affiliated to state institutions and the private to the market. As Shelly and Urry[30] remind us, however, such a division is not static, but fluid and hybrid, allowing the agents to move across the different realms and apply their knowledge of the rules in each realm.

As I argue below, the private realm, rather than being a static space, may encompass several layers, allowing the laity to navigate across these different layers. First, I show random examples of "private" matters penetrating the public realm, the aim of highlighting them being to show the complexity of the private sphere and the difficulty in drawing fixed boundaries between the "public" and the "private."

**Table 4.1** The public versus private realms

|  | Private sphere | Public sphere |
| --- | --- | --- |
| Interest | Individual | Community |
| Visibility | Privacy | Publicity |
| Logic | Emotion | Reason |
| Gender | Female | Male |
| Class | Poor and middle classes | Elite |
| Representative voice | Middle class | Elite |
| Visible topics | Social (domestic) | Politics/economics |
| Language | Vernaculars | MSA |
| Capital needed | Social, i.e. networking | Cultural, i.e. knowledge and education |
| Affiliation | Market | State |

## A private appeal to a privileged public

Fraser sees the private realm as being concerned with "private property" and "pertaining to intimate domestic or personal life."[31] In the
pan-Arab news media, the private may designate the local as well as
the domestic. Thus, while regional and foreign policies may be seen
as inherently "public" issues of regional concern, local politics may
be seen to be part of the private realm, along with domestic and
family affairs. For the Lebanese Ramez Maluf, "local media remain
for the most part the more significant influence on their audience,"
despite the abundance of regional and global channels available to
them.[32] He points to Western scholars' preoccupation with a handful
of "pan-Arab" channels, chief among them al-Jazeera, thereby
neglecting "394" other channels. This, he adds, is misleading, as
"these few stations are by no means in control of the market, which
is known to be fragmented, diversified, fickle, and loyal to programs
rather than to channels." Thus, Western scholarship tends to center
on the "shared," or "pan-Arab" rather than the local and particular,
as discussed in Chapter 3. I shall come back to this in Chapter 7, in
my discussion of Arab and Western media scholarship, but for now,
let me illustrate Maluf's point with random examples from pan-Arab
and local media, focusing on the interaction between readers/viewers
and media. These examples include one call-in TV program and the
letters-to-the editor pages in a number of pan-Arab and local
newspapers.

   The first example is from the regional channel al-Jazeera, and particularly from its most controversial call-in program, *The Opposite
Direction*. Shamri[33] provides a quantitative analysis of the program,
surveying thirty episodes broadcast during the period from 1997 to
1998. Shamri presents an overview of the topics of these episodes,
ranging from "peace with Israel," "Israel's relations with Turkey,"
"massacres in Algeria," "economic summit," "Yemen joining the Gulf
Cooperation Council," "Iran and the Gulf," "Kuwaiti-Iraqi crisis" to
"definition of socialism," "democracy and *shura*," and "definition of
capitalism." Few episodes from that period dealt with women's issues,
such as "women's freedom" and "polygamy." In general, the program
favored foreign policy issues rather than local or "social" issues. This
trend still continues, although, from time to time, the program picks
up a few "private/domestic" issues, such as the one on 12 December
2006 about the increase of cosmetic operations; a week later, the presenter acknowledged the various complaints he received from some

concerned viewers who saw that topic as "apolitical," and hence inappropriate for public debate!

The following week, on 19 December 2006, the program dealt with another "domestic" issue, namely the spread of music video channels in the Arab world, a phenomenon that the presenter said may be part of the Arab governments' conspiracy against their youth: "there are ministries of information and there are ministers of information whose main objective and task is to make into prostitutes the Arab youth and society." In particular, he referred to the ease of obtaining a license to launch a music channel while it may be harder to obtain a license for a news channel.

Ironically, the program host, Faisal al-Kasim, expressed a contrary view to that of favoring the grand political issue. In an opinion printed in MEB journal, al-Kasim lamented the absence of human issues in the pan-Arab media, wondering,

> Are not our societies crammed with hundreds of human and social issues that need immediate attention from the media? We are extremely fed up with news and programs about "imperialism," "Zionism" and "liberation issues." We should get liberated locally first before we get liberated from foreign colonialists. Our media should be harnessed to liberate the Arab people from their internal gladiators first.[34]

Yet, the presenter and part of his audience, as pointed out above, tend to define certain topics as "worthy" and others as "unworthy". The former category includes foreign policy issues – that is, Arab relations with Israel, the USA and Iran – or discussions around politico-economic concepts, such as capitalism or socialism. Thus, the public is clearly differentiated from the private in terms of topic (content); what is more, audience and media professionals alike seem to share this definition of the public realm.

Let us now turn to the letters-to-the-editor pages from the perspective of regional versus local press and the different topics brought up in these media. For instance, the letters page in the pan-Arab newspaper *al-Hayat*, on 28 December 2006, included two letters from two Arab intellectuals, one dealing with the situation in the Palestinian territories in relation to the internal struggle among the various Palestinian factions, the other presenting an overview of Egypt's role in the region and how Egypt's peace treaty with Israel affected that role. The pan-Arab rival *al-Sharq al-Awsat* had, on the same day, several letters and comments on news stories concerned with regional and global issues. Thus, one letter commented on the story of Hillary Clinton's plan to join the race for the American presidential elections, while another commented on the Palestinian–Israeli conflict and whether it would be resolved with Israel's releasing Palestinian prisoners. Others were concerned with the situation in Darfur, Iran's plan to develop nuclear weapons, and the increasing number of militias in Lebanon. *Al-Quds al-Arabi*, moreover, on the same day, had several letters, some of which had been written by intellectuals residing in Western countries. In fact, as indicated by Lynch (see Chapter 3), the majority of the letters to the editor published in such pan-Arab broadsheets stem from diasporic readerships; as mentioned before, the difference in readership, whether diasporic or local, is as important a part of the analysis of Arab media content as is the difference among the channels, that is, regional or local. As for the topics discussed, they centered on regional issues such as the political situation in Iraq, Saudi security measures on the borders with Iraq, comment on the recent speech by Palestinian leader Mahmoud Abbas, and yet another on the elections in Mauritania.

On the other hand, the letters pages in local newspapers have a different emphasis. The Egyptian local newspaper *al-Gomhuria* has a special section entitled *With the Public*, dedicated to letters from "the public" usually about complaints and individual pleas to officials. On 28 December 2006, this section included a letter concerning a plea to the Minister of Education for children of underprivileged families to be exempt from school fees. There was another letter, from a concerned husband, addressing the Head of the Union of Teachers, wondering why the Union refused to contribute to the cost of medical treatment for his wife, who had served the education sector for more than forty years. A third letter was also concerned with the educational sector, pointing out particularly the contradictions in the regulations for all public schools, such as the rule about using a laboratory for science classes (although most of the labs are unequipped), while another letter made a sarcastic statement about a governmental office employing more than 60 public servants and serving 800 pensioners and yet the office occupies one single 4 × 4m room.

Another local newspaper is *al-Ahram*.[35] The paper is usually packed with regional and international political news,[36] but its letters-to-the-editor section may at times reflect more "domestic" concerns. For instance, on 28 December 2006, *al-Ahram* had several letters indicating concern about the phenomenon of Egyptian "street children," following the news of the arrest of a gang that raped, abused and killed a number of those children. The debate was reminiscent of the commotion caused by the biographical novel, *For Bread Alone*, by the

Moroccan Mohamed Choukri, which was banned in several Arab countries for its "inappropriate" style, topic and characterization of Moroccan society. Yet, the phenomenon of street children and the abuse to which they are exposed is a problem that faces several Arab countries. In Egypt alone, more than one million children are classified as "street children" if they fulfill certain criteria:

> children working in areas where they cannot be seen or reached, such as home-servants or those who work in other areas that do not necessarily entail direct contact with the street setting, and those who are at risk or are vulnerable are added to the list.[37]

It is, then, not surprising that the laity and elites alike may show concern about this problem, which affects their daily lives, one way or another, perhaps even more than Iran's plan to develop nuclear weapons or Israel's possession of such weapons! It is striking that several of the problems that concern the daily lives of the lay majority are to be found not in the letters-to-the-editor sections in broadsheets but in the same sections in tabloids, such as the Egyptian tabloid *Crime News*.

In fact, crime news has proved very popular, and the reason, according to one editor of an Egyptian tabloid specializing in crime news, is that "people are bored with politics." A sociologist, on the other hand, justifies this popularity by claiming that readers achieve gratification in learning about others' hardship and use it as a strategy to help them to cope better with their own.[38] As mentioned above, *Crime News*, published by the Egyptian publishing house Akbar el-Youm, is an example of such a tabloid, and it is concerned primarily with the crimes and calamities of local people. The letters-to-the-editor page in this tabloid is dedicated to the humble people's complaints and personal pleas, and is even entitled *People's Complaints*. For instance, the letters published on 28 December 2006 were concerned with the daily lives of some underprivileged citizens. One of them sent a letter lamenting his chronic disease and appealed for the well-off to donate a certain amount of money to buy him a respiratory machine. Another letter is from a man who told his story of deprivation since childhood, and his fear that his two sons may face the same destiny. Due to his illness, he had to leave work, and had no other financial source to support him; his letter was directed to those who could help him and his family. Usually such letters include the addresses and telephone numbers of the senders. Thus, this tabloid may indeed serve as "pantheon of human behavior, morality, efficacy and circumstances," or as a "ritual moral exercise,"[39] but, above all, it also serves as a forum for the poor and deprived to present their appeals to the more privileged classes.

In sum, the focus of the pan-Arab media tends to center on regional politics rather than the immediate local concerns of each Arab society. Thus, for a news story to be deemed "worthy" it should deal with either the Islamic or the pan-Arab politico-religious sphere. In a pan-Arab outlet, such as al-Jazeera, the grand political issues are supremely newsworthy. One of the channel's top hosts, Yusri Fouda, justified this as follows:

> You are not talking to only a certain group, or a certain mentality or area, and you adopt a pan-Arab mentality; this is the number one criterion that will help you decide whether this news item would interest someone in Mauritania or affect someone in Somalia or Iraq or Morocco, i.e. is it too local? Or will other Arab people, whether in the Arab World or somewhere else, anywhere in the world, be interested in knowing a little bit more. This is criterion number one . . .We'll try to see the value; let's say there was a fire in Malaysia and five people were burned to death. Many considerations are going to be involved here: was it an accident? The husband was going to make some tea, he was ignorant, it was his first time in the kitchen, and it was all an accident. If this is the case, then maybe not. But maybe it was racially motivated. A Muslim did it to a Christian family, or it was politically motivated. Then the news item begins to gain significance. Maybe someone who lives in Egypt would like to know a little bit more about it, because we know that Malaysia has many Muslims living here, and there are some troubles.[40]

Anecdotally, I recall asking a female journalist at one of these pan-Arab media about the stories that occupied her at the time. She responded immediately that Iran's plan to develop nuclear weapons, or the "Iranian file" as she called it, was the most interesting story for her then. And when I asked why, she answered impatiently, "You see, Iran wants to develop these weapons, but the USA does not approve of it, so the USA threatened Iran with economic sanctions, but China, a member in the Security Council, would not support this decision. . ." I noted how a diverse country like Iran was reduced to being a protagonist acting against the antagonist USA, backed up by the guardian, China, and here I interrupted her and asked, "Would not you rather cover a story of more importance to the local audience in your country?" She gave me a look of complete disdain, saying that the repercussions of Iran's possession of nuclear weapons are far greater than the impact of the dreadful status of schooling or acute poverty in her country.

The implications of the narrow definition of newsworthiness among Arab journalists in pan-Arab media may not be confined to the newsrooms, and may influence audiences as well. So, this definition of worthiness can also be entrenched in the audience's minds even if they are exposed to other foreign channels with a different news diet. For instance, Gönül Gigilcim's exploratory study among a sample of Turkish viewers living in Norway showed the viewers' disapproval of the Norwegian channels' news diet, deeming it "trivial" for its focus on local issues such as schooling, pensions, binge drinking, and so on.[41] For this diasporic minority, it was unfathomable how the Norwegian media indulged in the "private realm" rather than presenting "more serious" topics, particularly about foreign policies. There are several analyses of the representations of ethnic minorities in European news as well as of the minorities' perception of this representation. However, analysts have yet to conduct surveys similar to Gigilcim's among local Arab audiences to form a qualified view of the interplay of journalists' perception of news versus that of their audiences.

## Layers of the private sphere

Elsewhere,[42] I have reviewed the context that gave rise to the proliferation of Arab tabloids. For instance, in Egypt, the tabloids flourished due to a loophole in the law that enabled the publishers to obtain their licenses. Also, establishing a tabloid has been regarded as a much cheaper business than launching a glossy magazine or a private television channel. But is the term "tabloid" an umbrella term that can be used to define any non-broadsheet in any country? The answer is no, as it was shown that, for example, Finnish tabloids are usually regarded as newspapers rather than as tabloids in the British sense of the word. This is due in particular to the Finnish tabloids' attentiveness to the political news rather than entertainment news, such as that found in the British *The Sun*.[43] The same can be said about Arab tabloids, which are also occupied with national political issues.

Indeed, I argue that "tabloid" is an all-inclusive term that does not account for the distinctions made among existing newspapers and tabloids. It can be argued, moreover, that a hierarchy of tabloidization exists on the Arab media scene, and, as I argue below, we may rather discuss the layers of the private realm as reflected in the local and tabloid press, depending on each local outlet's position vis-à-vis the "more serious" outlets. This hierarchy ranges from those papers concerned with "popularized politics," usually partisan newspapers, to those concerned with gossip and celebrities. For instance, a new tabloid newspaper in Morocco has reportedly managed to gain popularity and be compared with reputable and well-established dailies because of its weekly content of "sex, private life gossip, and society scandals."[44]

In some Arab States, such as Egypt, there are different kinds of tabloids and partisan press, with some concerned with politics rather than social issues, and others concerned with celebrity and private gossip. Table 4.2 presents this distinction among tabloids, with examples drawn particularly from Egyptian media outlets.

The first group comprises media outlets specializing in popularized politics. An example of this is the Egyptian weekly *al-Osboua*, which is regarded as a tabloid although its content is purely political. What has made critics describe it as a tabloid is perhaps its preoccupation (in line with the Egyptian party press) with political scandals, for example, the arrest of a mayor's son for forging a check.

The second group includes outlets specializing in the "official" private realm. An example of this is the Egyptian daily *el-Mesa*, which is an "evening newspaper."[45] The daily has diverse sections for political as well as celebrity news. Moreover, most of the political news is concerned with local issues. *El-Mesa* has been famous for its last-page section dedicated to letters sent by poor citizens (and edited by the

**Table 4.2** Examples of different local outlets

|  | Outlets specialized in popularized politics | Outlets specialized in the "official" private realm | Outlets specialized in gossip |
|---|---|---|---|
| Example | Egyptian weekly *al-Osboua'* | Egyptian daily *el-Mesa* | Tabloids such as *Crime News* and *Celebrity News* |
| Topics | Purely political | Political as well as celebrity news | Contrasting gossip about the famous with stories about the poor |
| Position vis-à-vis the formal public realm | Close | Middle position | Seceded |

journalists) asking well-off families for help. Apparently, this section has been so popular that *al-Osboua* has followed suit and inserted a new section called *Goodness Well*, concerned with similar issues.

Finally, the last group includes outlets specializing in gossip, such as the Egyptian weeklies *Akhbar al-Hawadeth* (*Crime News*) and *Akhbar el-Nogoum* (*Celebrity News*). The former, as the title indicates, is concerned with crime news and contains diverse sections about crimes, for example, a historical crime, crime of the week, international crimes, and so on. This tabloid has also a letters-to-the-editor section concerned with citizens' complaints and/or requests for help (as discussed above).

In fact, crime news seems to be more popular now among the Arab readership than previously, as the former editor-in-chief of the Jordanian tabloid *Sheehan* indicated. According to him, *Sheehan*'s readers used to be attracted to gossip and social taboos, but now, thanks to the abundance of satellite entertainment channels discussing various sexual and social taboos, the readers are now more occupied with crime news.[46] It has to be added here that crime news is usually a monopoly of the print media rather than of the broadcasting media, whether as news or debate.

If Habermas's critics argue for the existence of multiple publics or subaltern publics,[47] one can argue here that there is a multi-layered private sphere, including the family/domestic affairs, the poor and marginalized, popularized politics, and so on. The capital obtained by each player in the private sphere gains its currency through its intersection with the "formal" public sphere, as shown in figure 4.1.

Figure 4.1 shows the hierarchy of publicity and visibility in the private realm, depending on the topics of concern: at the top of the

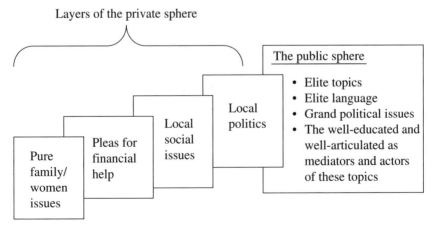

**Figure 4.1** Layers of the private sphere

hierarchy comes local politics, then social problems such as education and sexuality; at the bottom are the humble laity's pleas for help, as well as purely family/women's matters. The influence of journalists working in each type of media may then correspond to the position of their media outlet in this hierarchy, so those working with local political issues may enjoy a better status than do those working with women's issues. The most influential positions, on the other hand, would then remain the monopoly of those reporting on global political issues.

To be fair, Western news media (whether European or American), which provided the training and educational space for many Arab journalists in the new channels, have not really set a better example. There exists a gap between the national news and foreign news coverage in Western media. Thus, while the national news focuses on ordinary citizens' immediate and daily problems, the foreign news presents other nations only through a purely political window focusing on foreign governments, so ordinary citizens from the Middle East or other regions appear only in the background. Western news media do not give nearly as much coverage to those citizens as they do to their own Western citizens: their problems, their dreams, their culture, their struggle to get a job, their struggle to maintain an income, their struggle to educate their children, the deterioration of education in public schools, child labor, and so on. The result is twice as damaging. On the one hand, Arab journalists shore up their misconception of serious news as something to do with politics and governments and ignore the masses and their daily troubles, relegating them to "low level" journalism. On the other hand, Western audiences never really come to know Arab peoples as people, but rather only as governments. The difference is decisive. How often do we see Arabs represented in Western newscasts as ordinary citizens, sharing dreams and problems similar to those of Western citizens? How often have Western media taken up the social issues ignored in Arab news media? How often have Western newspapers mentioned Arab countries in their culture sections? Western news media can indeed take part in revolutionizing the news genre and journalistic traditions in Arab media if they dare revolutionize their own foreign news coverage and make it more pluralistic.

## Local is bad, global is good?

In her seminal analysis of Americans' apathy towards politics, Nina Eliasoph[48] blames the local media for framing activists' issues in a local context rather than portraying the activists as citizens who may have a say in national and global policy. She recalls how local reporters regarded their reporting jobs as dull and wished they were city reporters whose job is to "report on more important-seeming issues."[49] They ridiculed what they covered, which made them far from an ideal "Edward Murrow reporting on world-shaking events." Thus, Eliasoph seems to favor the in-depth analysis of "local" problems via an examination of their political roots and how they are related to an overall national or even global policy rather than to the pure interest in "a local individual's visible actions (handing the blanket to the homeless person, feeding the hungry person, for example)."[50]

However, what is presented in this chapter is the exact opposite case: here we have journalists who tend to frame issues in a regional/global context as a prerequisite for publicity and visibility. If issues are deemed local, they are per se unworthy of this visibility in high-ranking outlets. I am tempted to argue that Western scholars such as Eliasoph or Habermas tend to base their views on a rather Eurocentric attitude anchored in the solid history of the "politics of recognition," to use Charles Taylor's term,[51] and which has even been claimed to acquire an emotional character of self-realization.[52] In the Arab context, however, we have a public, or rather, we have fragmented and diverse publics, which are shunned out of serious debates communicated in an exalted language. The segments of the audiences who are willing and able to discuss these issues usually contribute to such forms while those who are unable to do so resort to low outlets, usually hidden in the inside sections of newspapers or in the drama and fiction of popular culture. The end result is the exaltation of the global (public) rather than the local (private).

In the American context, highlighted by Eliasoph, "Common sense considered the pubic sphere to be a place for dramatically airing self-interest and translating self-interest into short-sighted public policies; this folk definition of the public sphere kept most interesting debate out of public circulation."[53] However, the opposite is true in Arab media, where journalists tend to prioritize the grand political, that is, foreign policy and issues, pushing other local concerns to the fringe of the public debates. Thus, if Western scholars express their concern about the tyranny of the private over the public, Arab scholars should have the opposite concerns about the public tyranny of the private.

In addition, Eliasoph rejects the suggestion that popular talk shows, à la Oprah, may contribute to restoring Americans' faith in politics by discussing politics in a more popular frame. Rather, she stresses the urgency that citizens "*learn* how to connect their personal lives to political issues. A one-shot call to a radio talk show would be likely to reaffirm listeners' belief that political debate is bewildering and disembodied, that ideas come from nowhere and the people who care about politics just want to hear themselves talk at weird hours of the day and night."[54] But, again, this view assumes a certain type of public: an audience indulged in personal recognition, who are asked to balance the personal with the political. In the Arab context, however, we have diverse publics, the majority of whom *need* but do not *dare* to demand an equal share of recognition. It is only recently, as discussed before, and as part of their marketing strategy, that local terrestrial and private satellite channels have begun to highlight the malaise of these people as a marketing, rather than political, means to win the hearts and minds of people. Those publics, then, have begun to realize that their feelings do count, that these feelings may indeed have "an exchange value" in such media.

This is perhaps why talk shows like that of Oprah Winfrey have proved so popular in the region, particularly in Saudi Arabia, where a third of the population of 26 million people are women under the age of twenty-five.[55] One Saudi man recounted how his mother of seventy years was attracted to the program when she saw a photo of a burned young woman. The image aroused her curiosity and she asked her son to translate to her what the episode was about, shedding warm tears when she learned about that young American woman's accident. Above all, the program has helped Arabs in the Gulf to penetrate the real American society that is not covered by the political debates and current affairs programs.[56] In fact, the popularity of this show has driven several Arab female broadcasters to copy it; the Egyptian presenter Nashwa el-Roueni, for one, launched her program, *Nashwa*, on the Dubai satellite channel, presenting a panorama similar to that of Oprah, mixing social problems with interviews with celebrities. For this show, it was considered el-Roueni had a claim to the title "Oprah of the Arabs," a title she thinks her fans must have popularized.[57]

If, as argued in Chapter 1, the Arab media stand for a bridge that connects and separates the agents, it also stands for an elitist bridge. It forms a mental bridge that separates the intellectuals from the non-intellectuals, the privileged from the less privileged, in terms of the topics, style and subjects of the media genres. Elsewhere,[58] I have presented an example of this exaltation of those with "cultural capital," drawing on the Egyptian anthropologist Reem Saad's reflections on her experience with a documentary called *Marriage: Egyptian Style* produced for BBC2 in 1991.[59] The documentary dealt with divorce and used a humble Egyptian woman as an example. The woman was illiterate and had been abandoned by her husband. She recounted her problems with her grown-up children. The woman, who was not particularly good-looking, was speaking in her vernacular spiced up with slang words that revealed her social status. The documentary encountered huge criticism inside Egypt, where middle-class intellectuals used the press as a forum to insult the documentary-makers and the Egyptian anthropologist who helped them produce the show, claiming that the woman was far from representative of the true Egyptian mother, and that her lack of education and her use of slang words was a disgrace to the nation. Conversely, in Western societies, the elites and the laity alike do not become offended by humble or homeless people being the subject of news and debate programs. On the contrary, such an example would be appreciated as part of the media's duty to grant visibility to all classes in society. This also reflects the prevailing politics of recognition in Western societies, where the laity demands and gets the recognition it needs in the public realm.

From the above, it is clear that the power of the media lies precisely in two main factors: content and access. If the content addresses immediate problems in the national or local society, the media may contribute to its visibility in the public realm. Equally important is open access, enabling all factions and classes in society to take part in these debates.

One unique characteristic of Arab news media is that they are decentralized and dispersed across several countries, with audiences equally dispersed across the same geographical spaces. Yet, Western scholarship fails to take into account this striking interplay between local and regional media on the one hand, and between regional and global media on the other. Thus, far from naively exalting the pan-Arab media for focusing on the global and regional, we should perhaps look for the representation of the laity, or the lack of the same, in the same media. I encountered European scholars who expressed a wish that EU media may one day "attain" the sober level of pan-Arab media in binding the European laity. However, what they forgot to imagine is the kind of media this would be, if the focus were to be solely on EU foreign affairs, discarding local daily problems as unworthy, relegating them to popularized outlets.

## Conclusion

As I argue above, the content of the pan-Arab media is usually "elitist" in that it focuses on foreign policies rather than on immediate social problems and needs in local societies. Yet, the recent competition that resulted in an increase in the number of new media outlets, both print and broadcasting, not to mention Internet forums, has helped give the private and domestic a fair amount of visibility.

It has become viewed as common sense to believe that what distinguishes free from non-free media is the relationship between the media and political regimes. Thus, if the regime is a dictatorship, then the media will be used in concealing important and vital information from the public, or worse, twisting facts like the famous example of the radio channel *The Voice of the Arabs*. But, in my view, by not addressing the day-to-day and immediate problems of the people – and here I mean the humble and less privileged people as well as the emerging middle classes – the media conceal vital information by disregarding important debate issues.

Yet, for Western scholars, the problem with Arab media lies solely in the authoritarian regimes in several Arab States. Thus, the argument goes, if the regimes give journalists the freedom to publish what they want, then the news media would automatically contribute to reducing the social malaise. However, this view completely overlooks the way journalists themselves perceive their role in society and their evaluation of what is worth publicizing. This can indeed have fatal implications for the role of the news media in serving their audience and in contributing to the democratization of the region.

The exaltation of hard-core politics as one of the "serious" genres is usually valued as an essential part of "prestigious" journalism, which requires a fair share of cultural capital among its media professionals. Nevertheless, if those professionals do not strive to show the clear link between the local and the regional, the risk is that the laity may yield to rather simplistic narratives to account for this link. For instance, the obsession with news and views about the USA's formal relations with the Arab States, rather than reflecting on the American laity and their daily problems, may nurture a form of conspiracy narrative where the USA, as a whole nation, plays the role of evil antagonist. In the words of a popular talk-show host, the Egyptian laity, for one, has come to blame the USA for their daily problems. So, "If the price of oil rises, the USA will be the reason. And because we depend on the Americans for wheat, we blame the USA if the price of a loaf of bread rises; the lay Egyptian knows that the USA is the reason of all malaise."[60]

If, above, I have criticized some Arab channels for laying so much emphasis on "politicizing" their news, both national and foreign, rather than focusing on immediate social issues, I have to add here that

Western journalists from trendsetter organizations tend to "politicize" the Other as well. The result is that the audience rarely sees the Other as a fellow human being, but rather as a member of a politicized entity whose problems can be solved only by using political intervention. The result is a huge gap between the way Western journalists cover "local/national" news versus foreign news.

Indeed, there are sweeping generalizations in Western media in which Arabs are portrayed as a unified, rather than a diversified, group, usually defined as Muslims. In fact, in several Western countries, the term "Muslim" is not used to designate a religious background, but rather to define people as if it has become their "nationality." For instance, when the most senior police officer in Britain called for the further recruitment of thousands of "Muslim" policemen and women, the British media circulated the news without specifying what "Muslim" here means.[61] Does it imply that anybody born into a religion should always be defined by it? What if they are refusenik, or non-practicing, or simply do not care about religion? Why not define them by their ethnic or national background, regardless of their religious background? Would the media, or any politician, make the same announcement for the recruitment of Buddhists, Christians, Hindus or Jews into the police or the army?

Needless to say, these simplistic terms do not hold in a global society characterized by hybrid identities. Saghieh and Bechir hammer home the same point when they say,

> The immigrants and their descendants ... may have arrived as Pakistanis, Turks, Moroccans, Algerians, or Iraqis; it was only after they settled in the west that they were transformed into "Muslim communities". Such communities are, to a certain extent, a "virtual reality" that exists above all in the minds of western politicians, "experts" and journalists – and, of course, in the minds of their supposed and self-appointed "spokesmen".[62]

# Chapter 5

# Global Media, Global Public Sphere?

It is usually during the time of crises such as wars that the role of the pan-Arab news media comes to the fore in Western attention and debates. It is then that Arab coverage of conflicts and wars is put under systematic scrutiny and continuously compared and contrasted to coverage in European and/or American news media. It is also here that the "clash of voices" emerges as a hidden assumption behind the scrutiny of why news coverage has particular features in each cultural context. I have previously overviewed[1] the accusations exchanged between Arab and American professionals regarding the coverage of the Iraq War, where the central issue was those professionals' interpretations of the information – statements as well as images – on the war.

This misinterpretation of each other's media coverage is indeed proof of the increasing "reflexivity" in the new global media sphere, where media professionals constantly accentuate their professional and ethical differences. It also suggests the existence of a global media sphere where not only the events (what) are constantly under scrutiny, but also the way (how) they are mediated.

The accusations made against Arab news media by some Western journalists reflect a tension between two "interpretive communities."[2] Thus, analysis of the journalistic product from several communities may shed light on the difference between the values and the function of news in each community, and how the notion of "outsiderness" of the professional practices of one community vis-à-vis another is formed. Seeing journalists in Arab media institutions forming an interpretive community with its own practices vis-à-vis the Western journalists in, for instance, American media institutions helps to shed light on the struggle among these communities to shape the meaning of their journalistic practices and professional standards.

Moreover, the debate among journalists points to the issue of objectivity as an important characteristic of an ideal reporter. It is obvious that objectivity in this context – for example, in covering the recent war – is not merely a question of falsity versus accuracy (that is, whether Arab journalists, for instance, reported on the truth or whether they fabricated the news reports), but rather if, by zooming in on Iraqi victims, some Arab news media might be accused of agitating rather than assuaging the conflict between East and West, despite the fact that the reports presented a piece of reality. What is at issue here is the reporters' integrity as professionals in the heart of the conflict zone; or, to put it differently, the issue is about "which" part of reality is represented in the news and "how" it is represented. It is, then, expected that the journalist is not a typical observer, but rather "an ideal observer."[3] One important characteristic of such an observer, as defined by Matthew Kieran, is to balance between being impartial and yet attentive to human feelings and emotions, and thus "to understand characters from the inside."[4]

The aim of this chapter is to discuss the role of journalists as mediators and facilitators in a so-called "global public sphere." The following discussion centers on the role of Arab journalists in this new global space, and their visibility in a dominant power space. Central to this discussion is whether this new global space still upholds the notions of center versus periphery, and if, when applied to the field of journalism, we can talk about dominant journalistic practices. The field of journalism plays a central role in forming the modern public sphere, which lies precisely in its ability to serve as a platform for diverse voices as a basis for reasoned judgement. However, rather than viewing reason in universal (Habermasian) terms as the cornerstone of the (global) public sphere, I propose Bourdieu's view of reason as a "rule of the game," contingent to the field in which it is articulated. As argued in Chapter 1, Bourdieu's view enables us to see journalists as forming an "interpretive community." Central to this discussion are the power relations and the hybrid identities formed on the global media scene.

This chapter unfolds as follows: first, I discuss the general contours of the global public sphere, focusing on the flow of information as a prerequisite for rational participation in this sphere. Then, I discuss the role of Arab journalists in facilitating this participation, drawing in particular on the notion of hybridity, examining the role of journalism as a cultural bridge between a global Other and a local self. As I argue below, the role of journalists as mediators in this global sphere should take into consideration the way they form their identity, and the impact of this identity on the mediation of public debates. To illustrate my argument, I present an analysis of coverage of the Iraq War in four émigré pan-Arab newspapers to show 1) the hybrid roles of journalists, particularly in hybrid media such as the pan-Arab press, and 2) to further discuss the notion of hegemony in this global sphere. This analysis will be presented in more detail in Chapter 6.

As I argue below, hegemony is not, as Arab scholars view it, a question of information flow from center to periphery; rather, hegemony can be manifested in the distribution of power among actors in a global journalistic community. Based on this analysis, I argue that viewing journalists (worldwide) as one unified "interpretive" community excludes the articulation of difference and/or conflict among them.

## The global public sphere: a dialogic arena

The Habermasian notion of the public sphere as an arena for civil interaction and "rational discussion" has been used by several researchers and subsequently developed as a normative model of civil life that can be applied at a global scale. Simultaneously, the globalization of news communication has fueled further arguments in favor of a shared global sphere. Knowledge about, and the visibility of, distant events has sharply increased thanks to the proliferation of satellite television channels and the Internet. More specifically, what this notion entails is the ability of news media to render visibility to distant events beyond the spatial and temporal borders of the audiences' everyday life. Visibility, as John Thompson[5] argues, has thus become the main characteristic of this new public sphere.

The public sphere as an arena for civil interaction and "rational discussion" was subsequently picked up by several researchers and developed as a "normative model of exemplary civil life."[6] Ingrid Volkmer, for instance, argued that a new global public sphere exists, and that it "has become an extra-societal global sphere of mediation particularly enhanced by the Internet."[7] In fact, the Internet is regarded as a global mobilizer and infrastructure of public activities. Street,[8] for example, points to the use of the Internet among global activists to arrange demonstrations around the world (not to mention that the Internet has been utilized by international terrorist groups). Hjarvard, however, argues that the "globalization of economy, governance, and culture has not been accompanied by a similar globalization of the public sphere. Opinion formation is still very much tied to the level of national political institutions."⁹ What must be acknowledged here is that the increasing interconnectedness among world nations and the fast circulation of world news, including war and calamities, in transnational channels must indeed have an impact on public opinion both in the West and the East.

The notion of a global public sphere puts back on the agenda issues of communication flowing from "center" to "periphery," as argued in Galtung's classic account of structural imperialism.¹⁰ The emphasis then was on the structural dependency between the elite in the center and the periphery, pushing institutional practices closer to those in the dominant center, and hence promoting the latter's values. Abdel Rahman¹¹ sees the global communication revolution as serving the interests of the dominant cultures in the center by proliferating its values and attitudes while marginalizing the native periphery cultures. On the other hand, other scholars¹² point to the complexity of the interaction between dominant (center) and dominated (periphery), making it difficult to assume a linear or causal flow of values.

The flow of information is seen as the foundation for such a global space to prosper. It also means visibility of the Other (periphery) in the dominant power space (center). Thussu discusses the notion of contraflow as a means of giving the chance for the "subaltern to speak," showing that the "traffic is not just one way – from North to South."¹³ Volkmer suggests that there is no more center or periphery but a multidiscursive space of mediation where "autonomous" media systems operate, but no single actors dominate "the game."¹⁴ Yet, the global media scene is a site of contestation: a manifestation of power but also resistance, the hegemony of the center but also counter-hegemonic movements in the periphery. As I argue below, the view that the global media scene has no "dominant actors" excludes the power struggle among journalists (the media professionals) in shaping their professional identities, and what this struggle entails in terms of the articulation of difference among them.

## Arab journalism and modern polity

Journalism has come to play an important, yet ambivalent, role in forming the modern public sphere. On the one hand, Habermas¹⁵ relates the decline of the rational public sphere to the triumph of capitalism and the rise of mass media, which adds to the fragmentation of the public, now treated as mere recipients of mass communication and advertising. On the other hand, Thompson assigns the media institution a crucial role in the development of "deliberative democracy," where diverse points of view are made visible, and hence individuals can form "reasoned judgment."[16]

According to Dahlgren,[17] the analysis of the topics and social structure of a public sphere should be supplemented by an analysis of media institutions – for example, the organizational constraints, ownership, and the role of technology – as well as media representation, that is, symbolic and rhetorical representation, and division among genres. Habermas's later work[18] continued to build on the thesis that knowledge as discursively manifested in debates informs and feeds into our action. It is precisely here that journalism gains its paramount importance in mediating and facilitating this debate, by uniting spatially disparate publics into one public with shared interests. Information, then, serves as the basis for this debate: with "access to reliable information from a variety of perspectives, and a diversity of opinions on current affairs, citizens will arrive at their own views on important issues and thus prepare themselves for political participation."[19] Information, then, is a basis for enlightenment, and as such, the flow of news is seen as "a huge, huge gift."[20] It is also widely accepted that free information is a prerequisite for democracy, and is why some authoritarian governments restrict the free flow of information or exercise monopoly of information channels to keep their people in ignorance.[21]

The Arab public (or the Arab "street," as it is popularly called)[22] is assumed to fall as easy prey to the lack of professionalism of some journalists endeavoring to fuel anti-American attitudes.[23] For instance, Nisbet et al.[24] hypothesize that watching media known for their anti-Americanism may result in fostering this attitude towards the USA among Arab audiences. This view reflects a commonly held stance among many Americans that sees "al-Jazeera and the new Arab media as a fundamentally hostile force generating anti-Americanism and complicating foreign policy objectives in Iraq, Israel, the war on terror, and more."[25] The fear here is of the distortion of information, of violating validity and consensus as an integral part of a well-functioning (global) public sphere.

The same view, moreover, can be extended to the journalists as facilitators of this public debate. Zayani,[26] for instance, reminds us of the problems surrounded al-Jazeera's journalists and editors having their offices closed in Arab States following the airing of "daring" debates. In such cases, journalists are usually depicted as heroes who undertake a lot of trouble searching for the truth, enduring harsh confrontations with politicians and governments. This indeed consolidates the image of journalists as "watchdogs," an image cultivated by daring dispatches and investigative series.[27] Thus, the more trouble they face, the more glamour and glory they gain, which makes their credibility contingent on an amount of enmity with the established regimes. However, if journalists have not fulfilled this heroic role by merely repeating official statements, they are heavily criticized for falling prey to manipulative discourse.[28] We therefore tend to measure journalistic integrity based on media distance from governmental discourse.

This image triggers the Western image of a journalist as a "truth investigator," an image that has been merged into the Arab journalism field as a result of the vigorous process of hybridity (see Chapter 1). Hybridity in the news and debate genres in Arab journalism seems to provoke enthusiasm in the West as being a sign of enlightenment and progress.

## Hybridity in Arab media

Hybridity usually refers to the result of mixing two or more culturally differentiated signs into a new amalgamated sign, for example, Latino rock, Mandarin pop, Islamic fashion show.[29] Hybridity, then, is the process of integrating Western signs and practices (music or fashion) into the native fabric (particularly in the developing world, for example, Latin America, Middle East) in order to re-conceptualize a new (modern) indigenous identity. The process of forming this new identity utilizes the same Western tools: adapting advanced technology in news editing, live techniques, and even style and language have all been affected by this hybridization.[30] Hybridity cannot only be studied in texts and signs, such as music or news language; rather, it can also manifest in the role of mediators (musician, news anchor, educator).

Hybridity, argues Tomlinson, is a natural result of "the dissolution of the link between culture and place."[31] It is the free floating of cultural signs across geographic and cultural spaces, ready to be picked up, mixed and matched, according to local needs. Salman Rushdie celebrates this process: "Mélange, hotchpotch, a bit of this and a bit of that is how newness enters the world. It is the great possibility that mass migration gives the world, and I have tried to embrace it."[32] Conversely, hybridity can be seen as a threat to indigenous culture and tradition, and a triumph of one dominant culture.[33] Moreover, Kraidy[34] points to the increasing need to integrate hybridity into communication theory in order to analyze its impact, that is to say, whether the mélange is celebrated or whether it is masking cultural hegemony and suppressing the inequality behind it.

For our purposes here, the role of the media professional is of particular importance. In an Arab context, this role is not seen in essentialist terms, either anchored in the native culture or in the dominant (Western) culture. Rather, it is seen to be the hybrid product of amalgamating the two cultures. Media in the developing world are seen to, maybe unintentionally, restrict critical debates by "toeing the official line."[35] For instance, Thussu[36] points to such a hybrid media culture in India, where television news takes appropriate American formats and Indianizes them. Mimicking Western practices, however, is not done merely because the latter seem "effective," but because it is part of gaining power and accumulating capital in the local, native field. For instance, CNN products carry more "cultural capital" than the news of a local outlet,[37] and thus will enjoy a great deal of legitimacy. Arab news media, then, may have to adjust their practices in order to be measured by this Western yardstick; thus, the news genre itself develops to reflect these new practices.

Among his recommendations for press journalists, Abdel Nabi[38] stresses the importance of dealing critically with incoming news from international news agencies, and he proposes the establishment of an interdisciplinary committee to deal with the incoming news. In so doing, he stresses the importance of news professionals as mediators between cultures and ideologies, drawing upon their education and knowledge of the Other (that is, their cultural capital) to sieve out the incoming impulses and sort them according to their usability within a local context. Journalists should therefore master the dominant cultural signs in order to able to discern the values internalized in the foreign culture, and hence construct a less value-laden representation of reality to their audience. This coincides perfectly with the view of journalists themselves as "communicators of information" rather than interpreters of events.[39]

Although the West may be the main source of knowledge and information, hybridity is here seen as the ability to amalgamate the different pieces of information and interweave them into the main indigenous fabric. This final product then counteracts Western hegemony. The journalist is like the educated elite in general, a modernity facilitator: they know the Other's language, and can decipher the real meaning of external messages, read between the lines, sort out incoming impulses as being useful or useless for the modernization project of the indigenous culture. Ambivalence, then, is the main characteristic of the relationship with the West, as a source of inspiration for developing and modernizing media products. Arab journalists may at once positively identify with Western journalistic practice while negatively dissociating themselves from that very same practice. The positive identification serves as the basis for legitimacy and credibility, while the negative dissociation is an assertion of the autonomous role of journalism in its particular context. Previous cross-national studies[40] have argued that the conception of journalism may be unified cross-culturally. It is the Anglo-American model, in particular, that seems to dominate, as shown by a recent survey among Estonian journalists adopting the role of "watchdog."[41]

It was in this vein that Zayani argued that al-Jazeera, as one example of this hybridity, is "caught between two trends. On the one hand, the channel uses the best technical skills and journalistic practices that the West has to offer. On the other hand, it uses these means and practices precisely to advance ideas and views that contradict and doubt the Western narrative and interpretation of events and issues that are increasingly bringing the Middle East to the center of the world's news attention."[42]

The hybrid outcome, then, represents the moment of intersection between its own internal mission, for example, to educate, entrain and/or stimulate public participation, and the adaptation of external actors' practices depending on the latter's power in the field. This is roughly illustrated in figure 5.1.

One major critical position against the Habermasian public sphere rests on the implied assumption of identity as a fixed category, "formed once and for all in advance of participation in the public

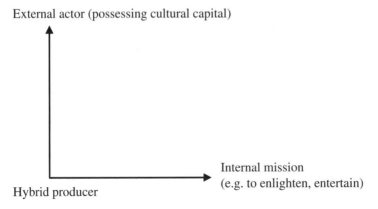

**Figure 5.1** Hybridity as intersection of exteriority and interiority

sphere."[43] As the issue of identity lies at the heart of the public sphere as a site for rational debate, it is imperative to inquire into the identity formation not only of the public (audience) participating in topical debates, but also, as I argue here, the identity of the journalists as facilitators of this debate.

Indeed, Habermas's notion of the public sphere does not account for the particular socio-cultural baggage that each member of the public carries prior to their participation in a public engagement.[44] Likewise, journalists, in their capacity as facilitators of public sphere production, encompass at once a professional/institutional identity and an individual identity grounded in their own indigenous culture. Thus, as Dahlgren argues, "Even one individual can encompass several (even contradictory) political positions at a particular point in time by virtue of multiple group identities or memberships,"[45] which further stresses the importance of identity politics as one major parameter for public participation. Analyzing the role of journalists as mediators and "cultural intermediaries" should therefore take into consideration the way they form their identity and the impact of this on the mediation of public debates.

"Cultural intermediaries" was the term used by Pierre Bourdieu[46] to refer to those engaged in the act of "presentation and representation," a concept that has received increasing attention among cultural studies scholars (see, for example, the issue of *Cultural Studies* devoted to the subject).[47] The study of news, according to this concept, will no longer center around a linear transmission model of information flow and production, but will shed new light on the role of journalists as intermediaries, articulating as well as connecting the production and consumption of news. This should be seen against the long-held notion of the journalist as "gatekeeper,"[48] as this presumes "that cultural items simply appear at the 'gates' of the media- or culture-producing corporation where they are either admitted or excluded."[49] This excludes, however, the intermediaries' engagement in sifting certain types of information and their endeavor to legitimize their own product and expertise. For instance, the use of correspondents, as I argue below, can be one indicator differentiating between journalistic products among Arab newspapers, adding legitimacy to the final product.

Journalism is usually associated with social responsibility, and research in journalism tends to focus on the same rule.[50]Although I do not oppose this view, my aim here is not to provide normative principles regarding the role of the press. The media, in my view, are but one part of the dialectical and multi-dimensional relationship between media and audience, and/or media and sources. If researchers expect journalists to act in a certain manner, they treat journalism as a notion that is taken for granted instead of questioning the foundation of journalistic practices and journalists' sense of professional identity. Social institutions should be analyzed according to their effects and consequences, but also according to the legitimacy of their foundation.

## The journalistic identity

Journalism is a process of making sense of reality.[51] It has now become common sense to view journalism as occupying a pivotal role in facilitating political debates, and hence a healthy public life. Journalists mediate a "sense" of reality to their audiences, and in so doing they entrench one main signifier of their professional identity as the public's confidant, a role long acclaimed by Joseph Pulitzer, who viewed journalism as "the most fascinating of all professions . . . Every single day opens new doors for the journalist who holds the confidence of the community and has the capacity to address it."[52]

At the heart of this role is the task of transmitting facts, exalting objectivity as the dominant norm, at least in the Anglo-American journalistic model.[53] The news, then, has become the manifestation of the "culture of factuality,"[54] where the real acquires a privileged status. American journalists now agree that scrutinizing governmental claims is an integral part of the journalistic mission. This imposes upon the Arab journalism field a desire to embrace objectivity while keeping a safe distance from subjectivity or indulging in emotion, thus parting company with an old stereotype of the Arab journalist as a mouthpiece and mere stenographer for political forces.

Particularly in covering wars and disasters, journalists feel urged to provide as many facts as possible, and they may end up prioritizing the announcement of figures and numbers even before tolls are counted. This, argues Seaton,[55] may be due to the fact that numbers, especially big numbers, attract the audience's attention to the size of disaster or tragedy reported on. Moreover, the news analysis conducted by van Dijk[56] showed that the news structure in various newspapers in the world was characterized not by differences, but by similarity. Thus, newsmen are engaged in a "textual ritual," producing detached and neutral texts for consumption by the reader.[57] Van Dijk[58] regards the use of figures and statistics as a rather rhetorical device in hard news because the audience has no chance to estimate its significance. Above all, figures are used as a symbol of objectivity of the news stories.

In fact, objectivity is seen to be an integral part of journalistic practice by being part of both the news as a product and of the role of its producer:

1. Part of the production process: adhering to the notion of objectivity, reporters should gather "factual information," and actively seek this information. They should also serve as eyewitnesses of the events, and thus secure the reliability of their information.
2. Part of the journalistic product/output: the news text (as genre) should present this objectivity by avoiding certain textual stratifiers usually related to subjective genres. Thus, the use of the first-person voice is not recommended in journalism textbooks.[59] Also, the text should usually present two points of view.
3. Part of the role of news journalist/text producer: journalists should serve as detached observers who can communicate the reality.

Moreover, at the heart of the journalistic mission is to monitor the political and social environment, with the aim of holding politicians accountable. However, some scholars[60] argue that the news media have accumulated confidence at the expense of the mistrust of politicians, increasing skepticism and cynicism among voters and encouraging a retreat from political participation. This is partly manifested in the increase of the amount of negative news during the past decades. While in the 1960s, American media, for instance, was used as a platform for politicians to communicate at length with their voters, the decades that followed witnessed an increasing awareness of journalistic power, pushing journalists to acclaim new tasks as auditors of the accuracy, integrity, and reliability of political statements.[61] This new role gained precedence thanks to the Watergate investigation, a breakthrough in the journalism profession and a consolidation of the new role. From the 1980s onwards, American critical journalism has turned into a routine criticism of politicians who now serve as adversaries to the journalists.[62] This has added to public disillusionment with political institutions, although, as Patterson argued, politicians do manage to redeem the promises they made during election campaigns.

This investigative power, then, finds its strength in seceding from politics, turning the "investigative arm" into the people's arm rather than the government's. This point was raised in recent debates following the 7 July bombs, and specifically a *Newsnight* interview with members of a radical Islamic sect (al-Ghurabaa). The British police asked the program to hand over material, as well as notes on the interview, thereby giving journalists "a passport that enables them to roam,"[63] asking people questions, scrutinizing the political power of the state. This identity then counter-balances the view of journalists as "interest-driven marionettes."[64]

Assigned the important role of mediator in the modern public sphere, the news media exert a great share of power by providing testimonies documenting such events as the violations of human rights in other countries, the breaking of political promises, and the violating of international conventions in war, thus institutionalizing the act of witnessing. Journalists then obtain a new role as eyewitnesses, documenting history while asserting the legitimacy of their position as auditors of political reality. Acting as a link between politicians and citizens enforces the position of journalists as gatekeepers, not only of information but also of feelings.[65]

Recent studies have further elaborated on the identity politics within the field of journalism. For instance, Van Zoonen[66] analyzed journalistic identity operating in a model based on two dimensions: gender and goal. The former is linked to the binary oppositions of masculinity versus femininity, while the latter is divided between institution versus audience as target. Van Zoonen then places "organizational identity" as lying between the tension of subjectivity (gender, age, education, ethnicity, and so on) and structures (profession, ethics, space, sources, and so on), and calls for the analysis of organizational "identity" rather than organizational "role," for the role concept is "too limited and too volatile to capture the particular mixtures of structure and subjectivity elements that come together in journalists' day-to-day performance."[67]

Furthermore, Carpentier[68] provides an analysis of hegemonic and counter-hegemonic construction of the identity of journalists using Laclau and Mouffe's discourse theory, which operates at two levels: the discursive and the political, where the former operates within a set of nodal points and the latter operates within the concept of hegemony. Identities are then determined by identification (or nodal) points, of which some enjoy a privileged position and then become naturalized. There exist, however, antagonistic identities as counter-hegemonic points of identification.

Carpentier places objectivity at one level, stressing factuality and impartiality and linking it to the autonomous identity of the journalist as "watchdog," juxtaposing at the other level subjective identifications of the journalist as commentator and ideologist. Thus, the journalist (and indeed any agent) can assume a position at any of these points without totally abandoning the hegemonic articulation of the professional identity.

In sum, what these studies show is that the identity of a journalist is based on a set of roles and identification points of objectivity (natural and impartial account of events) and subjectivity (interpreter and investigator of truth).

But how is the role of the journalist manifested in the news text? And would it be possible to illustrate this hybridity of roles (objective observer and reality interpreter) in the textual analysis of a sample of news? Above all, would it be possible to illustrate the hybrid role of pan-Arab media as Janus-faced, looking at both global exteriority and internal reality? To answer these questions, I present an exploratory study into news texts in an attempt to illustrate identity politics at work. In this sense, I adopt the research strategy that looks at practical examples, rather than grand theories, to reach new premises.[69] In the remainder of this chapter, I present the empirical sources of my case study, namely the émigré press as an example of hybrid media. In Chapter 6, I present the analysis in more detail.

## A journalistic milestone

The following analysis looks at the construction of identity in the journalistic product itself, that is, the news text. Crucial here is the means by which the identification points are established, asserting for instance the journalist and/or the media institution's voice, as well as the relationship between journalists and the sources they cover.

Rather than choosing any news texts at random, I focus on war news. War reporting, in particular, represents a critical incident that can be used by journalists to "air, challenge, and negotiate their own boundaries of practice. For instance, contemporary wartime reportage, as seen with the Gulf War, is judged against the experiences of reporting World War II and Vietnam."[70] In this sense, for journalists, "such discourse creates standards of professional behavior against which to evaluate daily news work."[71] I chose a sample of news texts published during the Iraq War in 2003 as a case study that illustrates the role of Arab journalists in the texts.

In particular, the analysis will focus on the hybridity of roles and discourses as manifested in the news texts, which are taken from the (London-based) pan-Arab newspapers as examples of hybrid (diaspora) media.

Recent studies on Arab news media tend to hypothesize about the role of the media based on a theoretical discussion rather than an illustration with practical examples from the various news and documentary genres.[72] I believe the intellectual endeavor should constantly move between theory and practice, or the abstract claim and the concrete example, as the only means for providing an unyielding basis for further debates.

News texts provide rich material for the study of ethics in news reporting,[73] the representation of national identity,[74] or examples of cultural hegemony.[75] In the same vein, I have chosen to confine the following analysis to the role of journalists as illustrated in news texts, and the relationship between journalists and their sources. This is not to say that textual analysis is in and of itself a sufficient method for revealing the identity politics at work; rather, such an analysis should ideally be backed up with relevant results from fieldworks among news producers.

Furthermore, the aim of the following case study is not to show positive, negative or neutral attitudes, towards the Allied Forces, for instance, as illustrated recently in a number of studies. I believe that this kind of coding can merely be used as a means by which to stress the negativity of the portrayal of a certain country or region, without really addressing the issues of why the negativity was there in the first place. This point is of particular importance in the recent debate about the Middle East, which receives a huge amount of aid from both the USA and the EU. One outcome of the 11 September 2001 attacks on the USA was that the US government decided to cut some of its aid programs, or to offer them only on the condition that the anti-American campaigns in the media were stopped. This is not the place to go into a lengthy discussion about the effect of these demands, but suffice it to say that the coding of positive, negative or neutral may possibly not reflect how the general audience responds to a negative or positive attitude in the news. For instance, suppose the coverage of the USA in the Arab news media was found to be 60 percent positive: would that then mean that most Arabs would also have positive attitudes towards the USA and its policies? The positive coverage of, for instance, development projects in the region could not be argued to impose positive feelings about the Arab governments in the region. Indeed, previous studies have shown that even in Western democracies such as Denmark, the news media, although positive on a particular issue, cannot necessarily influence the audience to act in a different way; for example, Jensen[76] showed that the majority of the Danish population voted against the referendum on the EU Maastricht Treaty, even though it was favorably reviewed in the Danish media.

The following analysis takes its point of departure from a sample of news texts about the Iraq War (2003 to present), with the aim of illustrating the diverse roles of journalists as manifested in the journalistic products (the news). The roles, sketched above, exhibit a hybridity or a mixture of identification pointers (objective versus subjective pointers), and the following analysis will expand on this hybridity of roles and discourses, as manifested in the news texts, from a sample of hybrid pan-Arab newspapers.

Let me begin first by briefly discussing the phenomenon of the émigré press as hybrid media combining Western techniques with native concerns, focusing on three particular dates in the coverage of the Iraq War.

## Émigré press as hybrid media

London and Paris, in particular, have been hosts to a number of the so-called pan-Arab newspapers. The phenomenon of publishing outside the Middle East region is not new, as its first wave began in the nineteenth century,[77] with journalists fleeing political and economic situations in their homelands; a second wave followed from the middle of the 1970s. In his comparison between the first and second waves, Abu Zeid[78] showed that the first wave included publications that fled to other regions, as well as others fleeing ethnic and religious conflicts in their own countries but remaining in the region, while the second wave has been confined to migration outside the Arab region. Some of the Arab newspapers in London (and probably other cities as well) are now returning to the Arab region in an attempt to minimize the high costs resulting from their operations abroad. In addition, the technology to which they managed to gain access in their Western headquarters has been made superfluous due to the globalization of technology in the whole world, including the Arab region,[79] despite the censorship that is still practiced one way or another in the Arab States.

Among these newspapers, three in particular have enjoyed a high circulation and represent a forum for important issues for Arab readers:[80] these are *al-Hayat*, *al-Sharq al-Awsat* and *al-Quds al-Arabi*. These, and the international edition of *al-Ahram*, are included in the following case study as representatives of the elite newspapers, and usually serve as suitable sampling material because the prestige media usually provide thorough coverage of foreign affairs in both news texts and commentaries,[81] thus serving as an agenda-setter for other news media outlets. Furthermore, prestige newspapers enjoy a good reputation that is in itself a motivation for their reporters to produce fair and balanced news reports.[82] The elite newspapers also appeal to "globalist" segments of readers, and thus they tend to include a more "global" approach than the local newspapers, not to mention that the prestigious press usually has a larger number of correspondents than the local press.

Additionally, some émigré newspapers (for example, *al-Hayat* and *al-Sharq al-Awsat*) are financed by Saudi businessmen who, in turn, tend to practice the policy of "carrot and stick" to control the opinions conveyed in these broadsheets.[83] *Al-Ahram*, however, is owned by an Egyptian public corporation, and *al-Quds al-Arabi* is the only Arabic newspaper in London with no Saudi sponsors, which makes it interesting to analyze both of these papers' content.

Indeed, the inclusion of these four newspapers responds to the recent call[84] for conducting such comparative studies in order to uncover differences in the content of Arab media. Let me begin, however, by presenting a brief overview of each newspaper included in this case study, pointing to its history, readership, and role on the media scene.

## Al-Hayat

*Al-Hayat* was established after the Second World War, accompanied by a modern plant. In the beginning of the 1950s, *al-Hayat* had the largest circulation registered for a non-Cairo-based paper at that time.[85] *Al-Hayat*, alongside *al-Sharq al-Awsat*, is regarded as the most prestigious and authoritative newspaper in Saudi Arabia. Although published outside the kingdom, these are both still subject to the same constraints as all local newspapers, that is to say, they may never attack Islam.[86]

The paper was founded by Kamel Mrowe (Lebanon) in 1946, but had to close in 1976 following the outbreak of the Lebanese civil war. The newspaper was re-launched in 1988 from London, with financing provided by the Saudi Prince Khalid bin Sultan.[87] The newspaper's editors regard the occasional banning of the newspaper in certain Arab countries as a sign of the newspaper's independence, although being banned in Saudi Arabia in particular may mean a tremendous loss for the newspaper.[88] *Al-Hayat* comes with a weekly supplement called *al-Wasat*, which was first launched as a separate magazine in 1992,[89] however the circulation and advertising sales remained weaker than that of *al-Hayat*. *Al-Wasat* means "in-between" or "in the middle", and the choice of the name was not accidental, as one Arab editor said: "this is the age of 'in-between'; between the end of a world order and a beginning of a new one . . . there is no longer right and left."[90] The magazine focuses mostly on Saudi and Egyptian affairs, ignoring even Lebanese issues.[91]

*Al-Hayat* is known for its neutrality in dealing with important Arab issues, except when it comes to issues sensitive to Saudi views. In terms of technical quality, *al-Hayat* is the closest to the forms of Western newspapers, for example, in its use of color photos. The newspaper offers a forum to various opinions, Islamists, pan-Arabists, and so on.[92]

Through my correspondence with *al-Hayat*, I was informed that the newspaper is seen as the most "objective and daring voice in the Arab international press." Furthermore, its aim is to make the newspaper the first choice for Arabs outside the region, and the second choice for Arabs inside the region, after their local daily.

As for its target audience, *al-Hayat* defines this as "Arabic-speaking, male, above 20, high education and high income," belonging to the intellectual elite, scholars, politicians, and the like. The newspaper is published in London and distributed in more than thirty-five countries and printed in nine different cities. Most of its journalists hold degrees in journalism and they are sometimes quoted in the Western press. The newspaper's circulation was 196,800 copies in 2002. Saudi Arabia is the largest market, receiving almost half of the daily printing (100,200 copies). Circulation in Europe (16,200 copies) equals that in the Levant countries (Lebanon, Jordan and Syria, around 16,750 copies). Egypt and the USA are the next two largest markets for *al-Hayat*, receiving 9,500 and 8,200 copies respectively.

### Al-Sharq al-Awsat

The newspaper was launched by Saudi Research and Marketing in 1978, from London. The company used the latest technology in producing the newspaper and appointed the former editor of *al-Hayat*, Jihad Khazen, as editor-in-chief. The newspaper is published simultaneously in several Western and Arab cities, for example, Cairo, Beirut, Frankfurt, New York and Marseilles. The views represented in the newspaper are diverse, with a readership that is claimed to exceed the circulation figures.[93] The newspaper is regarded as being the first Saudi newspaper operating from abroad. It claims the largest circulation among pan-Arab dailies, and includes a large number of advertisements.[94]

*Al-Sharq al-Awsat* has called itself the "Arab international newspaper."[95] It was founded by two Saudi men, Hesham and Mohamed Hafez, whose father and uncle both practiced journalism and opened a newspaper called *al-Madina* in 1937. The Saudi government turned the General Directorate of Broadcasting, Press and Publication into the Ministry of Information and assigned it the task of regulating press ownership. The committee recommended two solutions: limiting government advertising to one main publication (*Um al-Qura*, established in 1924) and compensating the rest of the publications via secret subsidies; or limiting newspaper ownership to organizations, leaving the government the right to license publications and appoint editors-in-chief. The Saudi government chose the second solution, which was adopted in 1963.[96] After the Saudi press laws changed, the brothers Hafez moved their business to London, where they bought the British Central Press Photo, and from there issued *al-Sharq al Awsat*, attempting to mirror the success of the *International Herald Tribune* as an international newspaper.[97]

The news content in *al-Sharq al-Awsat* focuses on Saudi Arabia, Egypt, Lebanon, Gulf and the Palestinian issue respectively. Most of its writers are either Saudi or Egyptian, followed by those from Lebanon and Palestinian areas.[98] The owners have asserted that they deliberately ignore Saudi news in order not to associate the daily with Saudi views. Abu Zeid[99] argues that the newspaper adopts the Saudi views anyway, although it seeks to be neutral (thus again reflecting the Saudi foreign policy of neutrality). The owners themselves refuse to call their newspaper, or any of their publications, émigré press, arguing that they never emigrated from Saudi Arabia. The reason they publish in London, the owners further argue, is to ensure a neutral view on Arab issues, claiming that each local edition reflects the national policy of the country from where it is issued. The main aim for the owners is to make the newspaper the "second choice" for Arabs living inside or outside the Arab world and for Arab tourists abroad.[100]

## Al-Quds al-Arabi

Launched in 1989, and run under the leadership of the Palestinian-born Abdel Bari Atwan, *al-Quds al-Arabi* has only a handful of reporters in London, and yet it has managed to play an important role among Arab expatriates.[101] One important feature of the newspaper is

that it dedicates one whole page daily to the translations of editorials
and features from Israeli newspapers. The paper does not rely on Saudi
money, which (according to Alterman)[102] has given it more freedom to
scrutinize Gulf politics, but instead depends on funding from the
PLO, and thus its freedom can be argued to be restricted by the policy
of its backers. Abu Zeid, for instance, argues that it serves mainly as a
mouthpiece for the PLO.[103] However, Ghareeb[104] argues that *al-Quds
al-Arabi* has sometimes been critical of the policies of the Palestinian
authority. He describes it as a "daring" newspaper dedicating large
amounts of space to Arab issues, and offering on its op-ed page a
forum for a diversity of views representing different Arab factions.
*Al-Quds al-Arabi* is usually seen as the "the most Arabist of Arab
newspapers."[105]

   *Al-Quds al-Arabi* is the fourth émigré newspaper printed in
London, following *al-Arab*, *al-Sharq al-Awsat* and *al-Hayat*. The
newspaper focuses on Palestinian issues and targets Palestinians
abroad and others interested in Palestinian issues.[106] The editor-in-
chief said once that, apart from himself, there was no other Palestinian
staff member, as the team consisted of different Arab nationals. It is
worth noting that the newspaper contains not more than one or two
advertisements (if any) per issue, which was the reason why Abu
Zeid[107] argued that it serves mainly as a mouthpiece for the PLO, who
contributed to its budget and thereby cast doubt upon its independence. However, in order to show the newspaper's objectivity, the
editor-in-chief referred to the frequent invitations he received from
various Western news media to comment on important Arab events,[108]
arguing that he would not have been invited if his newspaper was not
known for its objectivity.[109]

### Al-Ahram

The harsh political situation in Lebanon, including increasing pressure
by the Ottomans in the nineteenth century, forced many Lebanese
journalists to flee to other countries. Some fled to Egypt, which had
gained autonomy after 1831. These journalists fostered the profession
of journalism in Egypt, and even monopolized the publication of
newspapers, some of which still exist to this day, for example, the daily
*al-Ahram* and the weekly *al-Musawar*.[110] *Al-Ahram* was established in
1879 by two Lebanese brothers named Teqla.[111] It was launched as a
weekly paper, which became daily in 1881. It operated first from
Alexandria (until 1899), before moving to Cairo.[112] The two brothers

had French citizenship, which gave them freedom to criticize the Ottoman ruler (Ismail) of Egypt, a circumstance that sometimes resulted in closing *al-Ahram* temporarily.[113]

Since its birth, *al-Ahram* has claimed the role of being the main provider of information on vast local and foreign issues, not to mention analysis features on various subjects.[114] According to the historical account provided by Ayalon,[115] *al-Ahram* marked its objectivity by giving higher priority to reportage than to ideological views. However, according to Abu Zeid,[116] *al-Ahram*'s founders used the newspaper to express their political inclinations, as they did when the British army invaded Egypt in 1882 (for example, by welcoming the British general leading the British troops in to Egypt).

*Al-Ahram* belongs to a large publishing house, which is one of the four dominant publishing houses in Egypt.[117] *Al-Ahram* is published in an international edition, the content of which is based on the national issue printed from Cairo. According to Ghareeb,[118] some Arab newspapers issue international editions that are only copies of the national edition, and thus primarily address expatriates of the same nationality. *Al-Ahram*, however, reaches wider segments of Arabs abroad (namely in Europe and the USA).

The circulation of *al-Ahram* reaches around 900,000, ranking third at the national level and fifty-third at the international level.[119] Al-Ahram Publishing House publishes a number of other newspapers and magazines in both Arabic and foreign languages (English and French), for example, *al-Ahram Hebdo*, *al-Ahram Weekly* and other specialized publications in Arabic. The newspaper is usually included in media and communication studies involving the Middle East,[120] since it represents the mainstream and "widely read press."[121]

## Dates to remember in a global war

As I mentioned earlier, the analysis presented in Chapter 6 focuses on news texts about Iraq War. The war broke out on 19 March 2003 (or 20 March at c. 4.00 a.m. Baghdad time). The first operation was called "Operation Iraqi Freedom," targeting Saddam Hussein and other leaders in Baghdad. Approximately a week after the war broke out, international news media circulated the news of the first civilian causalities, which was supposed to contradict what the Allied Forces said about the war being a "clean war." The first report on casualties was on 27 March 2003, following the missile attacks on Nasr Market in Baghdad. One important date on the war timeline was indeed 9 April 2003, which witnessed the fall of Baghdad and US forces taking control of the city. Officially, the major war operations were declared over on 1 May 2003, although some battles are still going on to date between American forces and Iraqi rebels.

The following analysis will focus on front-page stories, since the front page can be seen as the newspaper's display window, viewing the new events that matter. Although the period stretching from the first day of the war (on 19 March 2003) until the "official" announcement of its end (on 1 May 2003) encompasses a wealth of news texts that can be used for our purpose here, I had to narrow the choice and therefore confine the analysis to a coherent sample from the following dates:

- 19 March 2003 – the day war broke out. The articles chosen deal with the preparation for the war and the American soldiers taking positions around the outskirts of Iraq.
- 27 March 2003 – the first civilian casualties among Iraqis. The articles selected here deal with shootings in civilian areas and resistance acts by Republican Guard troops.
- 9 April 2003 – the fall of Baghdad. The articles chosen for this day are about the American forces' efforts to control Baghdad, following air strikes on the Palestine Hotel, where almost all foreign journalists were based.

In general, the focus of *al-Quds al-Arabi* was on the war and its casualties from an Arab standpoint. Thus, the war is foregrounded as the main global event. The assemblage of articles shows a movement in space, moving between Iraq, Europe and the USA. The latter is particularly obvious in all spaces: in the Arab space due to the war, and the US efforts to help the Kurds control some small villages in Iraq. *Al-Sharq al-Awsat* maintained an "Arab" focus, giving the space to Gulf countries' statements, for example, Saudi Arabia, which were given less space in other Arab newspapers. *Al-Hayat* attempted to show an "all-round" view of the war, where the main focus was the ordinary Iraqi people, with interviews and quotes from both Western and Arab sources and with correspondents' reports from Baghdad and other cities. In contrast to both *al-Quds al-Arabi* and *al-Sharq al-Awsat*, the role of Egypt is foregrounded in *al-Ahram*. One simple explanation for this is that it is primarily a national newspaper, unlike the three other newspapers in this study, which claim a pan-Arab role, and thus it is predictable that *al-Ahram* reflects only the national government's views. However, it may be that the Egyptian press really sees

Egypt as the leader of the Arab nation, and highlighting this role is merely part of this discourse.

## Conclusion

As I have argued in this chapter, reason, in universal (Habermasian) terms, is not the only tenet of the global public sphere; rather, we should be attentive to the view of reason as a set of rules contingent to the field in which it is articulated. Accordingly, viewing journalists, cross-culturally, as one unified community excludes the articulation of difference among them. I therefore call for the analysis of power relations influencing the global media scene, and hence the significance of the analysis of the professional identity of journalists as mediators of global debates.

I examined the role of Arab journalists in facilitating on the media scene, drawing on the notion of hybridity, which assigns journalists the role of a cultural bridge between a global Other and a local self. The identity of journalists, as I have shown above, is based on a set of roles mixing objectivity (impartial narrative) with subjectivity (interpretation of truth). I will take these tenets as my point of departure in my textual analysis of Arab news stories printed during the Iraq War.

Above, I presented the empirical sources of this analysis, namely a sample of the so-called émigré press, based in London. In Chapter 6 I present my analysis in more detail, showing how the news texts reflect the position of Arab journalists vis-à-vis their Western counterparts.

# Truth Martyrs

Barbie Zelizer[1] argues that the incorporation of tools of humanistic inquiry, for example, narrative and literary studies in the analysis of journalism, contributes to the examination of the journalism profession and how the authority of this profession is constructed in order to hold the members of its community together. Assuming that discourse both constitutes the social world and is in itself a constitution of other social practices,[2] I shall seek to show how the news texts constitute the war event while simultaneously being reflections of journalistic identity and practices.

In particular, the following analysis will focus on the hybridity of roles and discourses as manifested in news texts taken from four émigré newspapers as examples of hybrid media. This is to illustrate the hybridity of roles (objective observer and reality interpreter). Throughout the news texts, reporters (or the news institution as a whole) serve as mediators between news sources and news audience. They also provide a means of mapping social reality, with the "collage of events"[3] from various parts of the world assembled together in a shared routine. News texts, then, contribute to the upholding of the narrative of journalism as profession.

The following analysis takes as its point of departure the view that sees identity as constituted through the processes of similarity and differences.[4] This is to say, for instance, that Arab journalists may be discursively designated a single identity with certain characteristics that supposedly bind all Arabs together while juxtaposing this identity to an opposite "Other," that is, non-Western journalists. Thus, for the relation identified by the shared traits to gain foothold it needs to be defined against an Other-identity. Actors then strive to "fix" these identities "locked into a specific relationship to the others."[5] The position assigned each actor is in tandem with a set of rules and expectations of what to do or say. As actors are "fragmented," possessing diverse identities at once – for example, journalist, woman, educated and nationalist – this gives rise to conflicting discourses.

Practically, Arab news professionals may be designated a professional identity of "journalists" characterized by certain attributes and globally binding them to others in the same profession while setting boundaries among journalists according to their position in a global professional hierarchy. This professional identity is based on the "*dialectic of identification*: how we identify ourselves, how others identify us, and the ongoing interplay of these in process of social identification."[6]

What I would like to stress in the following analysis is the means by which "external categorization may be received as legitimate," that is, how Arab journalists may adapt the same identity designated to them by their Western counterparts, while struggling to re-allocate this identity, thereby resisting being locked into a fixed category. Some Arab media outlets, as I ague below, may even work actively to re-brand Arab journalism. Central to this categorization are time and space,[7] for example, the position of Arab journalists vis-à-vis Western journalists. As I argue below, the news stories show dynamic pace in moving across spaces, and times, and this dynamism has indeed become an integral feature of the modern role of Arab journalist and reporter. Also, evoking certain memorial dates is, as I show below, vital to upholding of the narrative of one global "interpretive community" of journalists.

To unravel the dialectic of identification between Arab and Western journalists, I note the instances when Western or Arab news institutions are referred to in the Arab news texts. These instances are then categorized according to the role designated Western or Arab journalists, that is, watchdogs. One direct outcome of this analysis, as I discuss below, is to challenge the theory of hegemony as presented in the scholarship about Arab media. Hegemony, I argue, cannot be confined to the monopoly certain international news agencies exercise over the process of newsgathering. Hegemony, instead, rests on power unevenly distributed between Arab versus Western journalists, even though all principally belong to a single interpretive community. Moreover, this power distribution among news institutions defines the parameters of the global media sphere, which may no longer be monopolized by a few players but is nonetheless characterized by the struggle among media institutions in both Western and Eastern spheres to re-define their position in the global field.

I group the following analysis around particular themes or roles that were clear in the news texts, of which extracts will be presented below. To save space, the extracts presented have already been translated into English rather than presenting them in their original Arabic, followed by a translation. The overall themes are indeed in harmony with the roles of journalists as objective raconteurs of reality and investigators of truth, as discussed in the previous chapter.

I have to stress that the news texts sampled here can indeed be analyzed in a myriad ways. I choose, however, to confine this exercise to the role of journalists (Arab and Western) as manifested textually. In general, the following analysis shows the spread of three particular roles, as evident in the following extracts. These roles range from 1) onlooker, and 2) auditor, to 3) truth martyr.

As I show below, these roles were represented in the news texts not merely to reflect the identity of local versus pan-Arab journalists in the Arab journalistic field, but also to signal the position of both of these vis-à-vis global actors such as CNN. I also show how these roles spread across the examined newspapers, where two outlets seem to favor the first role and the other two seem to highlight the second role. All newspapers, however, adopted the third role, as a means to bind Arab journalists with their counterparts in other countries in one interpretive community.

## Journalist as onlooker

One important task of the journalist is to survey the "reality" of war, documenting the course of events as well as casualties and violations. The act of documentation is rendered legitimate by the incorporated details and figures, for example, the exact time that it took the Allied Forces to react, the exact size of the bomb, the date and time, and so on. As Gamson pointed out, "Facts have no intrinsic meaning. They take on their meaning by being embedded in a frame or story line that organizes them and gives them coherence, selecting certain ones to emphasize while ignoring others."[8] The use of facts and figures is indeed one objectifying strategy in news reporting, and the newspapers included in this study showed some similarities in the use of "bare facts" as an integral part of their news reports. These facts and figures should signal the neutrality of the news reporter/correspondent who acts partly as interpreter of events, but also partly as "stenographer," transmitting the exact details of the event to the readers, as illustrated in the following extract:

---

**Al-Sharq al-Awsat (9 April 2003)**

An American official said that the CIA received information from a "source in Baghdad" stating that Saddam and his two sons would be meeting with security and intelligence officials in a building in the Mansour quarter. Forty-five minutes after receiving this information, the American middle leadership in Qatar launched a B1 missile to throw four bombs, 2000 pounds each, on the building at 3 p.m. the day before yesterday, local time. The official said, "If Saddam was in the building, it is mostly likely that he is dead now." The official described the information as being "the most precise" about Saddam and his sons since the beginning of the war, with a raid on another civil compound in Baghdad where it was said that Saddam and his sons were hiding on 20 March. He said also that one or two days were needed before confirming the result of this operation and that the raid came after tracking Qusay's communications.

---

The journalists here re-tell the account of the shooting as faithfully as possible, recalling for instance the chain of command, "the American middle leadership in Qatar," rather than just referring to it as "American forces," and going through the steps of command: first receiving the information, then acting promptly (after forty-five minutes), then launching a B1 missile on a specific building at a specific time (3 p.m. local time). The official's statements are quoted at length, thus adding to the legitimacy of the account: "If Saddam was in the building, it is most likely that he is dead now." The incident is linked to a previous incident in the course of war, "where it was said that Saddam and his sons were hiding," which was dated to increase the sense of accuracy (20 March). Certain details, in sum, were carefully extracted to add to the authenticity of the journalistic account: the number of people killed or injured, the type of warplane (for example, an A10), weight of bomb, the precise distance (in km) and time (in minutes) in the description of military operations, and so on.

Knowledge, then, is the basis of a "true" representation of reality, and various sources exist for acquiring it. The journalist's role is to link the various sources and build up a true representation of the course of the war through referring to these very sources. The representation, however, is inherently hierarchical, for some sources appear as authoritative informants, while other sources provide doubtful utterances, which the journalist scrutinizes. In the extract above, the military sources are likely to provide precise and trusted knowledge due to their engagement and physical presence in the battlefield. They are not only reliable sources of information, they are also powerful sources that, in cooperation with other institutions (intelligence), cleverly draw on a network of informants to realize their target: "the CIA received information from a " 'source in Baghdad' stating that Saddam . . ." Notice that the "source in Baghdad" is in quotation marks, heightening the sensationalist value of the news piece.

The above news piece begins with several datelines (Kuwait, Moscow, London) and a couple of bylines (from correspondents in Washington and Paris), thus showing the dynamism in gathering and presenting the news. This dynamism, moreover, is enforced by the fast pace in moving among different time zones ("3 p.m. local [Iraqi] time"), a characteristic also shared in other news accounts:

---

### Al-Sharq al-Awsat (19 March 2003)

While the world awaits the first strike of war, the Iraqi leadership hurried yesterday to reject the ultimatum . . . which ends at 1 a.m. tomorrow, Greenwich time . . .

---

### Al-Ahram (19 March 2003)

Fleischer said that the ultimatum would end at 8 o'clock tonight, Washington time (or 3 a.m. Cairo time) . . .
    . . . On the Iraqi side, the official television announced yesterday the holding of an urgent parliamentary session at 10 o'clock this morning, local time . . .

---

The ultimatum given to the former Iraqi president is referred to in terms of diverse time zones (Cairo, Baghdad, Greenwich, and Washington time), making the journalists a group of "cosmopolitans" who freely and easily move across different times and spaces. In addition, the time zones represent a hierarchal representation of reality as well; thus, events are timed according to certain areas and not others (for example, Greenwich and not Malaysian time). Representation that follows this timing then accentuates this hierarchy in favor of seeing world events from a certain temporality, rather than translating the events into a local temporality.

The antagonism between these temporalities (local and global, where the latter is pre-assigned to certain time zones/spaces) is also reflected in the Arab satellite channels, where the times of different programs are usually announced in both Greenwich and Mecca times. Moreover, al-Jazeera, for one, sometimes announces programs only in Mecca time, thus enforcing a central (Arab) reference point, although a major part of its audience is said to belong to diaspora communities.

The dynamism in movement is enforced, as mentioned above, in the multiple bylines and datelines, emphasizing the role of journalists in managing multiple spaces. It was *al-Sharq al-Awsat* and *al-Hayat*, in particular, that sought to enforce this dynamism via multiple bylines (and not only datelines), stressing thereby the (new) role of correspondents as credible sources of information and knowledge, as well as their autonomy as media institutions with their own network of sources.

The news text further stresses this pace by moving constantly from one space to another, such as in the following extract, which begins in the USA, telling the reader about Bush's ultimatum (which was due to end), then shift quickly to other geographical spaces.

### *Al-Ahram* (19 March 2003)

As for the international reactions to Bush's speech, both France and Russia issued a harsh warning yesterday against using military power against Iraq . . . And on his part, the French president said that the war on Iraq is illegal . . . and in Beijing, the new prime minister said that his country would not give up on its efforts to solve the Iraqi crisis peacefully . . . and in Britain two ministers, of health and interior affairs, resigned in protest against the rigid policy of Blair's government . . .

This piece is initiated with a general dateline (world cities) and a general byline (*al-Ahram* correspondents), thus enforcing the institutional identity of *al-Ahram* rather than highlighting the names of individual correspondents dispersed in diverse spaces in order to gather the reactions to the event (here, the ultimatum). The text shows the fast pace in moving across diverse geographical spaces, from the USA, to France, to China and Britain ("the French president said . . . and in Beijing, the new prime minister said . . . and in Britain, two ministers . . . resigned"). Phrases such as "and in Beijing" are deployed to serve a double-edged function: to serve as a cohesion device while marking the shift in space and/or topic. Here is another example:

---

### *Al-Sharq al-Awsat* (27 March 2003)

Thousands of fighters from the Republican Guard troops and "Fedayeen Saddam" move from Baghdad . . . to stop the progress of the American forces towards the Iraqi capital. <u>And while a fierce battle went on yesterday</u> over the control of a bridge near Najaf, the Pentagon admitted that Iraqi forces destroyed an unlimited number of artilleries . . . <u>and in an indication of increasing pressures on American forces,</u> the Pentagon declared that the 4th Cavalry will move today from the USA to Iraq. <u>On the other hand</u>, it was known yesterday that lawyers/legal experts accompanied the American forces in order to discuss imposition of emergency laws. <u>On the other hand</u>, the spokesman of the middle management in the American forces refused to comment on the missile attack on a popular quarter of north-east Baghdad . . .

---

In the above extract, the news report marks a shift among different geographical spaces and temporalities. It begins with a present scene from Baghdad, where Iraqi fighters were getting ready to clash with American forces, then moves back to the past, reminding the reader of a battle that took place near Najaf, introducing a comment from the USA-situated Pentagon.

In English, words such as "still" and "but" or prepositional phrases can be used as initial markers, introducing adversative statements or for the purpose of shifting the topic/scene. In Arabic, on the other hand, to ensure cohesion among sentences in the news items, reporters are not content with using "*wa*" (or "and") as the only means for achieving this. Phrases such as "in Beijing" and "in Britain" mark the reporters' cohesion strategies in shifting to either another related topic or shifting the speaker/scene. One qualified explanation for using these markers was provided by a recent linguistic study on the language of news discourse in Arabic and English.[9] This study points to some important features characterizing these markers, such as "on the other hand" and "on his/her part," which usually occur at the beginning of the sentence. Their presence is not just a matter of stylistic variation, but is actually dictated by the rhetoric of news discourse as a genre, to the extent that an attempt to delete them would result in a distortion of the cohesion links within the news text.

Phrases such as "on the other hand" and "in an indication of increasing pressures" (above) mark the dynamic pace in moving from one event and one comment to another, stressing the role of the journalist as "onlooker," one that stands above the events and marks down their sequence, and yet maintains the power to move back and forth in space and time to add to this account of reality. Defined beforehand, these spaces are restricted to the political and military fields, gathering information and commentaries from authoritative voices there. However, journalists are not there merely to transmit statements made by the "authorities," but rather to question their reliability. It is here that the identity of the journalist as auditor and "watchdog" takes shape.

## Journalist as auditor

Prior to the expiry of the ultimatum issued to Saddam and his family, the Saudi royal family announced that it would not participate in the coalition formed by the USA, justifying this, as announced in a formal speech to the nation (*al-Sharq al-Awsat*, 19 March 2003), by its wish to protect the Saudi people and the Saudi interest. Nevertheless, the statements made by the royal family were not taken at face value, and doubt was cast over their credibility.

---

### *Al-Quds al-Arabi* (19 March 2003)

Riyadh hurried to declare that it is not participating in the war, which should end by applying decree 1551.
   But American media/press reports confirmed that American planes will be using Saudi bases in battles and that the Saudi grounds will be open for humanitarian and logistic operations for American forces inside Iraq.
   The reports said that the British forces will move toward Basra and will take over the control in the south generally, while the American forces will move directly towards Baghdad . . .

---

The announcement made by and in "Riyadh" is juxtaposed with American media reports that confirmed Saudi participation by allowing American forces to operate on Saudi grounds. Thus, credibility is hauled away from the politicians' statements and accrues instead in the transnational media's reports, thereby enforcing the latter's capital as sources of reliable information[10] (which at times may outweigh any doubt as to the type of sources or discourses upon which they draw). Thus, the international media reports were mentioned and quoted without questioning their credibility or the discourse they were appropriating. Even though *al-Quds al-Arabi* at times doubts American officials' statements (see below), it did not doubt the transnational media, for example, CNN, Reuters, AFP, BBC:

---

### *Al-Quds al-Arabi* (27 March 2003)

The television station <u>CNN</u> said that a huge queue of Iraqi Republican Guard troops left Baghdad yesterday evening (Wednesday), moving towards the American forces marshalling near Najaf city.
<u>The station said through its correspondent</u> who accompanies the 7th Cavalry: "A long queue of 1000 Iraqi mobile units, including perhaps trained artilleries and vehicles, left Baghdad and is moving towards Najaf."

---

Reports made by CNN (through its correspondent) provided a reliable "onlooker" view of the spectacle of war as it takes place in the battlefield, as well as in the minds of strategists. A similar view was shown in *al-Ahram*:

---

### *Al-Ahram* (19 March 2003)

Amidst the increasing expectations of waging the war, the <u>military correspondent of the BBC</u> <u>predicted</u> that military operations should start in the first hours of next Saturday, and said that the military leadership <u>preferred to postpone</u> the strike until the waning of the moon and darker nights, because the full moon in the next few days does not suit the land operations. The correspondent said that the ultimatum . . . ends by Thursday dawn, and <u>it is not appropriate</u> to launch military operations on Friday, which is a Muslim holy day. Therefore, the most <u>accurate calculations</u>, which take into account the weather forecast and expected heavy storms, point to Saturday dawn as a <u>suitable timing</u> for these operations.

---

Here, the BBC correspondent calculates and weighs up the incoming information, in order to form a prognosis of a future scenario ("the military correspondent of the BBC predicted that . . ."). His knowledge then is taken for granted, for his prediction is not based on pure speculation but on knowledge of military tactics a well as local tradition ("the military leadership preferred to postpone until the waning of the moon . . . because the full moon does not suit the land operations"). In addition, the correspondent weighs the pronounced political plan to launch a military operation right upon the end of the ultimatum against his own knowledge of the local tradition: as the ultimatum ends "on Friday . . . a Muslim holy day," he decides to abandon the possibility of launching war on Friday. Instead, he provides another prognosis based on "accurate calculations" of several factors, "which take into account the weather forecast and expected heavy storms," leading him to conclude that "Saturday dawn" would be the most "suitable timing for these operations."

Foreign media sources, moreover, serve as eyewitnesses at the heart of events, writing back home details of events unfolding, and their testimonials add to the process of making sense of the war, mediated via bodily sense.

### Al-Ahram (26 March 2003)

And after three hours of fierce fighting in Nasriya city, the American marine forces managed to cross a bridge over the Euphrates river . . . and the correspondent of the AFP said that the smell of "human flesh" spread in the skies of that city, which lies 375 km from Baghdad.

. . . The Iraqi president Saddam Hussein called upon the Iraqi tribes to resist the American and British forces . . . and urged them in a speech aired at the Iraqi television . . .

. . . The British Air Marshall, Brian Burridge, lessens the possibility of achieving fast victory, and rejected in statements to the BBC network Britain's intention to increase its forces . . .

The testimonial of the AFP correspondent is enforced by the bodily experience of "smelling" and "seeing," as the correspondent wanders in Nasriya, smelling "human flesh" and seeing its smoke "spread in the skies," wrapping this bodily experience in the objective narrative of the journalistic report by adding details on the exact location of the city ("which lies 375 km from Baghdad").

While the foreign media have access to local as well as foreign political sources, local media, on the other hand, are deployed mainly as channels of communication, or as a town crier through which messages could be disseminated to the citizens. Thus, Saddam Hussein used the local media to transmit a message to the Iraqi tribes ("urged them in a speech aired at the Iraqi television"), and a podium from which he can mobilize Iraqis. A similar strategy was used by other Iraqi officials:

---

### Al-Quds al-Arabi (27 March 2003)

. . . The [Iraqi] spokesman said <u>briefly on the Iraqi TV</u>, regarding Iraqi oper-ations during the past 24 hours, that a British plane was downed near Basra, and a Somoud missile was launched targeting al-Salem air base in Kuwait.

---

The Iraqi spokesman appeared on television, albeit "briefly," to issue updates on the course of the war and on the Iraqi resistance progress, using the media as a briefing stand from which he addressed the nation. Other pan-Arab media served the same purpose:

---

### Al-Quds al-Arabi (19 March 2003)

. . . and [Nagi] Sabry [former foreign minister] said in a press conference, which he held in the Iraqi capital and which al-<u>Jazeera satellite channel transmitted live</u>, "We did not ask for help from anybody, but we say to the Arab countries that their security is threatened."

---

The former foreign minister held press conferences, which received attention from regional media, for example, al-Jazeera, which trans-mitted them live. A word of caution is due here: some scholars[11] see the inclination of news media, particularly television, to report on or transmit press conferences live as a sign of using media to transmit hegemonic values and ideas. However, journalists from Arab satellite channels justify the endeavor to broadcast press conferences as part of the function of the Fourth Estate in giving voice to different political actors. For instance, al-Habib al-Ghoureibi, from an Abu Dhabi TV station, said that his station was striving to broadcast Arab and American press conferences during the Iraq War, giving equal times to both parties in order to emphasize the station's impartiality. The same view was supported by Faisal al-Kasim (al-Jazeera), who said that it was part of the channel's task to give the floor to all speakers.[12]

In sum, while Arab politicians use local media to transmit informa-tion, foreign media seem to scrutinize and evaluate statements.

Moreover, this may pinpoint the hierarchies that exist within the "journalistic field," so it is not only political discourses that flow within a hierarchy of power (where US politicians' statements, for instance, are placed higher than an Arab politician's), media discourses are also contingent upon the powers within the global journalistic field itself. CNN news discourses may occupy a more significant place in this field – vis-à-vis the discourses circulated by an Arab media outlet – and hence are more often quoted as reliable sources of information. According to Fandy, foreign media are usually associated with "trustworthy information," which is the reason that the Arab audiences trust foreign services such as the BBC more than their own, or, as he put it: "It is not that Arabs do not trust the media because it is foreign but that Arabs, like everyone else, are selective about what to trust and what not to trust."[13]

In contrast to *al-Quds al-Arabi* and *al-Ahram*, *al-Hayat* and *al-Sharq al-Awsat*, as mentioned before, were keen to publish the multiple bylines of their correspondents, thus enforcing its power as a news-gatherer. To further consolidate this role, however, references to other (foreign) media institutions were discarded, and statements made by foreign (American) officials were referred to directly in the news texts:

---

### Al-Hayat (19 March 2003)

. . . The <u>White House confirmed</u> yesterday its determination to send allied forces from 30 countries to Iraq to disarm its prohibited weapons . . . <u>American officials confirmed</u> that the USA "has showered" the soldiers in southern Iraq with pamphlets urging them to surrender . . .

<u>It was announced</u> in Washington yesterday that the Bush administration has formed an alliance to disarm Iraq "immediately" . . .

---

Rather than citing these sources' reports verbatim, reporters (and editors) interpret the incoming statements, as illustrated in the use of verbs such as "confirm" ("the White House confirmed yesterday . . . American officials confirmed that the USA . . ."), confining the direct quote to controversial parts of statements ("the USA 'has showered' the soldiers in southern Iraq with pamphlets").

Also, the information disseminated from Washington was transmitted using the passive rather than active voice ("it was announced in Washington yesterday . . ."), although Arabic news is usually reported in the active voice.[14] This further eliminates middle-man sources (foreign media) while bringing *al-Hayat* and *al-Sharq al-Awsat* correspondents closer to the main sources of power/knowledge.

### Al-Sharq al-Awsat (19 March 2003)

And it was noticed a collective fleeing from Arbeel city, the capital of the Iraqi Kurdish province and from cities and town near the fighting zone. . . Above this, the American spokesperson Ary Fleischer said yesterday that Washington had not yet seen any indication that Saddam would abide by the ultimatum . . .

Most of the statements come from American sources, which implies the acknowledgement of the USA as a military and political power. Hence, foreign statements are seen as more likely to shape future events and, more importantly, to be more closely scrutinized rather than local statements, which are rather predictable.

This power can be manifested textually in the use of tense to indicate the distribution of power among interlocutors. The Arabic newspapers, for instance, assigned present tense to the direct speech by American leaders, while citations by the Iraqi leadership were in the past tense. This could be a sign of the power assigned to American leadership in this conflict and is part of each newspaper's particular discourse in framing the Iraq War. Thus, *al-Ahram*, for instance, deployed the future tense in statements by foreign officials:

### Al-Ahram (19 March 2003)

Ari Fleischer, the White House spokesman, said yesterday, less than 24 hours after issuing the ultimatum, that Washington had not yet seen any proof that Saddam would give in to the ultimatum and leave Iraq. He explained that, even if Saddam Hussein and his sons leave Iraq, the Allied Forces will enter the Iraqi lands to ensure the disarming of the Weapons of Mass Destruction.

Fleischer said that the ultimatum would end at 8 o'clock tonight, Washington time (or 3 a.m. Cairo time), and that Bush is the one who will decide the time to begin the war.

The US government, then, has the will and power to determine future events, for example, whether there will be war, and whether

Saddam and his sons may stay in Iraq, and so on. Another example is the following extract, in which the White House spokesman tells the world media the future scenario prepared by the US government.

---

### Al-Sharq al-Awsat (19 March 2003)

On the other hand, Washington said that it did not see any indication of Saddam's abiding by the ultimatum and considered this to be "another mistake" committed by Saddam if he did not leave. While the American forces in Kuwait were getting ready yesterday for the attack, one of its leading generals said that victory in Iraq will happen "within days."

He said that Saddam's decision to stay in Iraq will be "another mistake committed by Saddam Hussein." He resumed, "My role does not include naming the countries to which he could flee." Fleischer said that the Allied Forces formed by the USA will enter Iraqi to disarm it, even if Saddam left.

The American ambassador to Iraqi, Zalmai Khalil Zad, said yesterday that the Kurdish Iraqi battalions will put themselves under American command in the event of American military operations being launched against Iraq.

---

This is a series of statements issued from Washington indicating the course of future events, determining what will be happening and evaluating the moves taken by the opponent ("did not see any indication of Saddam's abiding by the ultimatum and considered this to be 'another mistake' committed by Saddam"). One American authority was quoted asserting the victory even before it took place ("victory in Iraq will happen"), although his assertion that it will happen "within days" seems to be controversial, as it is the only bit of his speech that was put in quotation marks.

The USA's allies inside Iraq (Zalmai Khalil Zad) also acknowledged US power, confirming their intention to "put themselves under American command."

Thus, statements issued by the Allied Forces (concerning the overall war strategy) were quoted in the future tense, claiming the upper hand in the course of the war. Likewise, President Bush, in the following quote, promised his soldiers and the Iraqi people that the Iraqi regime "will be" punished, and that the punishment day is "near."

> ### Al-Sharq al-Awsat (27 March 2003)
>
> On the other hand, President Bush said yesterday that the war on Iraq was progressing but was still far from over. He added, at addressing the soldiers at McDowell air force base in Florida, "I assure you, and assure the Iraqi people who suffered for too long, that the Iraqi regime will be held accountable and that day is getting close."

In sum, the role of news media here is to orchestrate all the political statements available and to interweave them into a dynamic narrative, moving across spaces and temporality, and supporting this narrative with statements issued from abroad (particularly from the USA). *Al-Ahram* and *al-Quds al-Arabi* relied on foreign media institutions to deliver, comment and evaluate these statements, enforcing the role of journalists as "onlookers." On the other hand, *al-Hayat* and *al-Sharq al-Awsat* preferred to present the statements as indirect quotations, with no mention of the source, thereby emphasizing the role of their correspondents as newsgatherers (as shown in the multiple bylines at the beginning of each news piece) and enforcing the role of journalists as "auditor or watchdog." In fact, the former *al-Hayat* editor-in-chief boasted about the newspaper's dependence on *al-Hayat*'s own correspondents to cover international events, rather than drawing on the ready-made news packages provided by the main news agencies.[15]

## Journalists as truth martyrs

Examining the use of attribution in Arabic and English news on BBC Arabic radio, al-Shabbab and Swales[16] demonstrated the use of attribution features, not so much quoting Arab officials but rather quoting two other sources: the BBC correspondents and the news itself, for example, *al'anbaa' tufiid* (or "the news says"). This tendency is seen in the following text, where Arab newspapers tend to refer back to themselves as actors in the event:

> ### Al-Sharq al-Awsat (27 March 2003)
>
> "*Al-Sharq al-Awsat*" yesterday entered the Iraqi city of Safwan, accompanying the food and medical aid convoy coming from Kuwait to the city inhabitants, whose number is c. 2,000, under British guardianship.

This entails the presence of a newspaper as an institution and implies the capacity consecrated in a whole institution (rather than an individual) to cover the war. Also, another possible effect of "institutionalizing" the reporter/narrator role is to enhance the objectivity of reports by undermining the subjectivity of reporters as individual actors.

---

### Al-Hayat (27 March 2003)

However, the American deputy Secretary of State, Richard Armitage, confirmed that the American forces "will do all what it takes" in order to topple the Iraqi regime, even if they had to fight inside the cities. He said in an interview with al-Hayat, to be published tomorrow . . .

---

Previous research on Arabic journalistic discourse has shown that quoting sources adds authenticity to news reports.[17] Citations are thus a means of displaying the news institution's objectivity by presenting the opinions or statements uttered by one or several parties on a certain issue. Moreover, Fandy[18] argues that trust in Arab (and Islamic) societies depends on the model of *isnad*, where the chain of sources is identified to stand behind an authoritative utterance. Thus, as the Prophet's sayings (Hadith) are transmitted through a chain of authoritative sources, Arab audiences need to verify the information they receive. However, as shown above, the *isnad* was not a particularly important strategy for either *al-Hayat* or *al-Sharq al-Awsat*, who report the events in the passive voice and at times quote foreign officials without mentioning their names. Yet, in adding the institutional voice, as above, news media stress their own participation in the event, and hence the *isnad* refers to their institutions as *the* main source.

Journalists, then, are involved as active actors participating in the event unfolding before them. In their capacity as eyewitnesses, they seek to investigate the truth, a mission that may collide with the interests of certain political parties. For instance, on 8 April 2003, more than a hundred journalists residing at the Palestine Hotel in Baghdad came under fire from US forces, leaving three dead. The International Federation of Journalists (IFJ) condemned the attack and demanded an explanation, while the US forces declared the strike to be a mistake. The killing of the journalists, according to *al-Quds al-Arabi*, was prompted by US fears that the "media" would reveal US atrocities, and was therefore implicit proof of the trust placed in foreign and/or regional media institutions' capacity to expose political malice:

**Al-Quds al-Arabi (9 April 2003)**

The American spokesman in Silieh base in Qatar <u>claimed</u> that the bombing of the hotel came after an Iraqi sniper shot an RPG missile from the hotel lobby, but then he <u>corrected</u> his statement to say that the sniper came from inside the hotel.

<u>According to observers, the aim of the bombing of the hotel where the journalists resided . . . is to scare the journalists and force them to leave the Iraqi capital,</u> which would allow the American forces to commit more massacres without any media coverage.

Doubt was cast over the American political statement, which was reported on as a "claim," and the doubt was further stressed when the official "corrected" his statement later, indicating that the whole statement may have been a mere fabrication rather than a representation of facts. The main aim of concealing facts here was to "scare" journalists from reporting reality, thus juxtaposing politics as a truth masquerade and journalism as truth detection.

The news piece further bestows the status of martyrdom on journalists, which accentuates the role of the journalist as a fighter (for truth), ready to sacrifice their life for a noble cause.

**Al-Quds al-Arabi (9 April 2003)**

The strike, which was met with global astonishment and dismay, resulted in the <u>martyrdom of al-Jazeera correspondent</u> and <u>colleague</u> Tarek Ayoub, and a Reuters photographer, as well as the injury of a number of other journalists.

Al-Jazeera correspondent Tarek Ayoub was referred to as a "colleague," thus binding all journalists together as one "community." Indeed, it is when a group is addressed and constituted as one[19] that it emerges as an imagined community, by adding a "chain of equivalence" between the status of martyr and the rest of the group. Journalists, then, stand against an "irrational" agency (military power) that seeks to silence them. This takes for granted that world journalists were there to cover the war in a neutral and impartial manner, thus ironing out any "hegemonic intervention" in the final media representations in each country.

Both local and foreign journalists were part of this "interpretive community," as the journalists killed and wounded, although belonging to different countries and media institutions, were unified as one community, as "colleagues" searching for the truth and paying a huge price for it. In fact, Nick Gowing (from the BBC World Service) shares this view of "communality" when he refers to other journalists covering crises as "colleagues" who face hardships ("facing a failure to investigate and bring to justice"), although he also pointed to the question of safety and the fact that journalists did not cover any crisis, for example, Darfur, as intensely as they did in Iraq due to the difficult sectarian situation in Darfur.[20] I come back to Gowing's comments later in this chapter.

In addition, losing one's life in search of truth was acclaimed as an inevitable part of the journalist's profession:

### Al-Hayat (9 April 2003)

A tax is due in all wars, and every year media institutions count their victims, martyrs of truth, witnesses on innocent people's tragedies whose lives are crushed by the blind war machine and its angry fire. But what happened yesterday in Baghdad was different. The three colleagues, Tarek Ayoub (al-Jazeera correspondent) and two photographers from Reuters and Spanish TV, did not fall martyrs by friendly fire or by technical mistake. A foreign journalist said that he saw an American artillery target the Meridien-Palestine hotel in Baghdad and open five first at the hotel reception, then at the offices of the Qatari channel [al-Jazeera] as well as at the office of the Abu Dhabi channel.

Besides the inevitability of martyrdom due to mistakes caused by not following safety rules, for instance, this incident was different in that the news report above used the testimony of "a foreign journalist" as a proof that the firing was deliberate, thereby stressing the role of journalists as adversaries to political power, targeted by the latter in order to be silenced.

The "martyrdom" for truth is seen as an inevitable part of the journalistic profession, a due that has to be paid and counted "every year." The journalist here is the "eyewitness on innocent people's tragedies," whose testimony should be enclosed in a frame of trust.[21] Journalists, then, endeavor to render legitimate their testimony as part of the process of accumulating "cultural and symbolic capital" in a highly competitive field. This status is further enforced on satellite channels like al-Jazeera, where correspondents tend to appear in armed vests and army helmets when covering hot spots such as Lebanon (due to the current crisis), or Afghanistan, thus appearing as the new "heroes" who endured hardships for the sake of uncovering the truth.

As shown above, both *al-Hayat* and *al-Sharq al-Awsat* tend to profile themselves by stressing the network of their own correspondents, a role that is further enforced in news channels such as al-Jazeera, where the correspondent takes over the role of interpreter and evaluator. For instance, the day following the fall of Baghdad, al-Jazeera's main evening bulletin aired a report from the Iraqi capital that is quoted at length here to illustrate the (new) power of the journalist as eyewitness and evaluator:

> No other scene could look more like an end. The Palestine hotel battle, or the last scenes of the American–British war on Iraq, was not carried out by bombs or missiles, and no blood was shed, as happened on Black Tuesday [when journalists were killed and injured]. Between yesterday and today, it seems that many things have changed, and the press was no longer the number-two enemy of the Marines, as the scene has shifted from American blunder to inevitable victory. The American artilleries surrounded a hotel where the majority of the international media institutions rallied with no convincing objective but to transmit to the whole world the message that the Yankees have come to the heart of Baghdad.[22]

Here, the reporter narrates a story, setting the scene behind him where Saddam's statue was brought to fall as a symbol of the fall of Baghdad and the former regime. The reporter wonders about the other media institutions rallying around the American forces to help the latter transmit a message to the world, thus setting a distance between al-Jazeera on the one hand as a "mature" media institution, and other media outlets that fell into the American trap. Yet, the integrity of the journalistic profession is kept intact as a reference was made to "Black Tuesday," the day of the killing and injuring of three journalists from three different countries residing at the same hotel. The press was depicted as the "number-two enemy of the Marines," thus enforcing the role of journalists as truth-finders and martyrs. The reporter here is an observer as well as an evaluator of the American progress in the war (moving from "blunder to inevitable victory").

Moreover, the journalist acts here as an observer who communicates the scene to his audience. In fact, the word "scene" even enforces the journalist's role as a mediator who reconstructs the war scenes, which in itself an act of mixing fictional elements with real-life events. In sum, part of the interpretive community of journalists is seen to fall prey to the American political manipulation, yet the whole community is kept objectified in the reference to Black Tuesday, a commemoration day for the truth martyrs of the journalistic profession.

The above analysis therefore shows three different roles:

1. Journalist as onlooker;
2. Journalist as auditor/watchdog;
3. Journalist as truth martyr.

While two émigré newspapers (*al-Ahram* and *al-Quds al-Arabi*) drew heavily on the first role, two others (*al-Hayat* and *al-Sharq al-Awsat*) highlighted the second role. Yet, all four newspapers, and indeed other outlets as well, agree on the third role as that which binds all journalists, despite their cultural differences, together in one community.

To recap, the aim of the above analysis was to illustrate the roles of journalists, as an interpretive community, in documenting events and mining the truth, even if these tasks eventually lead them to "martyrdom." These roles evolve around two identification pointers, namely knowledge (observing and documenting) and truth (eyewitness and investigator), which can be roughly summarized in figure 6.1.

The "knowledge" axis represents the objective tasks related to observing and documenting reality, while the "truth" axis represents the subjective tasks of witnessing events and searching for truth. The truth axis would be the hybrid product of the incorporation of

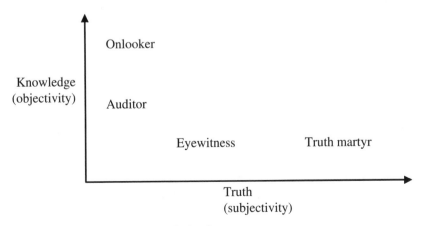

**Figure 6.1** The distribution of journalistic roles

Anglo-American journalistic practices. The roles of truth martyr and eyewitness are closely related to the core narratives of journalism as a profession, shared by members worldwide.

On the other hand, it can be argued that the knowledge axis represents the roles of journalists, to which a significant "cultural and symbolic capital" is attached. These are the roles distinguishing journalists worldwide, with some enjoying a higher capital than others. In turn, the amount of this capital determines the symbolic power of credibility associated with the journalists and media institutions acting as careful observers of facts. For instance, foreign news agencies such as Reuters or AFP were regarded as sources of reliable information (and truth) in al-Ahram and al-Quds al-Arabi. This axis also represents the struggle over credibility between national/regional media on the one hand and global media outlets on the other. This is a struggle over the re-definition of the position of local/regional on the global media scene. For instance, al-Ahram and al-Sharq al-Awsat did not mention foreign agencies, preferring instead to highlight the bylines of their own correspondents and stress their own role as newsgatherers. Clearly, the above identities do not represent a meticulous distribution of roles, as they rather overlap and compete, according to the events reported on.

The "interpretive community" of journalists exhibits a hierarchy of power,[23] much the same as in any other social field. For instance, Nick Gowing (from the BBC World Service) refer to journalists worldwide as "colleagues," thus indicating a shared identity, while reminding us of the hierarchy inside this community:

> in places like the Gulf, people who watch al-Jazeera, al-Arabiya and Abu Dhabi television and Kuwait television also go grazing, and they actually go to the BBC because they say they want to find out how it *really* is happening . . . But that is the anecdotal evidence we are beginning to get, even through the radicals in the Middle East . . . They are getting *a certain understanding* of the more radical ways of interpretation of news. But then they are turning to get a *different* view of the news. There is a very different matrix out there, so don't view it in a simplistic way.[24]

For Bourdieu,[25] social space can be compared to geographic space, so that the closer the agents in one space, the more features they have in common. Yet, "the truth of any interaction is never entirely to be found within the interaction as it avails itself for observation." In particular, Bourdieu points to what he called "categories of condescension,"[26] or the categories applied when the agents on a higher position deny the distance separating them from others below them, although the distance remains intact. So, Nick Gowing denies the difference that separates journalists worldwide, but the distance does not cease to exist. On the one hand, he acknowledges the role of other (for example, Arab) journalists as part of the global community of journalists, but on the other hand he stresses the differences among journalists according to their position in an overall hierarchy of power existing in this particular field (who is the most worthy of the audience's trust).

The above discussion aims at contributing to the debate on the global public sphere and the role of media in facilitating it. Central to this discussion are two factors: 1) the power of global media (at the top of the hierarchy), and 2) the ambivalence felt towards such media by their counterparts in developing countries (lower in the same hierarchy). Let me now elaborate on each point.

First, it can be argued that each Arab field (media, politics) derives its power from its position vis-à-vis similar Western fields. We tend to think of Arab media as expressing and influencing public opinion in a causal relationship. I argue, however, that trust and a positive image depend upon the message and messenger's place in the field. Here, the cultural capital of Western media has indeed become naturalized to serve as a yardstick by which other media, in developing countries, are measured. Critics of the Habermasian notion of the public sphere point to the idealized form of a public sphere in which social status is bracketed, and to this one can add that a normative global sphere equally brackets the cultural capital possessed by each participant/media institution. Such a global sphere is a site of struggle over legitimacy as well as visibility on the global media scene. Global media actors in particular enjoy a higher position in this power hierarchy, making truth and knowledge contingent upon the discourse and institutions producing it. The public sphere is not merely an arena for forming public opinion, but also for forming social identities. And by presenting journalists as one unified "interpretive" community, we exclude the articulation of tension among them.

Second, the hybrid role of journalists is characterized by ambivalence among media professionals (as well as audiences) vis-à-vis Western media. *Al-Ahram* directly referred to certain Western news media outlets in order to validate and render legitimacy to certain political statements, while other newspapers (such as *al-Hayat*) do not apply the same strategy. This is also seen in new satellite channels such as al-Jazeera, where the correspondents have become the main sources. Yet, al-Jazeera seems to acknowledge the credibility of the BBC while questioning the reliability of commercial outlets such as Fox News,[27] referring in particular to the recent criticism by Sky News of the public service BBC because the latter refrained from using the word "terrorist" in describing people accused of being so.

This ambivalence is even common among Arab media scholars; for instance, in his analysis of the Abu-Ghraib torture scandal, Khaffaf[28] depends upon quoting American news media, for example, CBS, *Washington Post*, *New York Times*, as the organizations responsible for sparking off a debate about the torture of Iraqi prisoners, and yet he sees the publication timing as part of a media collaboration with the politicians, particularly the Republicans, during the past elections.

## Conclusion

In general, the above analysis adds to the conceptualization of one important term in current communication research, namely "hegemony," and its impact on mediation as a basis for sound public debate. Hegemony is not a straightforward process, as some Arab scholars assume,[29] in which international news agencies exert power over the content of news circulated in local Arab news media, a view that denies the power relation. Rather, hegemony can operate via power distributed unevenly among actors in the same community. Thus, the role of journalists, as seen in international media such as the BBC and CNN, may be naturalized and entrenched in the local perception of journalism and its role in society. Quoting foreign media, as shown above, is part of the newspapers' strategy to brand and differentiate themselves vis-à-vis local newspapers that are more likely to cite local official statements.

This is not to suggest a return to an essentialist theory of hegemony in terms of homogeneity wiping out a pure original.[30] Rather, my aim here is to grasp the power relations in the hybrid identities formed on the global media scene. As Giddens[31] reminds us, power is not necessarily synonymous with coercion, but can be also associated with interdependence. Power then operates in a dialectic relation, despite the unequal distribution of power among the different actors. I do not propose to develop an action against such practices; my aim is merely to point out how power is proliferating in the field of journalism, for the analysis of communication is incomplete without the concept of power.

It is equally important to examine the ambivalent attitude towards Western media among Arab audiences, as Dahlgren argues: "The public sphere does not begin and end when media content reaches an audience; this is but one step in larger communication and cultural chains that include how the media output is received, made sense of and utilized by citizens."[32] In fact, research among diaspora audiences, for example, in Britain, shows that Palestinian audiences show less confidence in global media such as the BBC, while pouring confidence into pan-Arab news media such as al-Jazeera,[33] despite the fact that media outlets such as the BBC were seen as trustworthy news sources among audiences inside the Middle East.[34] Moreover, the poll undertaken by the Center for Strategic Studies, University of Jordan (2005) shows that the Arabs who were surveyed acknowledge the positive values in Western societies, but felt that these values are not reflected in foreign politics. The Western media were also trusted and seen as credible, at least in the UK and France, although the respondents demonstrated little knowledge of cultural life in Western communities in the USA, the UK or France.

So, where to go from here? From the above, it can be argued that analysis of the mechanism of the public sphere in an Arab context should operate at two levels:

1. at an Arab–Arab level, to analyze the strategies of legitimacy, hierarchy, and trust, as distributed among Arab media institutions and as illustrated in the audiences' attitude to these media;
2. at an Arab–Western level, where it is important to analyze the hierarchy and power relations among various regional and global media actors versus the view that sees a global sphere as devoid of center or hegemony.

If the above analysis shows the proliferation of Western media voices in Arab news texts, future research could perhaps look at the opposite trend, namely the incorporation and the image of Arab media voices in a Western context: when to quote Arab media and for what purpose, for example, showing a reaction to a Western political statement and illustrating the reaction in the Arab "street." If the Western media can be associated with trustworthiness and hence assigned a high "cultural capital," what then is the image of Arab media, for example, satellite channels, in the Western media? There exist several studies on the image of Arabs (portrayed as one homogenous group!) in American films[35] and news,[36] but there is a need to break down the image into specific groups in order to show how specific social identities, such as journalists, are portrayed (agitators, mobilizers, professionals, or adherers to the whim of the people).

# Chapter 7

# Arab Journalism as an Academic Discipline

The aim of this chapter is dual: it aims to provide an overview of the emergence of journalism and mass communication as an academic discipline in the Arab universities, while providing a critical evaluation of Arab as well as Western scholarship on Arab media. Clearly, this is an ambitious aim that needs a book-length treatment, and I would provide only a superficial account of this issue if I attempted to survey all Arab States. Therefore, I have chosen to confine my exercise to certain Arab States of the pioneering generations of Arab media scholars. My overall aim, then, is to show the gradual consolidation of journalism as an academic discipline.

The review would not be complete, however, without a discussion of the role of Arab academia in shaping the contours of the journalistic profession, and of how it sees its position vis-à-vis Western scholarship. I dedicate a large part of this chapter to a critique of the Arab methodology endorsed in Arab academic institutions, and the discussion concludes, albeit briefly, with an assessment of the claim that Arab scholarship may adhere to a particular "Arab" epistemology.

To round up, I juxtapose the contribution of Arab scholarship with that of Western scholarship on Arab media. As I argue below, Western scholarship, particularly the scholarship that emerged following 9/11, has not yet proven insightful in binding Arab media and journalism closely to social theories. I also conclude with a brief comparison between the roles of each scholarship vis-à-vis peer academics in the field (assumed to be autonomous power) and policy-makers (the political power).

## Rise of media education

The first Arab academic institution for the study of communication was established in Cairo in 1939.[1] Four years earlier, however, the American University in Cairo, a foreign institution, took the initiative in establishing a center for communication studies in 1935. The communication institute in Cairo, Cairo University, was the first Arab institute for the professional training of personnel for the newly expanding communications industry. Other Arab countries followed suit during the 1970s, with similar institutions for the study of communication and journalism. In many Middle Eastern countries, journalism formed part of the departments of Arabic literature and arts studies.

The main problem facing these institutions was the lack of trained and qualified teaching staff. That resulted in a decline in the quality of teaching and a shortage of research. The Department of Communication at Cairo University, which is the oldest Arab academic center in the region, witnessed an increase in the number of its students and was the only center in the region offering PhD degrees. However, the increase in the number of students resulted in an increase in the number of theses, and it became difficult for the staff to keep up with the new task of marking and guiding the students. Abu Bakr et al.[2] give the example of one professor from the center who, in 1976, had to supervise thirty-nine Masters theses and seven doctoral dissertations.[3]

The establishment of these departments also led to the need to attract qualified teachers from other disciplines such as sociology, history, and languages. Other departments have attracted those graduates with Masters and PhD degrees from other disciplines, but even this practice has not always resulted in raising the quality of teaching. Likewise, it has not proven fruitful to use media professionals to train communications students, especially in cases where those professionals were chosen not because of their qualifications but rather because of personal relationships and contacts.[4] Others cast doubts on the professionalism of the foreign trainers and wonder whether they simply accepted work in the Arab region because of their failure to get suitable teaching posts in their home countries.[5]

Awatef Abdel Rahman[6] referred to three pan-Arab seminars (Cairo 1976, Baghdad and Riyadh 1977, Algeria 1989) arranged to discuss the problem of the academic teaching of communication, of which the last issued a recommendation to conduct a survey on the state of this education. She presented some preliminary results that pointed to the existence of the then thirty institutions spread across seventeen Arab countries. She also highlighted the different ideological persuasions among those institutions, ranging from pro-French in the Maghreb countries, pro-American in the Gulf countries, Sudan and Yemen, and of the Islamic type in one institution in Saudi Arabia and one in Cairo (al-Azhar University).

Other scholars[7] saw the problem as being due to the poor planning of university journalism programs. In Algeria, for instance, where journalism was established as an academic discipline in 1964, the program concentrated on print media. Lacking equipment, the Algerian school did not offer courses in broadcast or television news editing, although the country needed more broadcasters than print journalists for its relatively illiterate population.

In addition, the lack of training materials in Arabic, combined with the students' insufficient knowledge of English, formed one more difficulty in accessing foreign-language books, not to mention the difficulty of those students acquiring suitable jobs in foreign news department.[8] The situation differed slightly in the Maghreb countries (Morocco, Algeria and Tunisia), where the students had access to French-language materials.

Realizing the urgent need for regional cooperation in the field of communication and journalism training, in 1979 the Arab Journalists Union took the initiative for establishing the first, and now the oldest, regional training center. First located in Cairo, then moved to Beirut, it did not receive regular funding, other than occasional support from the Iraqi government.[9] The need for regional centers had been realized already in 1976, though, when Arab deans and directors of communication departments met in Cairo and recommended the establishment of regional programs.

In addition, the first center for training in radio broadcasting was established in Egypt in 1957, and the establishment of another for television broadcasting followed in the early 1960s.[10] During the following decades, several centers were established in other Arab countries. The problem, however, was the disparity of the regularity of the courses offered and the number of students enrolled per year. Again, the lack of trained staff and well-written material in Arabic formed a difficulty for the development of that line of training. Sending trainees abroad, although an option for some centers, did not solve the problem of inadequate training. Trainees sent abroad felt the differences in the environment in their host countries, socially and culturally, compared to the Arab world; besides, the training offered was not geared to the needs of these students.[11] Since then, some have also warned against dependence upon foreign trainers lest the trainers merely copy the materials available abroad instead of designing new materials tailored to the needs of Arab trainees. One important characteristic of the materials available is that they are based on foreign, that is, Western, traditions, which, according to some Arab scholars, do not address the developmental needs of Arab trainees.[12]

Today, journalism and mass communication exist as well-established disciplines, particularly in old institutions in Egypt and Lebanon. The current generation of Egyptian media scholars is the fifth since the establishment of the Institute of Editing, Translation and Journalism in 1939.[13] We also see a new trend now in which several Arab media scholars maintain a professional link with the journalistic world by delivering journalistic tasks, usually as TV hosts and/or reporters to Egyptian and other channels.[14]

Recent years have also witnessed an upsurge in the number of private foreign universities. For example, in Egypt, following the model of the American University in Cairo, founded in 1919, foreign investors have found a new market servicing the 400,000+ students enrolling at Egyptian universities, especially given the indigenous universities' inability to accommodate such a huge number.[15] Profit, however, is claimed not to be the main drive behind these ventures, as one official from a foreign university in Egypt asserted, wondering why people would be "suspicious of private universities when we have thousands of students graduating from private schools each year?" The French ambassador to Cairo justified the establishment of the French University in Cairo by recalling how Mohammed Ali began his ambitious modernization project in the nineteenth century by sending envoys to France, who in turn "sent hundreds of teachers to Egypt." He added, "If you send your students abroad, they might lose contact with their home country and there is always the possibility they might never return;"[16] this, despite the fact that degrees from the French University are not automatically equivalent to those obtained in France. Moreover, the ratio of foreign to local staff differs across these foreign universities; for instance, one-third of the staff at the French university in Egypt are French and the rest are Egyptian, while half of the staff at the German university are Germans and the rest are local.

The process of establishment of communications departments in Arab countries was not subject to careful pre-planning; it took place arbitrarily without the universities addressing the serious consequences or even motivation, for example, the lack of trained labor and the needs of each country.[17] However, the increase in the number of these departments, and consequently the number of graduates, has meant that not all of them are guaranteed a suitable job in the communications industry. In fact, students are more inclined to major in subjects other than press journalism partly because they want to be guaranteed suitable jobs in the public service sector and partly because of their fear of getting into conflict with the governmental authorities that control the press, albeit indirectly.[18]

In Oman, journalism as an academic discipline in the Department of Mass Communication emerged in 1987–88, and although almost 280 students have graduated since then, few of them work in media organizations. The university was supported by an advanced broadcasting laboratory for training purposes, not to mention that the Department of Mass Communication has provided training to the local media.[19] Other Gulf countries are also moving towards expanding their educational services, including media courses. For instance, the wife of the Emir of Qatar, Sheikha Mouza, instigated the Education City in the capital Doha, where prominent American universities are represented, and there are plans to "select" other Western universities to be represented in the City.[20] A Qatari student at one of the Western campuses in the Education City endorsed the "hybrid" culture that results from the amalgamation of Western knowledge and Arab/Qatari culture, saying, "Although we study in . . . an American atmosphere, we adapted a special culture . . . a new culture in the middle between these [American and Qatari cultures]."[21] Likewise, Dubai launched Dubai Knowledge Village "to complement . . . Dubai Internet City and Dubai Media City."[22]

Yet, a large number of the employees in the communication industries in the region are not necessarily graduates of these departments, and need only fulfill certain requirements such as mastering the written variety of Arabic as well as foreign languages.[23] This emphasizes the importance of "personal contacts" in accessing the field of media and journalism, and once inside the field, new journalists learn the "craft" of journalism through the daily routines.[24] This situation, however, necessitates the existence of on-the-job training for novice journalists. In fact, the lack of adequate training is seen by some officials and media specialists as one of the real reasons behind what some call the "deterioration of the Arab press." They also relate the problem to the absence of role models, since the older generation of veteran journalists are claimed to be uninterested in passing on their experience to the younger generation.[25]

Even journalists who graduated from journalism schools express a wish to undertake tailored, on-the-job training. For instance, a survey among a sample of Algerian journalists showed that a significant percentage of them (around 48 percent) wanted to have additional training or a refresher course.[26] Even among those who graduated from the journalism school in Algeria, who were asked if they were well-prepared by the school to practice journalism, approximately 80 percent were not satisfied with the education they had received. Overall, Algerian journalists expressed a belief in combining academic education with non-academic experience as an important precondition for a career in journalism.[27]

Also, in Saudi Arabia, hands-on practice and non-academic experience were looked upon as very important assets. Some Saudi journalists wanted a clearer link between the academic curricula and the daily practice of journalism.[28] Unlike Algerian journalists, and indeed journalists from other poor Arab States, Saudi journalists had the privilege of traveling abroad more than once, and overall they were satisfied with their work conditions. Yet, the expansion of the media scene and the introduction of new TV and satellite stations have also contributed positively to the educational level of journalist, as illustrated in the new "academies" launched by media institutions (see Chapter 2).

## Difficulties in research and staffing

The difficulties faced regarding professional communication training in the Arab region[29] extended to the field of communication research. A combination of various factors, such as a lack of funding, the reluctance of publishers to publish that type of research, and the lack of adequate equipment and material to carry out the research, contributed to the decline of research.

Several Arab scholars have criticized the existing research, particularly among audiences. Awatef Abdel Rahman,[30] for instance, pointed out that most of the existing institutions have been part of the governmental administration and hence sought to apply only the government's policy. For Mohamed Kirat,[31] moreover, the lack of audience analysis in Algeria makes it difficult for Algerian journalists to adapt to the needs of their readership, whose only feedback is expressed in letters to the editor.

In addition, there are specific obstacles for academic researchers in certain Arab States. Commenting on his experience in conducting a survey among print journalists in Algeria, Kirat said the majority of administrators, planners and officials did not see the point of carrying out the survey in the first place, with several of them expressing a cynical attitude towards the outcome of the research: "You think you are going to change the world with your findings that we already know? You don't have to go through all of this; we know our problems and weaknesses."[32]

Kirat wrote that it was difficult to obtain a permit or authorization for research from the Ministry of Information in Algeria,[33] which forced him to rely on personal contacts to administer parts of the research. Some journalists were even hostile to the researcher and refused to answer the questionnaire, or refused to return it on the grounds that they did not like the questions, thereby reducing the large sample of 1,200 respondents to a mere 75.[34]

However, the difficulties facing researchers seem to depend on the country covered and the status of both journalists and researchers there. For instance, in his survey among Saudi journalists, Tash[35] reported on the ease of conducting personal interviews with all editorial staff in the seven Saudi dailies. He was then able to talk personally with more than eighty journalists representing all seven newspapers in Saudi Arabia.

The difficulties in carrying out this kind of research seem now to have diminished, however, thanks to the increasing number of media and journalism departments as well as the number of media outlets who now commission such studies. Also, the increasing number of academics who complete their graduate studies abroad has contributed to the expansion of journalism departments. For instance, Hadidi[36] showed in her survey among media academics in Egyptian universities that the percentage of young academics (fellow researchers) studying abroad has increased, particularly among those in radio broadcasting departments. The USA was by far the most popular study destination for those academics (65 percent), while France, which ranked as number two on the list of countries of study, was chosen by 14 percent.

## Arab methodologies

In his survey of the weaknesses and strengths of Arab social science, Ibrahim[37] mentioned the "lag of methodologies" as one apparent weakness. He comments, "Much of the current Arab social research still follows methodological tools and techniques which lag a few decades behind their counterpart in advanced countries. Not only is it more descriptive than inductive, but also *more qualitative than quantitative*"[38] (my emphasis). This evaluation, however, does not hold compared to the number of Arab media analyses/studies that I have reviewed and that are based on quantitative rather than qualitative methods. This may be because part of the media research in Arab academia is conducted in the faculties of humanities, and although social scientists are now part of the teaching cadre in media departments in Arab universities, Ibrahim's account does not include the humanities research.

Recently, an Arab media scholar, Atef al-Abd, collected the major academic studies on audience surveys and presented an analysis of over one hundred of these studies carried out between 1985 and 1986.[39] He pointed out to the increasing number of research papers carried out not only by communications departments in the Arab faculties, but also by other departments, for example, political science, humanities, education, and so on.

Al-Abd[40] argues that the main aim of the research was to assist the communication process and facilitate development plans. To achieve this, researchers applied research to evaluate programs and measure their effectiveness in order to evaluate the success or failure of the communication plan. The survey showed the prevalence of the quantitative method of research, particularly in field study and content analysis.[41] The majority of this research, part of which included MA and PhD dissertations, was done for "practical" reasons, for example, to measure the success of certain programs,[42] the degree of the dependence on foreign sources of news, or the role of the radio and TV in educating peasants. Another example is the role of news agencies, particularly the world's largest news agencies,[43] which has been seen as the most important and consistent factor in the analysis of news coverage.[44] News provided by international news agencies about the Arab region is estimated to include factors of "foreign propaganda" and not just sheer news. Although some scholars look distrustfully at the role of international news agencies as the major source of news,[45] others interpret the increasing dependence on these sources as an indicator of openness in the dependent country.[46]

The prevalence of the quantitative method may be due to two factors. First, it may be due to Arab academic dependence on foreign curricula, particularly those developed in the USA, where such analysis techniques may still prevail. For instance, the American journal *Journalism and Mass Communication Quarterly* reports on research that mostly uses content analysis as a main research method, beside other "meta studies" that analyze how the content analysis method has been applied in previous research. Second, Arab scholars may adhere to the positivist philosophy of science in regarding knowledge as that which can be observed and analyzed value-free by the researcher. Such analyses use sophisticated validity methods (statistical tools) to emphasize objectivity, which again seems to be a decisive element in research design and reporting in Arabic academia.

In his extensive study on the Arab mind and epistemological thoughts, al-Jabri[47] points to the traditions of Arab philosophers such as Ibn Khaldun to place great emphasis on causality and scientific methods in pursuing the "truth."[48] Thus, Ibn Khaldun's idea of elevating scientific method from everyday perception shares some resemblance with Comte's ideas, which laid the foundation for the positivistic traditions.[49] Here, everyday perception is subject to misinterpretation, while reliable theory has to be based on observable facts. Moreover, al-Jabri[50] also notes that there is a lack of epistemological stability in Arabic thought, given that Arabic thought was analyzed not according to particular epistemological paradigms but according to ideological choices. I come back to al-Jabri's views on a "shared" Arab epistemology later in this chapter, and I will also discuss the American influence; but before that, I present in the following section the contours of the positivistic paradigm as it developed in Western media scholarship.

## The positivistic paradigm

The scientific tradition of positivism defines knowledge as that which can be explained through direct observation and experimentation. This view, however, reduces knowledge to only that which can be observed or seen, not to mention that it isolates the objects of analysis in the course of observation. Indeed, the accumulation of "facts" about the "observable" event is a practice preached by positivists in the beginning of the twentieth century. Positivism seeks to obtain "objective" knowledge by adhering to the facts about reality and by conducting empirical studies to verify observations.[51] However, as Fay[52] argues, if this were true, then the telephone book would be the most scientific publication in the world, because it includes only facts about reality. Positivism is closely identified with empiricism, or the belief in the pre-existence of facts available for the researcher prior to formulating his/her theories.

Thus, positivism cares little about the "inner lives" of people/ agents, or their subjectivity.[53] The methods associated with this theory are usually quantitative, based on a large pool of data, aimed at "generating hypotheses, measuring social facts and discovering the causes of events so that laws are generated."[54] Equating collecting "facts" with being objective is thus a belief in the exclusion of subjectivity and subjective experiences in order to reach the "objective truth."[55] The possible definition of objectivity here is that it is "the cognitive state of lacking a priori categories and conceptions, desires, emotions, value-judgments, and the like which necessarily mislead and thereby prevent attaining objective truth."[56]

   Reporting on an accident, for instance, not only entails "factual" details about this event but also involves a selective interpretation of what "has really happened," or, as Fay puts it:

> Imagine yourself being asked to describe an automobile accident you just witnessed by confining yourself just to the facts about it. The result would undoubtedly be an incoherent jumble of descriptive statements. If your only guide is to confine yourself just to the facts you have no way of distinguishing significant facts from insignificant ones. Consequently you would have no way of sorting facts into appropriate levels.[57]

   This empiricism related to positivistic research has been regarded as "naïve objectivism" that ignores the complex relation between concepts and reality.[58] Even the facts collected in such analyses are "seldom objective or neutral in any definite sense. To be at all understandable they always comprise earlier, more or less hidden, everyday and/or scientific conceptualizations. That is, facts are theory-dependent and theory-laden."[59] Social researchers have continued to operate according to the positivistic principles, albeit in an unacknowledged manner, in their view of science as the discovery of universal laws or in their attempts to anchor research in the same methodologies.[60]

   Constructivism has been applied as one analytical approach in social scientific research, and in the study of journalism, and it indeed "constitutes an overall horizon or approach rather than a concrete research strategy."[61] The reason for this is the emergence of new realities, for example, the new world order at the political level, or the new medical technologies that deemed ethically challenging, and thus it is not sufficient to account for these new developments using old categorization conventions. Now, researchers are challenged to account for the change of categories and concepts themselves, as well as how they have been historically constructed.[62] Knowledge is no longer monopolized by the academic field, and indeed knowledge, as a factor, is becoming incorporated in other fields (such as management), where the accumulation of knowledge and the way of managing it has recently been the center of much attention. Every scientific endeavor entails a question about ontology (asking "what" a concept means, presuming its existence) versus epistemology (the cognition of that concept, or asking "how" this concept is perceived and how its meaning is constrained).[63] This kind of constructivism is deeply rooted in various contemporary theories, for example, post-structuralism, feminist studies and critical psychology. It seeks to question the taken-for-granted assumption about reality or the "natural" and the pre-given. Constructivism as a research framework has been applied in so-called "interpretive" research based on the qualitative method of analysis rather than quantitative methods, thereby favoring the examination of concepts and the way they are constructed in people's minds.

But if constructivism has penetrated Western journalism research while the number of Arab academics in Western universities has been on the increase, why has not constructivism found a base in the Arab research tradition? One plausible explanation, as I argue in the following section, is related to the validity usually associated with positivistic methodologies.

## Arab critique

Abdel Rahman[64] commented on the tendency of Arab researchers to "stuff" their research papers with figures and statistics rather than seeking to reveal a deeper analysis of issues specific to Arab audiences and media professionals. For her, the problem with media scholarship in the Arab universities is due to three factors:

1. The evaluation of research is done according to foreign, mostly American, standards;
2. The fact that journalism schools depend heavily on foreign, particularly English-language, educational material;
3. The tendency among Arab researchers to apply Western theories and methods rather than to illuminate the specific Arab context.

For Abdel Rahman, Arab researchers, at least in Egypt, want to raise their research to the level of applied and natural sciences.[65] Moreover, another point, which Ibrahim[66] raised and which I find relevant to my remarks on Arab research tools, is what he called "irrelevant conceptualization." By this he means that Arab social scientists have slavishly followed Western-developed theories, particularly Marxism and Functionalism, without attempting to develop variant theories more suitable for the Arab context. Those researchers are usually more concerned with the contribution that media institutions make to Arab society and its needs, and are less concerned about historical analyses, not to mention that their research tends to see the audience as passive recipients of media messages.

There is also the fact that most researchers have themselves been educated in the West, particularly the USA. Ibrahim,[67] for instance, said that the 1950s and 1960s, which witnessed the independence of several Arab States, was a period of exporting Arab PhD students to the USA. Moreover, Sabagh and Ghazalla showed that, although many Arab social scientists acknowledged the shortcomings of Western theories, "they continued to depend on them."[68] That was the period that followed the inception of mass communication research in the USA. The American research was then behaviorist in nature, concerned mainly with the effect "powerful" media have on audiences and public opinion. According to that view, media were "deterministic stimuli; a perception that is simultaneously accompanied by a hoary pessimistic image of man as primarily an automatic responder to such stimuli."[69] Here, audiences are seen as *Homo Mechanicus*, or "essentially weak, and the media as essentially all-powerful."[70] Such views were apparently taken at face value among Arab scholars, who, in their capacity as educators, passed them on to the new generation of researchers.

But why has this positivist paradigm found such a solid base in Arab research? Could there be a particularly Arab epistemology that endorses this paradigm? In other words, can we identify a particular epistemology that is unique to Arab media and journalism studies? If so, how would this influence the definition of journalism and its role in society, and specifically its position vis-à-vis political power on the one hand and the laity on the other?

To provide a thorough answer to these questions is beyond the scope of this chapter. But what I can briefly touch upon are attempts by two Arab scholars, namely Muhammad Abed al-Jabri and Muhammad Ayish, to define such an epistemology, indicating rather their shortcomings and failure to account for the differences and tensions that may be present in the academic field, preferring instead to base their analysis on the assumption of similarity among Arabs in terms of traditions and practices. In so doing, their accounts seem to be political in nature, aimed at endorsing rather than challenging the presence of one pan-Arab ideology.

## Al-Jabri's pan-Arab project

For al-Jabri, the imperative question that merits analysis is this: why has Arab thought stagnated since the *Nahda* (Renaissance of the nineteenth century), with the result that Arabs feel inferior to their Western counterparts? He set off to trace the genealogy of the main themes in Arab thought, focusing in particular on "the Age of Recording" (eighth century), and he takes it as a point of reference, rather than taking the pre-Islamic era or even the era of Mohammed. In so doing, he aims at unraveling the "epistemological" system that characterizes Arab thought rather than providing a critique of Arab ideologies. In particular, al-Jabri[71] points to three epistemological systems in Arab thought:

1. *Bayan*, or system of indication;
2. *Erfan*, or system of illumination;
3. *Burhan*, or system of inferential evidence.

*Bayan* dominates linguistics and theology; it is based on rules used to interpret discourse, thus its main aim is to analyze the relationship between an utterance and its meaning. Knowledge here was "explicatory" and *bayan* scientists would not pursue an analysis of the mechanism or causality but rather feel content with what al-Jabri terms contingency. *Bayan* is very much associated with the rise of the Arabic language, which was spoken by the nomadic people and was regarded as the language of the Koran. In brief, *bayan* as an epistemological approach is concerned with the relation between discourse and meaning, and knowledge production here is merely based on explaining and digesting that meaning according to a priori rules of interpretations. This, says al-Jabri, reduces the independency of reason as a superior faculty.[72]

*Erfan* is based on gnosticism and hermeticism, or on the manifest (*thahir*) knowledge of the latent (*batin*). There are no rules guiding it, as in *bayan*, but it is knowledge based on similarity, which why al-Jabri could not see the value of it to the development of rational thought. The researcher here would be concerned with the use of personal knowledge to reach the truth, which reduces the truth to an individual interpretation, differing from one person to another, rather than being a universal truth. Al-Jabri gives the example of interpreting Koranic verses among, for example, Shiites, and demonstrates how each interpretation "is considered by its owner as the truth."[73] Thus, there is no consistent causality between the object of study and the interpretation.

Finally, *burhan* is based on Western rationalism, which depends on causality and deduction rather than on intuition and individual interpretation. *Burhan* is based on interferential logic; hence, al-Jabri saw in it a suitable epistemological basis for the sciences. *Burhan* depends on man's cognitive qualities to produce knowledge, although, according to al-Jabri, *burhan* was not necessarily adopted in the Arabic-Islamic civilization to serve the production of knowledge for knowledge's sake, but to serve certain religious and ideological interests.[74]

For al-Jabri, the three epistemological systems can overlap, although each system can dominate the works of certain thinkers, such as Ibn Rushd or Averroes, who adopted the system of demonstration, *burhan*.

Al-Jabri's classification here follows, to a large extent, Foucault's notion of "episteme," and in fact *erfan* and *burhan* may correspond to Foucault's epistemes of the Renaissance on the one hand, and the classical and modern age on the other: where the former sees the world as a set of rules to be interpreted according to the "divine code," the latter marks the rise of science, which is based on observation. This line of thought developed even further in the modern age, where knowledge was not to be derived from nature or God, but from "man."[75]

Clearly, this rather brief overview of al-Jabri's epistemology does not do justice to the richness of his works. However, going into detail about Arab epistemology in general terms is beyond the scope of this chapter, So for my purpose here, I am merely interested in using al-Jabri's thinking to justify the trends in Arab media research. Applying his typology to Arab media research, one can argue that contemporary media research is close to the *bayan* episteme in as much as it is concerned with *explication* of the *representation* of a phenomenon rather than with discovering the underlying mechanisms that (re)produce it. For instance, several Arab studies are more concerned with the issue of representation of particularly the Arab image in Western discourse, for example, studies by Musallam and al-Daqdouqi,[76] to mention but two.

Despite its richness, al-Jabri's ambitious project cannot be taken at face value, as is pointed out by a number of his critics, who challenge the very foundations of al-Jabri's epistemes. The main opposition view is that, although al-Jabri deliberately avoids the analysis of Arab ideologies, he ends up in a purely ideological quest searching for the means to "unify" Arabs. His pan-nationalist thinking seems to interfere with his more sophisticated project of tracing the genealogy of Arab epistemology, as the main aim of his works is to find a solution for a renewed pan-Arabism rather than to open up new paths of critical theories. Also, he deliberately links all Arab cultures together as one unified object of study, thereby seeing each one of them as part of the totality rather than as an object of study in and of itself.

His goal, then, was "to make a link between Arab rationalism and the possibility of a scientific/capitalist revolution in the Arab world."[77] Al-Jabri's vision is not, as several early twentieth-century Arab thinkers proposed, to secure progress and modernization through hybridizing the native culture with European ideals; rather, his vision is to maintain both cultures as distinctively separate, because, in his view, the adoption of such ready-made views constitutes an impediment rather than an aid to forming the unique "Arab reason." In sum, what al-Jabri offers, briefly, is not a choice between going back to traditional elements of thought or adopting foreign elements; rather, he calls for a change of epistemological methodology. According to Abu Rabi', al-Jabri's vision is to emancipate "contemporary Arab Reason and, on the whole, contemporary Arab thought and culture from the shackles of both the Western and Islamic traditions."[78] Abu Rabi' adds another crucial point, namely the fact that al-Jabri was rather selective in his genealogy and disregards, for example, the role of Shiite intelligentsia as well as of Sufi sheikhs.[79]

Leaving aside al-Jabri's attempt to pin down a unified Arab epistemology, I will now sketch another attempt to fulfill the same task, namely that outlined in an article by Muhammad Ayish.[80]

## An Islamic epistemology

To begin with, Ayish's approach was rather less sophisticated than al-Jabri's. Ayish divided the works published in Arabic into six categories according to their themes: propaganda, development communication, historical accounts, news flow, professional work, and theoretical work.[81] The latter, he regrets, "failed to generate theoretical frameworks powerful enough to account for the varying realities of modern Arab communications."[82] I agree with him that a large part of Arab studies can be categorized as descriptive and administrative research rather than a solid theoretical contribution to the field of media studies, but we part company with regards to this theorization of a shared Arab/Islamic epistemology, as I find such an account theoretically and methodologically weak.

Ayish's main purpose is to provide "a normative framework for understanding communication, in its most general sense, in the Arab-Islamic traditions."[83] Ayish's theory, in a nutshell, sees the epistemological roots of Arab communication research lying in two important, albeit contradictory, epochs in the Arab region: 1) the pre-Islamic era, in which "tribal law" prevailed, and 2) the Islamic era, with its values and attitudes. The marrying of the two contradictory "life worlds" is manifested in a set of binary opposites or themes, according to Ayish.[84] These are individualism versus conformity, transcendentalism versus existentialism, rationality versus intuition and egalitarianism versus hierarchy. The result is a communication system that serves a dual purpose: "integrating the individual into the community and/or liberating him from the shackles of conformity to a collective system."[85]

This perspective, however, lacks a solid methodological and historical basis. Unlike al-Jabri, who endeavored to offer a genealogy of "Arab Reason" in several volumes, moving through different historical periods and authors, Ayish's perspective is based on sweeping and unqualified generalizations. For instance, in dealing with the pre-Islamic era, Ayish refers to the tribal code that prevailed among Arab societies at that time, and in so doing, only re-"affirms" Arab unity without even acknowledging the differences among Middle Eastern societies in the pre-Islam era. The tribal code may indeed have prevailed in Arabia, but it did not necessarily do so in Egypt or Lebanon, where the nucleus of modern communication was found in the late eighteenth century.[86] This was why some Egyptian intellectuals, such as Taha Hussein, sought to establish "a transhistorical link between modern European Reason and ancient Egyptian Reason,"[87] rather than with Arabian/Islamic or pre-Islamic reason.

Second, the dual role of communication as formulated by Ayish does not seem at all contradictory, for it is an integral part of the media as a system of generating meaning; for example, European media seem to bind Europeans into one imagined community while asserting the individuality of each state. In fact, one main characteristic of the mediated meanings provided by the media is, as Silverstone puts it, that they "move across space, and across spaces. They move from the public to the private, from the institutional to the individual, from the globalizing to the local and personal, and back gain. They are fixed . . . in texts, and fluid in conversations."[88]

Furthermore, Ayish notes that the French-oriented communication research in North African countries (particularly in Morocco, Algeria and Tunisia) has been more critical, linking communication with culture and politics.[89] Yet, he does not provide a single example of such research, for example, which universities fostered this type of research, in what language it was published (Arabic or French or both), its use of methodologies, how far it reached into other Arab media institutions, and so on.

Finally, Ayish sees the pre-Islamic and Islamic culture as a totality, when in fact it is immersed in the particularity of different pre-existing cultures. What is more, this view does not do justice to the fact that most of the founding fathers of the press came from Christian backgrounds, particularly from Syria and Lebanon.[90] Can we then claim that the Islamic or pre-Islamic heritage had been completely integrated into those pioneers' values? Would not such a claim wipe away the articulation of the differences among diverse social groups?

As I said before, the inquiry into the epistemological root of Arab epistemology, and into whether we can indeed speak of shared roots, deserves a book-length account. The brief overview presented here, however, is meant to open the door for future debates on this issue. The Arab epistemological root is obviously an issue that is still under scrutiny and gives rise to heated debates among Arab scholars. For our purposes here, it is important to confine the discussion to the epistemology adopted in "media and communication" research and, as pointed out above, this line of research seems to lean on a positivistic rather than, for example, a constructivist paradigm.

The above explanations do not seem useful in explaining the amount of administrative research in Arab scholarship. I am therefore inclined to agree with Abdel Rahman[91] that one main reason for this is the American influence. Yet, I am also tempted to suggest another explanation, which lies in the role of the media researcher vis-à-vis the political field of power. For instance, Arab media researchers may need to justify their research to policy-makers, which drives them to "stuff" their research with statistics, thereby stabilizing the results to conform to the predictability needed for policy planning. Central here is the role of the intellectual and whether it should be "to speak the truth to power," as formulated by Edward Said.[92] In other words, should the researchers support certain nationalistic and ideological plans or work autonomously for the sole purpose of producing knowledge and contesting produced knowledge?

## Role of academia

Intellectuals can be defined as those who produce knowledge and possess sufficient cultural capital to grant them social recognition.[93] Moreover, intellectuals are active agents operating according to a set of rules unique to their field. Bourdieu's formulation of field theory, again, allows the interpretation of the field as a dynamic space, where agents engage in a struggle over resources, and may even bring together those with similar interests. Here, "Struggles are not just about material gain but also symbolic and this capital is invested in, for example, citation, invitations to speak and book reviews."[94]

For Bourdieu, agents are operating in an overall field of power, with each agent struggling to attain and maintain their power/position. Agents do not calculate their actions, as they are guided by their social habitus, which generates their practice and representations. This habitus is transposable, which allows the agents to act across different fields[95] (see Chapter 1). Some Arab academics, for instance, pursued leading government positions, such as in Jordan, where the term "*ustadh mustawzir*" (or "professor seeking to become a minister") is used to designate a professor who actively arranges symposia and public lectures as well as constantly appearing in the local media.[96] Moreover, the cultural capital of the Arab researcher is not necessary related to wealth or social class, but rather to the amount of knowledge possessed by the researcher, and hence their power. For instance, the former Dean of the Faculty of Arts at Cairo University, Abdel-Aziz Hammoudah, used to pride himself of coming from a humble, "peasant" background and, as his colleagues remarked, he "worked his way up the social and academic ladder with unyielding stamina and great determination."[97] Living in an "American-styled villa" in a rich Cairo suburb, Hammoudah was not regarded "as an aficionado of American culture"; he did not lose sight of his mission, which was "to serve Arab and not foreign culture." In fact, academics like Hammoudah served as cultural counselors in Arab embassies in Western countries, and Hammoudah himself was Egypt's cultural attaché to the USA at the beginning of the 1990s.[98]

In developing nations, intellectuals gain an additional task, namely one in which "the construction of a broader, academically trained elite came to be seen as proof of the maturity and the capacity for self-reliance of the independent state."[99] Intellectuals here are living proof of the successful hybridity between "developed" and "developing," East and West, as usually they obtained their higher education degrees from abroad, thus enjoying the seeds of Western-style training[100] sown in their native origins.

What characterizes this type of researcher is their political rather than epistemological derivation; for instance, studies on the news flow seem to be a criticism of "Western" power and a call to increase the Arab presence on the global media scene rather than being a scientific contribution to theories on "culture flow." This in turn consolidates a certain image of the Arab media researcher as a link between laypeople (the less knowledgeable) and political power; in other words, it points to a certain role of the "intellectual" in those Arab societies where the intellectual's role is to gain knowledge of the West and use this knowledge to "reveal" Western hegemony on the global media scene. Another part of this role is to survey and document a trend for the sake of offering recommendations to the policy-makers and/or media professionals.

There are examples of "ideologically" grounded Arab research; Hadidi,[101] for instance, had a set of questions that she sent to a number of Egyptian academics in media departments. Among the questions was the following statement to which fellow academics were asked to respond: "Media is a Western science and there is no use in studying it but in the West or by following Western methods/curricula in Western languages." This statement, in my view, forces the respondents to answer in the direction desired by the researcher. More than 64 percent disagreed with this statement, but this, in my opinion, is because it is formulated to be negated and not to inspire new insights or explain real tendencies among academics. Rather, the statement appealed to the respondents' nationalistic pride, which might explain the large percentage of those disagreeing with the statement, not to mention the "do not know" percentage. The researcher concluded that there was indeed a need to "Arabize" the curricula and expand the Arabic research base.

Such an ideologically-grounded study shows that the main duty of a researcher is to contribute to their country's overall development policy rather than to interrogate knowledge, and the duty of a typical Arab university is to serve the national and regional interest. In this respect, the social sciences, "generally regarded as luxuries," seek public and academic legitimacy by competing with natural science in finding utilitarian solutions to social and technological backwardness.[102]

When the study of social sciences took root in the 1950s and 60's, the period of independence of several Arab States, social theory was said to transform Arab societies and to help them keep up with the developed world, making it the dream of sociologists "to become the ideologist or adviser of the new ruling elite."[103] Some disciplines, such as anthropology, were even rejected if they were not seen to offer much to Arab unity. Thus, while sociology claims to be concerned with Arab society, anthropology, usually associated with the study of primitive societies, "cannot become Arab because Arab society is not primitive."[104] Likewise, the study of folk history may not be taken seriously as it adds little to Arab unity, and Shami mentioned one example of a monograph on urban community that was rejected for publication because it added little to the concepts of "Arab identity and unity."[105]

Moreover, the inclination to produce administrative media studies could also be the result of funding policies that may prevent some Arab media scholars from applying for more "interpretive" studies, choosing instead to resort to administrative research as a means to secure funding. Finally, researchers also compete for funding from Western developmental funds, which in turn set the standards for research methodologies. Abdel Rahman accuses some of those researchers of adopting different methodologies just to gain access to these funds,[106] thereby using their research as a product to help them to accumulate material wealth rather than to produce knowledge.

Seen against this backdrop, it can be argued that the administrative research was used to move academia closer to the political field of power and funding while legitimating its position vis-à-vis other well-established disciplines such as the natural sciences. I need to stress again, however, that the debate around Arab epistemology is still ongoing and the above discussion is only meant to spark this debate further. But if there are shortcomings in Arab scholarship, let us now turn to Western scholarship on Arab media to analyze its contribution to this field.

## Western scholarship: a role model?

Middle Eastern scholarship in Western universities used to be in proportion with the "military" and strategic position of the region in relation to certain Western countries. In an article published in 1977, George Haddad, for one, acknowledged that the upsurge in publications on the military history of the Middle East since the 1930s, both in the USA and the UK, was due to the "strategic importance of the Middle East."[107] Some of the academic research carried out then was even funded by intelligence bodies, for example, Harvard's Center for

Middle Eastern Studies, which was established in the 1950s "to provide policy makers with better information on the Middle East."[108] Likewise, Beinin referred to the Washington Institute for Near East Policy, established in 1985, as one institute that had exerted a great influence on US policy in the middle East, with the WINEP associates appearing as media pundits and serving as policy advisers to the administration. Thus, the ultimate goal for researchers then was to serve as an adviser to both the media and the policy-makers. Associates, however, sought the academic affiliation, as it gave a kind of legitimacy to their position.[109]

The period following the 9/11 attacks on the USA has witnessed a renewed upsurge of publications about the Middle East, and particularly about Arab media. Thus, the number of books about Arab media produced during the past few years alone has probably surpassed the number of books produced in the past two decades altogether. Yet, I believe most of the recent works have followed the conventional path of appealing to policy-makers rather than to academia. As such, knowledge about Arab media is still insufficient: for instance, the issues raised and the questions posed in this volume have, for whatever reasons, never been posed before in Western scholarship.

In this section, however, I argue that the amount of scholarship has not particularly added much to our knowledge about (or pre-conception of) Arab media. What is more, Western scholarship focusing on Arab media may share the behaviorist attitude expressed in Arab research, as discussed above. It may also be isolating itself, either deliberately or involuntarily, from mainstream Western media scholarship, which has undergone a revolution during the past three decades.

Indeed, there is an abundance of studies primarily addressing Western policy-makers rather than peer colleagues, in as much as these studies are more concerned with a certain political agenda rather than with contributing to the field of media studies, for example, by offering new insights on the applicability of Western media theories to the Arab context. I would rather not single out specific titles, but a simple look at the websites of international bookstores should reveal the huge number of studies whose concerns range from propaganda and news flow, to monitoring the situation of Arab media in the same way as reports by specialized NGOs. A trendy line of research now is public diplomacy, with advice to policy-makers (particularly the American administration) on how to win the trust of the Arab laity. Others focus on the authoritarian regimes, adopting an almost "hands-off, cuffs-on" attitude to direct policy-makers to the "free," harmless media that should be left alone versus those outlets that precariously rally the masses as part of an overall tactless political agenda. In sum, the numerous projects examining pan-Arab media, whether broadcast or print, tend to resemble the equally numerous monitoring projects supported by governments and NGOs rather than seeing the Arab audience, and indeed journalists, as active agents. They also focus on only a handful of media outlets, ignoring the others[110] (see also Chapters 3 and 4).

In my view, one significant shortcoming of recent Western scholarship is that it deliberately overlooks the vast number of publications and theses by Arab scholars. As part of a sound research agenda, Western scholars must review and analyze Arab scholarship, at least to understand the research trends there. Also, works in Arabic, particularly with the huge expansion of private educational institutions and private academies specializing in journalism and mass communication, may provide Western scholars with a wealth of findings rather than them having to "reinvent the wheel" every time they embark on a research project about Arab media. This is an ethical issue for any researcher, namely to present the "Other" view as well, particularly if they master the Other's language; had I, for instance, chosen to specialize in American Studies, it would have been expected of me that I survey existing works by American scholars rather than confining my exercise to works published in a certain language or in a certain country.

Elsewhere,[111] I have criticized one of these scholars, namely William Rugh, for his negligence of the available body of research written by Arab scholars in Arabic. Rugh ignores the vast number of works done by Arab scholars and the theses written at Arab media faculties, when he states in his book that his primary data was collected from informal conversations with consumers rather than by the systematic analysis of media content, for such "a study has not yet been done, and would be an enormous undertaking."[112] I pointed then to the vast number of studies by Arab scholars on Arab media content, with which Rugh should have been acquainted.

Other scholars have followed Rugh's footsteps and deliberately disregarded Arab scholarship. For instance, in a footnote to her article on the development of Arab journalism, Naomi Sakr maintains that she depended mainly on Western (English-language) sources because, and she refers to Ayish[113] (discussed above), "seminal theoretical work on the subject in Arabic is lacking."[114] Therefore, she had to depend on literature coming "mainly from outside the Arab region." This is rather a simplistic statement for several reasons. First, Ayish dedicated part of his article to a review of some recent Arabic scholarly works, so there were at least some works that were worth reviewing, and on which Sakr could have drawn. Second, Ayish's article was not without faults, as discussed above, which should have been clear to Sakr. Third, as a media scholar, Sakr carries a responsibility to interrogate the academic knowledge rather than taking any work at face value. Thus, she could have reviewed relevant works in Arabic to confirm or refute Ayish's views. Last, but not least, Sakr has not really defined the criteria needed for a scholarly work to be classified as "seminal," and hence worth citing.

I could also here mention Marc Lynch, whose work is discussed in more detail in Chapter 3, and who, to write his book, despite a rich database of media content, depended on merely two books in Arabic and a vast bibliography of works in English. Assuming that Western scholars possess the necessary language skills and sufficient knowledge about the region's culture, one may wonder how they have never become acquainted with Arab media scholarship, or whether they have deliberately chosen to disregard it.

To be fair, two groups of Arab scholars may be cited in Western scholarship: 1) those who publish in English, and 2) native Arabs who received their education and/or who reside in the West – in that order. Even those diasporic researchers seem to adopt the same strategy, preferring to cite "authoritative" Western voices than to challenge the status quo.

Moreover, for the Lebanese sociologist Salim Nasr, Arab scholars have "limited expertise . . . about countries in the Middle East other than their own."[115] Yet, Western scholars who specialize in Arab media are sometimes labeled as "region experts," even if their expertise covers only one or two countries. Usually, the Arab countries covered in such studies are selective, while other states, such as Yemen, Oman, Libya, Sudan, and Algeria, may be excluded from the equation. Adopting, once more, Bourdieu's terms, we can see academia as a field in which

Field activity becomes a shared territory where members are able to use the space to create meaning through taking action such as publishing a book, and through describing and labeling action in particular ways by how they respond to that book. Therefore knowledge production takes place within the complex networks that are developed within existing power structures, such as the university, and are themselves a powerful structure through who is and is not included.[116]

Following Bourdieu's notion of knowledge,[117] agents compete for recognition and capital. The academic field, in particular, is assumed to enjoy relative autonomy, meaning that the agents within this field compete to produce and interrogate the produced knowledge rather than to gain political or commercial recognition. But this is not always the case in Western scholarship, which may compete more for political recognition (or external capital) than for internal capital among media scholars. Mainstream media scholarship, on the other hand, tends to accept the knowledge produced in the "sub-field" concerned with Arab media, as a kind of area studies, even if the main aim is to deliver a politically correct message hailing the vulnerable institutions (al-Jazeera) against the Goliath (USA). Mainstream media scholars therefore avoid questioning the produced knowledge or interrogating it.

In turn, Western scholars who have specialized in Arab media tend to borrow ready-made Western theories and apply them verbatim to the Arab context rather than challenging these theories or offering new ways to apply them. They then end up in the same trap into which Arab scholars have fallen, namely exporting theories wholesale to the Arab context without questioning their applicability to the object of study.

What they offer instead are rapid solutions to rapidly-posed questions from policy-makers, complete with policy recommendations, rather than being concerned with carrying out longitudinal analyses as individual building blocks in the project of Arab media research. Scholars then position themselves closer to the political arena than to academia, driven by short-term achievements, while their position in academia serves as a means to gain legitimacy and recognition. Clearly, there is nothing wrong in having a strong link between academia and political power, at least to feed the latter with qualified views on Arab media, but the link would prove flawed if it turned the academics into political advisers generating quick explanations rather than steadily interrogating the produced knowledge in their field.

The inclination to prioritize the demands of policy-makers over the knowledge production field is perhaps due to the intersection of the fields of politics and academia, where the former exerts a great pressure on the latter. For instance, public research councils that control research funding may indeed regulate the direction of Middle Eastern studies by confining research grants to projects dealing with post-9/11 key words, namely "terrorism," "religion (read: Islam)," or "public diplomacy." These kinds of projects are given higher precedence over others that do not directly address these key terms because they are supposed to fill the "gap" of knowledge felt after the 9/11 attacks, seeking solutions to the problem of how to harness some Arabs' inclination to fundamentalism!

Maton[118] distinguishes between the use of internal and external legitimating languages in the academic field: internal to address peer colleagues in the field, and external to address others outside the field.[119] Although his analysis was confined to the legitimacy of Cultural Studies, it can be used as a starting point to analyze the position of Western versus Arab scholars vis-à-vis the internal field (peer colleagues) and external field (politics and media). Arab scholars, then, would be situated in the middle of the continuum between internal and external means of legitimacy, where their aim is to gain sufficient recognition internally among peer colleagues while gaining legitimacy externally, for example, serving the development plans of their governments and justifying the significance of their research to gain funding. On the other hand, Western scholars specializing in Arab media would prioritize the external rather than internal legitimacy, if they confined their goal to serving as media pundits or political advisers.

Finally, juxtaposing the roles of some Western scholars with those of Arab media scholars strikes a chord with the relation between Arab journalists and their Western counterparts, as discussed in Chapter 6. If Western journalists seem to dominate the production of norms and professional standards, such as objectivity, so too do Western scholars who place themselves higher in the hierarchy of the intellectual field vis-à-vis their Arab counterparts, even though scholars from both spheres are, in principle, part of the same "interpretive community" of academia.

## Conclusion

This chapter reviewed the inception of journalism and mass communication as an academic discipline in Arab universities. It showed how Arab media scholarship has been consolidated in Arab academia by the amount of scholarship produced by generations of researchers. As I argue above, a shared characteristic between media educators and elite Arab journalists is that they both represent the hybrid product combining elements from East and West without losing sight of their primary mission towards their indigenous culture. The Arab scholarship, however, was not without limitations, as I pointed out in relation to the Arab scholars' tendency to value administrative rather than critical media research.

The last section in this chapter turned its gaze towards Western scholars on Arab media, only to show the monopoly of Western scholars in setting the standards in the academic field, for example, whom to cite, the object of analysis, and so on. In so doing, Western scholars tend to discard Arab scholarship, as if it were non-existent, while capitalizing on their new role as media pundits or policy advisers rather than autonomous knowledge producers.

This is not to deny the richness of Western scholarship, for example, anthropology, politics, religion, gender, and so on, which has indeed proven insightful for our understanding of the region. But my critique is limited only to research on Arab media and its contribution to mainstream media scholarship. One final comment is also due here: the above critique addressed Anglo-American scholarship in particular, as it serves as the source for the widely circulated literature on this field, not to mention its visibility on the global academic landscape compared to the work of other scholars who publish in languages other than English.

The above critique was meant to act as a provocation to both Arab and Western scholars and as a call for scrutinizing the aims and rationale of the numerous projects on Arab media. The provocation will only serve its purpose if it results in a joint debate among scholars in both spheres.

# Conclusion

No one doubts the importance of the media in the contemporary world,
but they are only one part of a much more complex set of social institutions that it is the object of sociology to study.

Anthony Giddens[1]

Rather than offering a coherent thesis, the previous chapters provided
pointers to future scholarship of Arab media. I would like to summarize these pointers in these concluding remarks, but let me first summarize the main themes and arguments of the previous chapters.

First, as I argued in Chapter 1, media as well as education have
served as the main building blocks in the modernization projects in
several Arab States. While education was meant to spread a new sense
of progressive identity, media was supposed to spread a sense of local
as well as pan-Arab belonging. However, those modernization plans
have not reached their goals, simply because they were based on essentialist views that saw indigenous cultural identity as a fixed entity that
would not be altered by mixing with other cultures. More importantly,
those plans discounted the ability of the laity, as well as intellectuals,
to constantly reflect on their actions and continuously work towards
improving their position in the social hierarchy. Media here play a
decisive role in that they serve as a bridge among cultures as well as
social classes.

Second, education has become an integral part of the cultural capital
of news professionals. Indeed, as I argued in Chapter 3, language
politics play a crucial role in the national and pan-Arab public sphere,
in as much as they partly reflect the power struggle among different
media players to attract a larger share of the audience. They also
partly reflect the potential impediment the laity experiences in trying
to access the public sphere. In Chapters 3 and 4, I summed up this

struggle by pointing to the limited access experienced by the laity as a result of the dangerous mix of an aloof style with distanced topics.

Third, I argue that Arab news media can be presented as a hierarchical system comprising serious versus lesser genres; local versus regional outlets. The hierarchal system is enforced by symbolic barriers, defined according to the total "capital" assigned to each media outlet and/or genre. Mapping out this hierarchy among local and regional outlets may help reveal a deeper mechanism in the development of the Arab media scene rather than merely romanticizing certain media outlets as liberal or autonomous without accounting for their position in this hierarchy and how this position has historically developed and influenced modern journalistic practices.

Fourth, the division or hierarchy among journalists does not operate merely locally or regionally, but also globally. Thus, while Arab journalists may be designated a professional identity that binds them globally to others in the same profession, they are separated by symbolic boundaries from Western journalists according to the position of each party in this global professional hierarchy. One acute consequence of this global hierarchy is that truth and knowledge may be made contingent on the institutions that produce them and the position of each institution in this power hierarchy. Rather than accepting, or again romanticizing, the global field of journalism, we should look deeper at the tension brought about by the articulation of difference between Arab and Western (Anglo-American) journalists.

## The scholarly endeavor

These themes, which have been explored here but not fully synthesized, ought to be prioritized in Arab and Western media scholarship. However, as I argued in Chapter 7, parts of the Arab media scholarship are still tied to an administrative rather than a critical research agenda, while parts of the Western scholarship of Arab media is still revolving on the policy-makers' orbit rather than focusing on interrogating knowledge. I have also been particularly critical of the tendency among several Anglo-American scholars to discard Arab media scholarship, which is reflected in their sparse reference to Arab works while capitalizing on their role as media pundits or policy advisers.

Professor Anthony Giddens[2] has recently called for sociology to get back to work and explain the vast social change occurring on many levels, both locally and globally. I share this view, in that I call for social theorists and Arab media specialists to "synthesize" rather than holding on to narrow specialisms. This is crucial if we really want to understand the complexities of the recent developments on the Arab media and social scenes. The core message of this volume is to point at rather forgotten and ignored issues, chief among them being language, power, hierarchy, and the ambivalence towards local versus regional identities, or between regional/local and global identity. Future research needs to look not only at the questions posed in this volume but also to explore a myriad of other new ones: for example, if the previous chapters focused on journalists as "social agents," future research could shed new light on the role of journalists as "moral agents" and how news producers, and indeed consumers, define the "moral distance" between them and us in their mediation.

I personally raised some of the issues discussed in this book in various open seminars and symposia involving Arab and Western scholars, as well as media professionals. The reactions differed between Western and Arab audiences. While a few Western scholars and journalists accused me of propagating nationalism in a world that *ought to be* anti-nationalist, several Arab journalists accused me of diverting attention away from what really matters by exposing private concerns in public. I also felt that those Arab journalists preferred to hold the debate at the "us versus them" level, which, in my view, represents a sort of denial to see the picture from within. In return, Western media professionals and audiences in search of a remedy tend to look at the outer layers of Arab problems rather than seeking a deeper understanding of these problems. The result is that the vast majority of journalistic accounts, and even the majority of academic accounts, inflict a typified identity upon all Arabs, leading observers to eventually wonder why things have not changed much in Arab societies, despite the media, political and economic attention that Western governments are pouring into the region.

## The road ahead?

At the heart of this book is my firm belief that local and pan-Arab media can be analyzed as a social field, an institution that should be synthesized by acknowledging its links to other social institutions. This is also an institution that can, and should be, analyzed vis-à-vis Anglo-American journalistic culture. I believe the analysis of the Arab journalistic field is, in and of itself, interesting as the basis for future debates on Arab society and media. In this spirit, I have already embarked on this task and the results will be duly published. Yet, comparing and contrasting this field with its Western counterparts may indeed prove invaluable for media scholarship, now open to the pulses and changes brought about by the increasing interconnectedness among nations. This comparative exercise, however, should also value the study of particular journalistic practices.

For this to happen, there is a need, whether we like it or not, for a stronger communication link between Arab and Western scholarship. Arab scholars' works should be made available to Western scholars and students, and should serve as the bedrock for future studies. We also need more in-depth analyses among Arab journalists and audiences. Otherwise, we will keep compiling abstract theses on what happens at the periphery of the Arab media field.

# Notes

## Introduction

1. Zelizer, 2004: 49
2. Ibid.: 60
3. Ibid.: 62ff
4. Ibid.: 77
5. Ibid.: 78
6. Ibid.: 80
7. Curran & Park, 1999:11
8. Benson, 2006
9. Benson & Neveu, 2005: 9
10. Bourdieu (1998) cited in Benson, 2006: 189
11. For example, Benson, 2000
12. Ibid.
13. Benson, 2006: 190
14. Auter et al., 2004
15. Benson, 1998
16. Eliasoph, 2004: 297
17. Ibid.: 301
18. See, for example, Schudson, 2005: 219
19. See Benson & Neveu, 2005: 16

## 1. Media: The Bridge to Globalization

1. Haenni, Patrick & Tammam, Hossam (2005). "Chat Shows, Nashid Groups, and Lite Preaching: Egypt's Air-Conditioned Islam." Available at: http://mondediplo.com/2003/09/03egyptislam
2. Göle (2000) cited in Pieterse, 2001: 222
3. Robertson, 1992

   4. Waters, 2001: 5
   5. Tarabishi, 2000
   6. Abdel Rahman, 2002a: 8
   7. Ibid.: 10
   8. Waters, 2001
   9. For example, Waters, 2001; Abdel Rahman, 2002a; Giddens, 1991
  10. Scholte, 2002: 8
  11. Al-Kahtani, 2000: 8ff
  12. Ibid.: 91
  13. Abaza, 2003: 4
  14. Abdel Rahman, 2002a
  15. Cited in al-Kahtani, 2000: 105
  16. Ibid.: 106
  17. Cited in Hindkær, 2001: 61
  18. Cited in Hindkær, 2001: 27
  19. Havrilesky, 2003
  20. Al-Jabri, 1997
  21. Ibid.: 136f
  22. Ibid.: 143ff
  23. Ibid.: 148 – my translation
  24. For example, Barber, 1995; Waters, 2001
  25. Hall, 1992
  26. *Al Bayan* (2004). "Islamic Cola kindles enthusiasm in Britain" (in
       Arabic), 8 March 2004.
  27. Shabkashi, Hussein "Fullah and Barbie: Clash of Civilization:
       Commentary" (in Arabic), *Al-Sharq Al-Awsat*, 23 May 2004
  28. Wheeler, 2001
  29. Al-Kahtani, 2000: 2
  30. Abaza, 2004
  31. Cited in Al-Kahtani, 2000: 122f
  32. Rachty & Sabat, 1987: 18
  33. Adams, 2006: 514
  34. Ibid.: 515
  35. Giddens, 1984
  36. Sewell, 1992
  37. Ibid.: 11
  38. Ibid.: 4 – emphasis in original
  39. Ibid.: 9f – emphasis in original
  40. Giddens, 1991: 1ff
  41. Ibid.: 16ff
  42. Ibid.: 32 – emphasis in original

43. Giddens, 1984: 5
44. Thompson, 2005: 87
45. Robertson, 2001: 462
46. Waters, 2001: 186
47. Lash & Urry, 1994
48. Meleis, 1982: 439
49. Eickelman, 1992: 845
50. Reid, 1987: 52
51. Ibid.: 51
52. Kamrava, 1998: 67
53. Ibid.: 68
54. Hourani, 1991: 391
55. Ibid.: 392
56. Lloyd, 2002: 156
57. Cited in Reid, 1987: 53
58. Rizk, Yunan Labib (2003). "*Al-Ahram* – A Diwan of contemporary life," *Al-Ahram Weekly* (Chronicle 523), 4–10 December 2003, Issue No. 667 (accessed on 2 October 2006)
59. Cited in Reid, 1987: 61
60. Lamont & Lareau, 1988
61. Ibid.: 158
62. Ibid.
63. Ibid.: 163
64. Abu-Lughod, 2005: 209
65. Abaza, 2004
66. Abu-Lughod, 2005: 76ff
67. Ibid.: 105
68. Ghannam, 2002: 135f
69. Siebert, 2002: 51
70. Ibid.: 52
71. Ibid.
72. Racy, 1982: 395
73. Ibid.
74. Al-Faisal, 2006: 416
75. Kamrava, 1998: 68
76. Eickelman, 1992: 650
77. Ibid.: 651
78. Kraidy, 2003
79. http://www.thedohadebates.com/
80. Fonda, Daren (2006). Dubai Inc. *Time*, NY: 13 March 2006, Vol. 167, Issue 1, pp. 38–40

81. Chaker, 2003
82. Quinn, 2001: 153
83. Cited in Sullivan, 2001a
84. Sullivan, 2001b
85. Abu-Lughod, 2005:198
86. Abaza, 2003: 5
87. Arebi, 1994: 16; Kazan, 1993
88. Abaza, 2001: 108
89. Ghannam, 2002, ch. 3
90. Abaza, 2001: 116
91. Ghannam, 2002
92. Quoted in Shehab, Shaden (2005). Mission impossible. *Al-Ahram Weekly,* 27 January–2 February 2005, Issue 727
93. Abu-Lughod, 2005: 72
94. Gordon, 2003: 76
95. Ibid.
96. Ibid.: 75
97. Ibid.: 78
98. Tester, 2001: 128f
99. Joseph & Stork, 1993: 23
100. Bayat, 1997: 59
101. Ibid.: 55
102. Abu-Lughod, 2005
103. Hourani, 1991: 384
104. Yacobi & Shechter, 2005: 499–505
105. Al-Hamzah, 2005: 289
106. Bayat, 1997: 58
107. Ibid.: 54
108. Abaza, 2001
109. Bayat, 1997: 55
110. Hadj-Moussa, 2003: 455
111. Bayat, 1997: 57
112. Thompson, 1995: 212
113. Lull, 1990
114. Thompson, 2005: 213
115. Hamdy, 2004.
116. Galal, 2004
117. Abaza, 2001: 118.
118. Shahine, Gihan (1998). "The double bind," *Al-Ahram Weekly*, 1–7 Ocotber 1998
119. El-Gawhary, 1995: 27

120. Ibid.

121. Fargues, 2003

122. Hourani, 1991: 386

123. Abaza, 2001: 117

124. Abu Odeh, 1993

125. Andijanai, Nahid (2004). "Saudi female university graduates in a mission to find jobs: 'Had I known my end, I would not have started'," *Al-Sharq al-Awsat*, 18 June 2004 (in Arabic)

126. Faqir, 1997: 169

127. Al-Medwahi, Omar (2004). "If the women asking to drive cars were like those participating in the intellectual forum, I would not hesitate permitting it," *Al-Sharq al-Awsat*, 16 June 2004 (in Arabic)

128. Zuhur, 2003: 21

129. Cited in a radio series by Magdi Abdelhadi, Middle East Affairs analyst, for the BBC World Service. Available at: http://www.thechangingworld. org/archives/wk39.php

130. Zuhur, 2003: 32

131. http://news.bbc.co.uk/1/hi/world/middle_east/1874471.stm

132. Yamani, 2000

133. Meleis, 1982: 443

134. See al-Arabiya's website: www.alarabiya.net: Egypt: university-educated women raise a case to permit them to belly dance, 16 June 2006 (accessed on 12 December 2006)

135. Levinson, 2006

136. See Mellor, 2005a

137. See Tash, 1983

138. Abu-Lughod, 2005: 10

139. Ibid.: 81

140. Turkestani, 1989

141. Abu-Lughod, 2005: 160

142. Abaza, 2003: 5

143. Usma Anwar Ukasha quoted in Abu-Lughod, 2005: 154

144. Chaker, 2003: 5f

145. Cited in Hadj-Moussa, 2003: 458

146. See Mellor, 2005a

147. Cited in Hadj-Moussa, 2003: 459

148. Abu-Lughod, 2005: 49

149. Yamani, 2000: xvii

150. Ouis, 2002: 316

151. Ibid.: 320

152. Ibid.

153. Yaquobi, 2004
154. Ibid.
155. Hassan, 2005
156. A news report adds that 20 percent of the patients are men and most of them seek anti-ageing treatment. See http://news.bbc.co.uk/go/fr/-/hi/arabic/world_news/newsid_4253000/4253012.stm
157. *Middle East Broadcasters Journal* (MEB), April–May 2006: 19–22. Available at www.mebjournal.com
158. Wahbi, 1996
159. See Abu-Lughod, 2005: 174
160. Al-Effendi, Abdel Wahab (2004). "Al-Azhar latest scandal and Egypt's need for appropriate symbols," *Al-Quds Al-Arabi*, Vol. 15, Issue 4545, Saturday/Sunday 3/4 January 2004: 19 (in Arabic)
161. See Amr Khaled's website: http://www.amrkhaled.net/
162. Read, for example, the interview with Dr. Heba Qotb in *Arabiyat* on 30 August 2004. Available at http://www.arabiyat.com/magazine/publish/article_528.shtml (in Arabic) (accessed on 12 December 2006)
163. http://www.smartsway.tv/about-ar.php
164. http://www.suwaidan.com
165. Ibrahim, 1997
166. Beck, 1992
167. Ghannam, 2002: 77

## 2. The Arab Journalistic Field

  * An earlier version of this chapter was presented at the Media Change and Social Theory conference, St Hugh's College, University of Oxford, 6–8 September 2006
1. See, for example, Zayani, 2005; Rugh, 2004
2. Sharkey, 2003
3. See, for example, Tash, 1983; al-Rasheed, 1998; and recently Ramarprasad & Hamdy, 2006
4. As, for example, in Sakr, 2005
5. Bourdieu, 2005: 33
6. Matheson, 2003
7. Mellor, 2005a
8. Bourdieu, 1984; 1991
9. Zelizer, 1993/1997b
10. Bellah et al., 1985: 153
11. Zelizer, 1993/1997b: 407
12. Bourdieu, 1998

13. Tester, 2001: 23
14. Bourdieu, 1984; 1992
15. Benson, 1998: 479
16. Benson, 2000: 8
17. Bourdieu & Wacquant, 1992: 133 – emphasis in original
18. Benson, 2000: 12
19. Hovden, 2001
20. Bourdieu & Wacquant, 1992: 101
21. According to Yasmine Abdallah, the presenter of the daily program *Good Morning Egypt* (on the Egyptian Satellite Channel, ESC), 80 percent of the interviewees in her daily program are either politicians or political analysts (Ezzi, 2004: 198).
22. Benson, 2000
23. Mellor, 2005a: ch. 3
24. Rugh, 1987; 2004
25. Abu Bakr, 1985: 18
26. Yet, it was not really until the 1960s that those Gulf countries developed a more sophisticated printing culture, in terms of both content and form (see Mellor, 2005a).
27. Tash, 1983: 51
28. Sreberny, 1998: 178
29. See Mellor, 2005a, for a fuller discussion
30. See, for example, Mellor, 2005a
31. "The Centrality of Live Talks in Arab Satellite Broadcasting," at http://www.faisalalkasim.net/forum/viewtopic.php?p=183&sid=5a721dd99bc807925e83f6dbed92e055 (accessed on 12 June 2006)
32. Tibi, 1997
33. Kienle, 1995: 54
34. Cited in Kienle, 1995: 65
35. Potter, 1961: 35
36. Tibi, 1997: 203
37. Tibi, 1997: 203
38. Fandy, 2000
39. Taweela, 2002
40. Fandy, 2000
41. Nasser, 1979
42. Tibi, 1997: 211
43. Turkistani, 1989
44. Sakr, 2001a
45. Ghareeb, 2000; Ayish, 2002
46. Lakoff, 1991

47. See Mellor, 2005a, Introduction
48. Rugh, 1987: 16
49. See Mellor, 2005a
50. Ibid.
51. For a fuller discussion on these factors, see Mellor, 2005a
52. Ayish, 2001
53. Davies, Humphrey (2003). "CNBC Arabiya – the debut," *Transnational Broadcasting Studies*, 11, available at www.tbsjournal.com/CNBC_Debut.html
54. Ayish, 1991
55. Soloway, 2003
56. Habermas, 1962/1989
57. See Street, 2001: 41ff
58. Ramarprasad & Hamdy, 2006
59. Kraidy, 2005
60. Cited in Ezzi, 2004: 157
61. *Al-Sharq al- Awsat* (2005). "Why the Moroccan presenter has not succeeded in conquering the Arab channels?" *Media Supplement*, 18 June 2005 (in Arabic)
62. Ibid.
63. Badry, 2006
64. Ellis, 2000
65. Ibid.: 176
66. Cited in Lynch, 2006: 4
67. Lynch, 2006: 4
68. Henry et al., 2003
69. Ibid.: 307
70. Kraidy, 2005
71. Ibid.
72. Sakr, 2001a; Rugh, 2004; Lynch, 2006
73. Suleiman, 2003
74. Qandil, 1999
75. Al-Jammal, 2001
76. Jenkins, 1996
77. Benson, 1999
78. Hannerz, 2004: 21
79. Ibid.: 3
80. Willnat & Weaver, 2003: 413
81. See Mellor, 2005a
82. See Mellor, 2005a; Ayish, 1991
83. Ezzi, 2004: 168

84. Mellor, 2005a

85. See Mellor, 2007

86. Ezzi, 2004: 169

87. Zayani, 2005: 10

88. Ezzi, 2004: 188

89. Al-Qadry & Harb, 2002

90. See also Mellor, 2005b

91. Zeinab Hefni (2003). "Opinion," *Al-Sharq al-Awsat*, 21 June 2003 (in Arabic)

92. Dajani, 1992

93. Abdel Rahman, 1989: 18

94. Abdel Rahman, 2002a: 46

95. Kirat, 1987

96. *Al-Hayat* (2006). "Young men refuse to engage with them because they are free: Algerian young women enter the profession of trouble at the expense of their private lives," *Youth Supplement*, 5 June 2006 (in Arabic)

97. Sensenig-dabbous, 2000: 15

98. In fact, female correspondents now serve as the new heroes who expose themselves to danger, particularly in covering the Palestinian–Israeli clashes. See http://islamonline.net/arabic/adam/2003/06/article08.shtml (in Arabic) (accessed 14 June 2006)

99. According to the Kuwaiti daily *al-Qabas*, young TV female presenters have a huge fan base among Arab youths and men who now use the chat sites on the Internet to exchange views on certain presenters. See Mohamed Hanafi (2006). "Satellite presenters, the new dream women," *al-Qabas*, 9 April 2006 (in Arabic).

100. Al-Jazeera star host Faisal al-Kasim, presenter of the controversial debate program *The Opposite Direction* (molded after the American *Crossfire*), recalled the times when he was overwhelmed by young Arabs, which made him feel like a pop star or an Arab Michael Jackson! See Faisal al-Kasim's article, "The centrality of live talks in Arab satellite broadcasting," at http://www.faisalalkasim.net/forum/viewtopic.php?p=183&sid=5a721dd99bc807925e83f6dbed92e055 (accessed on 12 June 2006)

101. Al-Jack, Sanaa (2000). "A high percentage of Lebanese journalists enter the election battle to win a seat in the parliament," *Al-Sharq al-Awsat*, 24 August 2000 (in Arabic)

102. *From Washington*, 4 December 2006. Available at www.aljazeera.net/NR/exeres/71691781-C297-40BB-BBE6-B5595CB7556F.htm (in Arabic) (accessed on 20 December 2006)

103. Wu & Weaver, 1998: 517
104. Wright, 2004
105. *MEB Journal* (2006). "Kuwait University struggles to groom young broadcasters." Available at www.mebjournal.com (accessed on 30 June 2006)
106. Al-Qadry & Harb 2002
107. Ibid.: 96ff
108. The report, undertaken by UNESCO, is called "Training of Mediterranean Women Journalists." Recommendations, and a brief description of that study, are available at http://www.unesco.org/webworld/highlights/women_media_050799.html
109. See Sakr, 2001b
110. Abdel Rahman, 2002a: 154
111. Abdel Rahman, 2002a.
112. Al-Qadry and Harb, 2002
113. See Mattar, Shafika (2003). "Jordan's Husseini created a new beat: Honor crimes." Available at http://www.womensenews.org/article.cfm/dyn/aid/1321/context/jounalistofthemonth
114. The Kuwaiti Qabas quoted one of those young admirers who likened Marilyn Monroe to one Arab TV presenter called Shuair al-Quesi, adding that both stars being born on the same day (31 May) was proof of their resemblance. Mohamed Hanafi (2006). "Satellite presenters: the new dream women," *al-Qabas*, 9 April 2006 (in Arabic)
115. "I am not only a program presenter. I present both debate programs and the news bulletin," said al-Roumhei. *Al-Sharq al-Awsat*, TV supplement 28 March 2003 (in Arabic)
116. Hamidi, 2004: 214
117. Cherribi, 2006: 127.
118. Hannerz, 2004: 95
119. http://islamonline.net/arabic/adam/2003/06/article08.shtml (accessed on 12 June 2006)
120. Ibid.
121. Al-Qadry & Harb, 2002
122. Mohamed Abu Zeid (2004). "Ibrahim Helal: The governments that fear the flow of information deal with the media as an enemy," *Al-Sharq al-Awsat*, 4 September 2004 (in Arabic).
123. For example, al-Rasheed, 1998; Kirat, 1987; Ramarprasad & Hamdy, 2006
124. Al-Rasheed, 1998: 57
125. Weaver, 1994: 148
126. Kirat, 1987

127. Al-Rasheed, 1998: 63ff
128. Al-Jammal, 2001: 60
129. Turkestani, 1989: 249
130. Abdel Nabi, 1989
131. Al-Qadri, Nahawand (2005). "Models of Innovative Experiences of Young Media Women Between Conservative and Open Surroundings." *Al-Raida*, Vol. XXI–XXII (106/07), Summer/Fall 2004–5: 88–91
132. Cited in Ezzi, 2004: 156
133. http://www.aljazeera.net/Portal/training%20center
134. Al-Jammal, 2001
135. Ibid.: 59
136. See the report of the Stanhope Centre for Communications Policy Research, "Study of Media Laws and Politics for the Middle East and Maghreb." Available at http://www.internews.org/arab_media_ research
137. Al-Jammal, 2001: 65
138. Mellor, 2005a
139. Al-Rasheed, 1998: 58
140. See Abu Zeid, 1993; Mellor, 2005a
141. Ezzi, 2004: 152
142. Hannerz, 2004: 148
143. Dubai Press Club, http://www.dpc.org.ae/ar/aja/aja.html. This should also be seen in light of the United Arab Emirates, particularly Dubai, promoting itself as an Arab cultural center, hosting Dubai Media City (launched in 2001) as well as inaugurating the Dubai Film Festival in 2004–5
144. See http://www.mebshow.com/. It has to be added, however, that although this information is valid at the time of writing, due to the current situation in Lebanon the award may not proceed as planned.
145. Kasim, Faisal (n.d.). "The centrality of live talks in arab satellite broad-casting." http://www.faisalalkasim.net/forum/viewtopic.php?p=183& sid=5a721dd99bc807925e83f6dbed92e055 (accessed on 12 June 2006)
146. Abu Zeid, 1993: 283
147. Benson, 1999
148. Bourdieu, 2005: 39

## 3. Journalism as a Beacon for Democracy

1. For example, Rugh, 1987; Koeppel, 1989
2. Alterman, 2000
3. For example, Zayani, 2005; Sakr, 2001a
4. Dahlgren, 1995:

5. Lynch, 2006
6. For example, Calhoun, 1992
7. Fraser, 1992
8. Ibid.: 132
9. Benhabib, 1992
10. Dahlgren, 2006: 275
11. Schudson, 1992
12. Van Zoonen, 1998a: 187
13. Calhoun, 1992
14. Habermas, 1992: 427
15. Eliasoph, 1998: 11
16. Ibid.
17. Lynch, 2006: 32
18. Ibid.
19. Ibid.: 33
20. Ibid.
21. See Mellor, 2005a
22. Lynch, 2006: 49
23. Van Zoonen, 1998a: 188
24. Dahlgren, 2006: 281
25. Ibid.: 10
26. Lynch, 2006: 80f
27. Cited in Ezzi, 2004: 192f
28. See "What Readers Know" (2005). Available at http://www.journalismorg/node/511/print, and Lewis, 1994
29. Karam, 2007
30. Abu Darwich, Layal (2006). "Hannibal fails to conquer." *MEB Journal*, April–May 2006. Available at www.mebjournal.com
31. Lynch, 2006: 10
32. Mellor, 2007
33. For example, Tester, 2001; Höijer, 2004
34. Shiblak, 1996: 39
35. Lesch,1991: 17
36. Shiblak, 1996: 39–43
37. Abou-Habib, 2003: 67
38. Ibid.: 68f
39. Ibid.: 70
40. Ibid.: 72
41. Each foreign laborer, including those from neighboring Arab countries, must have a local sponsor or *"kafeel,"* who issues the laborer's visa and claims full legal and economic responsibility for the laborer.

In return, the laborers are tied to their *"kafeel"* and cannot change employer once they are in the host country (see, for example, Longva, 1999)

42. El-Gawhary, 1995: 27. El-Gawhary mentioned the incident of punishing an Egyptian doctor working in Saudi Arabia with eighty lashes, following the doctor's complaint that his son was raped by a Saudi school headmaster

43. Khalaf and al-Kobaisi, 1999

44. Michel Aoun is a former Lebanese army chief, from the Christian Maronites. He was forced into exile in 1990 after the Syrian-Lebanese forces defeated his six-month rebellion against the Syrians

45. The phrase "the General" in Arabic is *al-Emad*. If the definite article is deleted (*al-*), the remaining word sounds like a male name

46. Dahlgren, 2002: 17

47. Wyatt, Katz and Kim, 2000

48. Eliasoph, 1998

49. Ibid.: 13

50. Dahlgren, 2002: 18

51. Lynch, 2006: 63

52. Ibid.: 34

53. See also Cherribi, 2006, for a critique on Lynch's view of the religious programs on al-Jazeera

54. Lynch, 2006: 76

55. Dahlgren, 2002: 6

56. Fraser, 1990: 57

57. Ibid.: 125 – emphasis added

58. Fraser, 1990: 127

59. Cited in Ezzi, 2004: 139

60. Fraser, 1990: 64

61. Ibid.: 127

62. Ibid.: 62, 66

63. Haas & Steiner, 2001: 125

64. Ibid.: 135

65. Splichal, 2006: 695

66. Mellor, 2005a

67. Cited in Swales, 1990: 36

68. Swales, 1990: 24

69. Ibid.: 52f

70. Mellor, 2005a

71. Hafez, 2002: 242; al-Jammal, 2001: 69

72. For example, Ennaji, 1995; Haeri, 2003

73. Mellor, 2005a

74. Cited in Habib, 1985: 97

75. Habib, 1985: 103

76. Ibid.: 135f

77. Ibid.: 157

78. Ibid.: 173

79. El-Khoury, 2005: 315

80. Ibid.: 339

81. Fairclough, 1992

82. Ibid.: 204

83. See Mellor, 2005a, for a lengthy discussion on the role of MSA in the news media

84. Mahfouz, 1991: 82

85. Cited in the Kuwaiti newspaper *Al-Rai al-Aam*, 7 January 2006. Available at http://www.alraialaam.com/07-01-2006/ie5/special.htm (in Arabic) (accessed on 24 June 2006)

86. El-Khoury, 2005: 289

87. Cited in Ezzi, 2004: 187

88. Suleiman, 2004: 37

89. El-Khoury, 2005: 145

90. Ibid.: 262f

91. Ibid.: 298

92. Suleiman, 2004: 43

93. El-Khoury, 2005: 306

94. Cited in Suleiman, 2004: 44 n16

95. El-Khoury, 2005: 308

96. *From Washington*, 4 December 2006. Available at www.aljazeera.net/NR/exeres/71691781-C297-40BB-BBE6-B5595CB7556F.htm (in Arabic) (accessed on 20 December 2006)

97. Whitaker, Brian (2005). "New Mubarak means same old problems, say opponents," *The Guardian*, 7 September 2005

98. Al-Qassas, Jamal (2005). "Presidential candidates support their campaigns with a *new look*," *Al-Sharq al-Awsat*, 18 August 2005 (in Arabic)

99. The phrases such as "We suffocate" (*Itkhanaqna*) or "We watch you" (*shay'finkou*) may not sound particularly informal in English, but they were written as they were pronounced in the vernacular to mark their informality and hence conversationalist style

100. El-Khoury, 2005: 318

101. Ibid.: 324

102. Ibid.: 325f

103. Said, Edward (2004). "Living in Arabic," *Al-Ahram Weekly*, Issue 677, 12–18 February 2004. Available at http://weekly.ahram.org.eg/print/2004/677/cul15.htm (accessed on 2 October 2006)

104. Shanor, 2003: 115


## 4. The Dichotomy of the Public/Private Sphere

1. Fraser, 1990: 71
2. Jawad, 2002
3. Mellor, 2005a
4. Hannerz, 2004: 84
5. Ibid.: 133
6. Schudson, 1982: 99
7. Ibid.: 102
8. Ibid.: 108
9. Fouad, Matar (2001). "From Journalism to Ministry," *Al-Sharq al-Awsat* (editorial), 16 May 2001 (in Arabic)
10. Bekhait, 1998; Abdel Nabi, 1989; Abdel Rahaman, 1989
11. Abu Bakr, 1985
12. Abdel Rahman, 2002a
13. Ibid.: 156
14. Cited in Ezzi, 2004: 194f
15. Al-Manar TV is owned by the Lebanese Hezbollah and it began its terrestrial broadcasting in 1991 and by satellite in 2000
16. Ezzi, 2004: 174.
17. *From Washington*, 4 December 2006, available at www.aljazeera.net/NR/exeres/71691781-C297-40BB-BBE6-B5595CB7556F.htm (accessed on 20 December 2006) (in Arabic)
18. Ibid.
19. Ibid.
20. Muqalled, Diana (2006). "When there is no place for the non-political in the media." *Al-Sharq al-Awsat, Media supplement*, 3 December 2006 (in Arabic)
21. Al-Kasim, Faisal (2005). "Humanizing the Arab Media," *MEB Journal*, November–December 2005: 42. Also available at www.mebjournal.com
22. "Arabiske medier er for passive!" Available at www.amnesty.no (in Norwegian)
23. Farrag, Najib (2006). "Few of the dispatches on the economic situation in the Palestinian media." Available at http://ammannet.net/look/eom/ (in Arabic) (accessed on 3 January 2007)

24. Omar, Mohamed (2006). "On the press and the naked bread." Available at http://ammannet.net/look/eom/ (in Arabic) (accessed on 3 January 2007)
25. Abdel Nabi, 1989
26. Fandy, Mamoun (2005). "The facile media and self-deception," *Al-Sharq al-Awsat*, 3 October 2005 (in Arabic)
27. Sheller & Urry, 2003: 107
28. Ibid.
29. Ibid.
30. Shelly & Urry, 2003
31. Fraser, 1990: 71
32. Maluf, Ramez (2007). "Looking Closer to Home," *MEB Journal*, January/February 2007. Available at www.mebjournal.com (accessed on 23 January 2007)
33. Shamri, 1998
34. Al-Kasim, Faisal (2005). "Humanizing the Arab Media," *MEB Journal*, November–December 2005: 42. Available at www.mebjournal.com
35. It is worth mentioning that *al-Ahram* prints an "international" edition, distributed from London and other European cities, but the content tends to be similar to the local edition
36. See Mellor, 2005a, for a discussion of Arab news values.
37. From the UN report "The Rapid Situation Assessment of Street Children in Cairo and Alexandria, 2001." Available at: http://www.unodc.org/pdf/youthnet/egypt_street_children_report.pdf
38. Abu Zeid, Mohamed (2005). "Crime newspapers in Egypt . . . between reality and fiction," *Al-Sharq al-Awsat*, 27 November 2005 (in Arabic)
39. Dahlgren, 1988
40. Cited in Salamandra, 2003
41. Gigilcim, 1992
42. Mellor, 2005a
43. Pantti, 2005
44. *Al-Sharq al-Awsat*, "Opinion," 24 June 2001 (in Arabic)
45. See Mellor, 2005a
46. Al-Jazeera program *Kawa'lees* (*Backstage*), aired on 31 July 2005. Full script can be downloaded from www.aljazeera.net (in Arabic)
47. For example, Fraser, 1992
48. Eliasoph, 1998: 213
49. Ibid.: 226
50. Ibid.: 228
51. Taylor, 1994
52. Furedi, 2003
53. Eliasoph, 1998: 255

54. Ibid.: 260

55. El-Rashidi, Yasmine (2005). " 'Oprah' is Attracting Young, Female Viewers to TV in Saudi Arabia," *The Wall Street Journal*, 1 December 2005: B1

56. From al-Arabiya's website: "Oprah. . .presents 'a different American' to the Arabs." Available at http://www.alaraibua.net/Articles/2004/08/22/2862.htm (in Arabic). The article is followed by feedback from Saudi Arabia, and other viewers, particularly women, who were fascinated with the show and its presenter

57. Taha, Alaa (2006). Nashwa el-Roueni: "Bad luck haunted me in Nashwa show," *Al-Qabas*, Vol. 35, 11858, 8 June 2006 (in Arabic).

58. Mellor, 2005a

59. Saad, 1998

60. Mahmoud Saad cited in al-Jazeera program, *From Washington*, 4 December 2006. Available at www.aljazeera.net/NR/exeres/71691781-C297-40BB-BBE6-B5595CB7556F.htm (in Arabic) (accessed on 20 December 2006)

61. See, for instance, the BBC news story" Met 'needs 2,000 Muslim officers'," Available at http://news.bbc.co.uk/1/hi/england/london/4122972.stm

62. Saghieh, Hazem & Bechir, Saleh (2005). "The 'Muslim community': A European invention," *OpenDemocracy*. Available at http://www.opendemocracy. net/conflict-terrorism/community_2928.jsp

## 5. Global Media, Global Public Sphere?

1. Mellor, 2005a
2. Zelizer, 1993/1997b: 402
3. Kieran, 1997: 53ff
4. Ibid.
5. Thompson, 2005
6. Schudson, 2003: 67
7. Volkmer, 2001: 67
8. Street, 2001
9. Hjarvard, 2001: 19
10. Thussu, 2000: 64ff
11. Abdel Rahman, 2002a: 28ff
12. For example, Hannerz, 1997
13. Thussu, 2000: 206
14. Volkmer, 1999
15. Habermas, 1962/1989
16. Thompson, 1995: 257f
17. Dahlgren, 1995: 11ff

18. Habermas, 1981/1984–7
19. Dahlgren, 1995: 9
20. Amanpour cited in Mindich, 1998
21. Keane, 1991: 22
22. See Eickelman, 2002. Referring to the Arab public opinion as "Arab street" indicates its passivity and exposure to manipulation, not to mention its lack of leadership (Eickelman, 2002: 40)
23. See Rugh, 2006
24. Nisbet et al., 2004
25. Lynch, 2006: 6
26. Zayani, 2005
27. For example, Zelizer, 1993/1997b
28. For example, Hallin, 1986
29. Pieterse, 2001: 220–2
30. For example, importing and assimilating English words as well as phrases into the Arabic news language (see Mellor, 2005a)
31. Tomlinson, 1999: 141
32. Cited in Tomlinson, 1999: 142
33. Pieterse, 2001: 224
34. Kraidy, 2002: 317f
35. Thussu, 2002: 211
36. Thussu, 2005: 131f
37. Ayish, 1991
38. Abdel Nabi, 1989
39. Bekhait, 1998
40. For example, Splichal & Sparks, 1994
41. Lauk, 1996
42. Zayani, 2005: 30
43. Calhoun, 1996: 461
44. Dahlgren, 2006: 275
45. Ibid.: 270
46. Bourdieu, 1984
47. For example, *Cultural Studies*, Volume 16(4)
48. Shoemaker, 1991
49. Negus, 2002: 510
50. Dahlgren, 1989: 3
51. Hartley, 1996
52. Quoted in Whittle, 2005: 54
53. Schudson, 1978
54. McNair, 2005: 27
55. Seaton, 2005

56. Van Dijk, 1984
57. Almeida, 1992: 260f
58. Van Dijk, 1988
59. For example, Fedler et al., 1996
60. For example, Cappella & Jamieson, 1997
61. Patterson, 1993
62. Ibid.
63. Whittle, 2005: 54
64. Van Zoonen, 1998b: 124
65. Mellor, 2007
66. Van Zoonen, 1998b
67. Ibid.: 138
68. Carpentier, 2005
69. See Flyvbjerg, 2001; Chouliaraki, 2006
70. Zelizer, 1993/1997b: 406
71. Ibid.
72. With the exception of Lynch, 2006
73. Chouliaraki, 2006
74. Wodak et al., 2000
75. Kraidy, 2002
76. Jensen, 1998
77. See, in particular, Abu Zeid, 1993
78. Ibid.: 454ff
79. Ghareeb, 2000
80. Alterman, 1998
81. Wells & King, 1994: 653
82. Lacy, Fico & Simon, 1991: 366
83. Ghareeb, 2000
84. Alterman, 2000
85. McFadden, 1953: 22
86. Wright, 2004; Alterman, 1998
87. Alterman, 1998: 10
88. Khazen, 1999
89. Alterman, 1998: 11
90. Abu Zeid, 1993: 135
91. Ibid.: 140
92. Ghareeb, 2000
93. Alterman, 1998: 7ff
94. Ghareeb, 2000
95. Abu Zeid, 1993: 215
96. Tash, 1983: 40f

97. Abu Zeid, 1993: 215f
98. Ibid.: 216
99. Ibid.
100. Ibid.: 217f
101. Alterman, 1998: 12
102. Ibid.
103. Abu Zeid, 1993: 281
104. Ghareeb, 2000
105. Lynch, 2006: 12
106. Abu Zeid, 1993: 281
107. Ibid.
108. Ibid.: 283
109. The implication of this view, then, is that the yardstick of measuring objectivity is based on Western criteria, for example, the messages and guests for whom the Western news media provide space. It may also indicate an implicit hierarchy of media institutions in which the top places may be occupied by the most globalized and internationalized institutions, such as the BBC and CNN, whose credibility will also benefit those who appear in their news stories, for example, as sources
110. Dajani, 1992
111. Abu Zeid, 1993: 42
112. Ayalon, 1995: 43
113. Abu Zeid, 1993: 42
114. Ayalon, 1995: 43
115. Ibid.: 43ff
116. Abu Zeid, 1993: 48
117. Amin, 2001: 25f . The four publishing houses are al-Ahram, Dar Akhbar al-Yum, Dar al-Tahrir and Dar al-Hilal
118. Ghareeb, 2000
119. Topoushian, 2002: 22
120. For example, Dajani, 1989; al-Jammal, 1990
121. Weimann & Brosius, 1991: 338

## 6. Truth Martyrs

1. Zelizer, 1993/1997a: 25
2. Fairclough, 2002: 309
3. Giddens, 1991
4. Jenkins, 2000; Laclau & Mouffe, 1985
5. Phillips & Jørgensen, 2002: 25
6. Jenkins, 2000: 7 – emphasis in original

7. Jenkins, 2004: 25f.

8. Gamson, 1989: 157

9. Khalil, 2000

10. For example, Ayish, 1991

11. For example, Thussu, 2004

12. Cited in Ezzi, 2004: 137

13. Fandy, 2003: 390

14. Abdelfattah, 1990: 62ff

15. Abu Zeid, 1993: 392ff

16. Al-Shabbab and Swales, 1986: 38

17. Ibid.

18. Fandy, 2003

19. Laclau & Mouffe, 1985

20. This rather contradicts the view that journalists are there to uncover the truth, if their presence is conditioned by the amount of safety granted by military or political forces. Source: Nick Gowing's speech and Q & A from the Alistair Berkley Memorial Lecture held at the LSE on 21 March 2004. Available at http://www.crisisstates.com/download/Berkley/Berkley2.pdf

21. See Mellor, 2007

22. Cited in Ezzi, 2004: 125

23. Bourdieu, 1998

24. Nick Gowing's speech and Q & A session from the Alistair Berkley Memorial Lecture, held at LSE on 21 March 2004 (emphasis added). Available at http://www.crisisstates.com/download/Berkley/Berkley2.pdf

25. Bourdieu, 1989

26. Ibid.: 16

27. Ghassan Ben Jeddou, presenter of al-Jazeera program *Hewar Maftouh* (*Open Dialogue*), asked one of his guests about the credibility of certain news media, saying, "Which is more credible media. . . is it Fox News and Sky News at the expense of other media? As you know, there has been an argument lately between Sky News and BBC, with the former criticizing the latter for not using the word 'terrorists'." Source: *Open Dialogue*, al-Jazeera, 19 July 2005 (in Arabic)

28. Khaffaf, 2005

29. For example, Abdel Rahman, 2002a

30. Pieterse, 2001

31. Giddens, 1979

32. Dahlgren, 2006: 274

33. Miladi, 2006; Matar, 2006

34. For example, Ayish, 1991
35. Shaheen, 2003
36. Asi, 1981

## 7. Arab Journalism as an Academic Discipline

1. Abu Bakr et al., 1985
2. Ibid.
3. Ibid.: 45
4. Ibid.: 217
5. Ibid.: 218
6. Abdel Rahman, 1991
7. For example, Kirat, 1987: 64ff
8. Ibid.: 45
9. Abdel Rahman, 1991: 48
10. Ibid.: 46
11. Ibid.: 47
12. Al-Jammal, 2001
13. Abdel Rahman, 1985: 62; Abdel Rahman, 2006
14. For instance, Hanan Yousef is a presenter at Egyptian official television while serving as a lecturer in international media at an Egyptian university. Likewise, Naila Hamdy, a TV correspondent, is affiliated to the American University in Cairo, Egypt
15. Rashed, Dena (2005). "To learn or not to learn," *Al-Ahram Weekly*, Issue 759, 8–14 September 2005
16. Tadros, Mariz (2002). "The Europeans are coming," *Al-Ahram Weekly*, Issue 575, 28 February–6 March 2002
17. Al-Jammal, 2001: 213
18. Ibid.: 216
19. Al-Hasani, 2006
20. See Flamini, Roland (2003). "A thirst for knowledge in Qatar," *Washington Times*, 3 December 2003
21. Cited in a radio series by Magdi Abdelhadi, Middle East Affairs analyst, for the BBC World Service. Available at: http://www.thechangingworld.org/archives/wk39.php
22. See www.kv.ae
23. Turkestani, 1989: 249
24. Ibid.
25. These reasons were raised in a convention for media officials held in Kuwait in June 2003 and reported on in *Al-Sharq Al-Awsat*, 22 July 2003, by Samir Attallah (in Arabic)

26. Kirat, 1987: 157f
27. Ibid.: 162
28. Tash, 1983: 127ff
29. Abdel Rahman, 1991
30. Abdel Rahman, 1989: 174f
31. Kirat, 1987: 63
32. Ibid.: 137
33. Ibid.: 138ff
34. Ibid.: 141
35. Tash, 1983: 114
36. Al-Hadidi, 1996
37. Ibrahim, 2000
38. It is not possible to provide a page number for this quote since I down-loaded the whole report from the Internet in HTML format. The link to this report, as mentioned in the reference list, is http://network.idrc.ca/ev.php?ID=32206_201&ID2=DO_TOPIC
39. Al-Abd, 1993: 6
40. Ibid.: 5
41. Ibid.: 16
42. Ibid.: 27
43. The studies cited here refer to AP, Reuters and AFP
44. For example, Rachty, 1978
45. For example, Abdel Rahman, 1989; Al-Jammal, 1990
46. For example, Dajani, 1989
47. Al-Jabri, 2000; 2001; 2002
48. See, for instance, al-Jabri, 2000: 564f
49. Fay, 1996
50. Al-Jabri, 2002: 43f
51. Fay, 1996: 72
52. Ibid.
53. Filmer et al., 2000: 25f
54. Ibid.
55. Fay, 1996: 201f
56. Ibid.: 202
57. Ibid.: 73
58. Danermark et al., 2002: 17
59. Ibid.
60. Jensen, 2002: 261
61. Dahlgren, 1989: 7
62. Andersen, 2003: ix
63. Ibid.: x–xi

64. Abdel Rahman, 2002b: 177ff
65. Ibid.: 179
66. Ibrahim, 2000
67. Ibrahim, 1997: 549
68. Sabagh and Ghazalla, 1986: 374–8
69. Mendelsohn, 1974: 381
70. Ibid.: 380
71. Al-Jabri 2000
72. Ibid.: 74
73. Ibid.: 290
74. Ibid.: 384
75. Danaher et al., 2000: 20f. See also http://aljabriabed.net/
    t10_arabIslamic_ philosophy.pdf
76. Musallam, 1986; al-Daqdouqi, 2001
77. Abu Rabi', 2004: 279
78. Ibid.: 283
79. See ibid.: 287
80. Ayish, 1998
81. Ibid.: 33
82. Ibid.: 33
83. Ibid.
84. Ibid.: 40
85. Ibid.: 45
86. See, for example, Hourani, 1991
87. Abu-Rabi', 2004: 269
88. Silverstone, 1999: 15
89. Ayish, 1998: 34
90. Ayalon, 1995: 52ff
91. Abdel Rahman, 2002b
92. Cited in Karabel, 1996: 205
93. Karabel, 1996
94. Gunter, 2002: 11
95. Ibid.: 10
96. Shami, 1989: 650, n5
97. Selaiha, Nehad (2006). "In memory of Hammoudah: A true intellectual
    of peasant stock," *Al-Ahram Weekly*, Issue 811, 7–13 September 2006
    (accessed on 21 October 2006)
98. Other intellectuals, however, fled to the same Western hemisphere from
    accusations of apostasy, such as the famous Egyptian professor of litera-
    ture, Nasr Hamed Abu Zeid, who fled to the Netherlands. Abu Zeid
    found himself in the public eye and amidst a public lawsuit demanding the

separation of Abu Zeid and his wife on the grounds that his Muslim wife could and should no longer be living with an apostate, a title he got following the submission of his controversial research judged to be violating the tenets of Islam (see, for example, Abou el-Magd, Nadia, (2000). "When the professor can't teach," *Al-Ahram Weekly*, Issue 486, 15–21 June 2000

99. Blommaert, 1997: 131
100. Ibid.
101. Al-Hadidi, 1996
102. Shami, 1989: 650
103. Ibrahim, 1997: 550
104. Shami, 1989: 653
105. Ibid.
106. Abdel Rahman, 2002b: 183
107. Haddad, 1977: 83
108. Riggins, 1985: 33
109. Beinin, 1993
110. See Maluf, Ramez (2007). "Looking Closer to Home." *MEB Journal*, January/February 2007. Available at www.mebjournal.com (accessed on 23 January 2007)
111. Mellor, 2005a
112. Rugh, 2004: 250
113. Ayish, 1998
114. Sakr, 2005: 153, n1
115. Nasr & Hajjar, 1997: 16
116. Gunter, 2002: 8
117. Bourdieu, 2000: 111ff
118. Maton, 2000: 152
119. Maton (ibid.: 152) also adds another axis to his analysis of the language of legitimation, namely the discursive versus social. While the former addresses knowledge producers within the field, for example, via conference papers, the latter addresses the institutional field of reproduction, such as lectures and textbooks.

## Conclusion

1. Giddens, Anthony (2006). "A call to arms." *The Guardian*, 26 November 2006, Available at http://commentisfree.guardian.co.uk/ anthony_giddens/2006/11/ post_682.html (accessed on 20 February 2007)
2. Ibid.

# References

Abaza, Mona (2001). "Shopping Malls, Consumer Culture and the Reshaping of Public Space in Egypt." *Theory, Culture & Society*, Vol. 18(5): 97–122.

Abaza, Mona (2003). "Who is Afraid of Disneyfication? A Response to Sonja Hegasy." *OpenDemocracy*, 23 October 2003, available at www.openDemocracy.net

Abaza, Mona (2004). "Advertising History." *Al Ahram Weekly*, Issue 697, 1–7 July 2004.

Abdel Nabi, Abdel Fattah (1989). *Sociology of News* (in Arabic). Cairo: Al Arabi Books.

Abdel Rahman, Awatef (1985). *The Difficulty of the Developmental Media in the Arab World*. Cairo: Dar el-Fikr al-Arabi (in Arabic).

Abdel Rahman, Awatef (1989). *Studies in Egyptian and Arab Press – Current Issues* (in Arabic). Cairo: Al Arabi Books.

Abdel Rahman, Awatef (1991). "Arab World," in Nordenstreng, Kaarle & Michael Traber (eds), *Promotion of Educational Materials for Communication Studies*. Report of phase I of UNESCO/IPDC Interregional Project by IAMCR/AIERI, available at www.uta.fi/textbooks/index.html

Abdel Rahman, Awatef (2002a). *Issues of the Arab Region in the Press in the 20th Century* (in Arabic). Cairo: Al Arabi Press.

Abdel Rahman, Awatef (2002b). *The Critical Theory in Communication Research* (in Arabic). Cairo: Dar el-Firk al-Arabi.

Abdel Rahman, Awatef (2006). Personal communication with the author, 15 November 2006.

Abdelfattah, Nabil MS (1990). *Linguistic Changes in Journalistic Language in Egypt, 1935–1989: A Quantitative and Comparative Analysis*. Unpublished PhD dissertation. University of Texas at Austin.

Abou-Habib, Lina (2003). "Gender, Citizenship, and Nationality in the Arab Region." *Gender and Development*, Vol. 11 (3): 66–75.

Abu Bakr, Yahya et al. (1985). *Development of Communication in the Arab States – Needs and Priorities*. Paris: UNESCO.

Abu-Lughod, Lila (2005). *Dramas of Nationhood*. Chicago: Chicago University Press.

Abu Odeh, Lama (1993). "Post-colonial Feminism and the Veil: Thinking the Difference." *Feminist Review*, Vol. 43: 26–37.

Abu Rabi', Ibrahim (2004). *Contemporary Arab Thought: Studies in Post-1967 Arab Intellectual History*. London: Pluto Press.

Abu Zeid, Farouk (1993). *Arab Émigré Press* (in Arabic). Cairo: Alam Al Kotub.

Adams, Matthew (2006). "Hybridizing Habitus and Reflexivity: Towards an Understanding of Contemporary Identity?" *Sociology*, Vol. 40(3): 511–28.

Al-Abd, Atef (1993). *Audience Research in the Arab World* (in Arabic). Cairo: Dar Al Fikr Al Arabi.

Al-Daqdouqi, Ibrahim (2001). *The Image of Turks in the Arabs' Minds* (in Arabic). Beirut: Center for Arab Unity Studies.

Al-Faisal, Turki (2006). "Saudi Education in the Global Economy." Address delivered to Town Hall Los Angeles Meeting, Los Angeles, California, 21 March 2006. Vital Speeches of the Day, 15 April 2006, 72, 13: 414–16.

Al-Hadidi, Mona (1996). "Gatekeepers, in Saad Labib (ed.)", *Proceedings of the Symposium on Media in the Arab World* (Cairo, 23–4 November, 1996) (in Arabic). Cairo: ALESCO.

Al-Hamzah, Khaled (2005). "The Image of the City in Modern Arab Painting: Artists Recreate Their Own Cities." *Journal for Cultural Research*, Vol. 9 (3): 281–99.

Al-Hasani, Abdulmonam (2006). "Teaching Journalism in the Arab World: Recent Obstacles and Future Plans in Oman." Paper presented at the IAMCR conference, Cairo, July 2006.

Al-Jabri, Mohamed Abed (1997). *Issues in Contemporary Thinking* (in Arabic). Beirut: Center for Arab Unity Studies.

Al-Jabri, Mohamed Abed (2000). *The Constitution of Arab Reason*, 6th edition (in Arabic). Beirut: Center for Arab Unity Studies.

Al-Jabri, Mohamed Abed (2001). *Critical Study in the Arab Ethics*, 1st edition. Beirut: Center for Arab Unity Studies.

Al-Jabri, Mohamed Abed (2002). *The Constitution of Arab Mind*, 8th edition (in Arabic). Beirut: Center for Arab Unity Studies.

Al-Jammal, Rasem M. (1990). "Foreign news in Arab newspapers" (in Arabic). *Al Mustaqbal Al Arabi*, 135/13.

Al-Jammal, Rasem M. (2001). *Communication and Media in the Arab World*, 2nd edition (in Arabic). Beirut: Center for Arab Unity Studies.

Al-Kahtani, Sulaiman A. H. (2000). *Globalization or Americanization: A Comparative Analysis of Portrayals of Globalization in United States and Arab Mainstream Newspapers During the 1990s*. Unpublished PhD thesis. Howard University.

Almeida, Eugenie (1992). "A Category System for the Analysis of Factuality in Newspaper Discourse." *Text*, 12(2): 233–62.

Al-Qadry, Nahound & Harb, Souad (2002). *Female and male journalists in the television* (in Arabic). Beirut: Arab Cultural Center & Lebanese Women Researchers.

Al-Rasheed, Anas (1998). *Professional Values: A Survey of Working Journalists in the Kuwaiti Daily Press*. Unpublished PhD thesis. Southern Illinois University.

Al-Shabbab, Omar & Swales, John (1986). "Rhetorical Features of Arab and British News Broadcasts." *Anthropological Linguistics*, 28, 1: 31–42.

Alterman, Jon B. (1998). *New media, new politics? From satellite television to the Internet in the Arab world*. Washington Institute for Near East Policy.

Alterman, Jon B. (2000). "Counting Nodes and Counting Noses: Understanding New Media in the Middle East." *The Middle East Journal*. Washington, Summer 2000, Vol. 54, Issue 3: 355.

Amin, Hussein (2001) "Mass Media in the Arab States between Diversification and Stagnation: An Overview," in Kaj Hafez (ed.), *Mass Media, Politics & Society in the Middle East*. Cresskill, NJ: Hampton Press.

Andersen, Niels Åkerstrøm (2003). *Discursive analytical strategies: Understanding Foucault, Koselleck, Laclau, Luhmann*. Bristol: The Policy Press.

Arebi, Saddeka (1994). *Women & Words in Saudi Arabia: The Politics of Literary Discourse*. New York: Columbia University Press.

Asi, Morad (1981). "Arabs, Israelis, and TV News: A Time-Series, Content Analysis," in William Adams (ed.), *Television Coverage of the Middle East*. Norwood, NJ: Ablex.

Auter, Philip, Arafa, Mohamed & al-Jaber, Khaled (2004). "Who is Al Jazeera's Audience?" *TBS Journal*, Issue 12, Spring 2004, available at www.tbsjournal.com/html12/auter.htm (accessed on 5 January 2007).

Ayalon, Ami (1995). *The Press in the Middle East: A History*. New York & Oxford: Oxford University Press.

Ayish, Muhammad (1991). "Foreign Voices as People's Choices: BBC Popularity in the Arab World." *Middle Eastern Studies*, 27, 3: 374–88.

Ayish, Muhammad (1995). "Potential Effects of Direct Satellite Broadcasting on National Television Systems in the Arab Region." *Journal of Humanities and Social Sciences*, 11: 394–426 (in Arabic).

Ayish, Muhammad I (1998). "Communication Research in the Arab World: A New Perspective." *The Public*, Vol. 5(1): 33–57.

Ayish, Muhammad (2001). "American-Style Journalism and Arab World Television: An Exploratory Study of News Selection at Six Arab World Satellite Television Channels." *Transnational Broadcasting Studies*, 6, Spring/Summer.

Ayish, Muhammad (2002). "Political Communication on Arab World Television: Evolving Patterns." *Political Communication*, 19: 137–54.

Badry, Fatima (2006). "Positioning the Self, Identity, and Language: Moroccan Women on the Move," in Susan Ossman (ed.), *Places We Share: Migration, Subjectivity and Global Mobility*. Lanham, MD: Lexington.

Barber, Benjamin (1995). *Jihad vs. McWorld*. New York: Times Books.

Bayat, Asef (1997). "Un-civil Society: The Politics of the "Informal People." *Third World Quarterly*, Vol. 18(1): 53–72.

Beck, Ulrich (1992). *Risk Society: Towards a New Modernity*. London: Sage.

Beinin, Joel (1993). "Money, Media and Policy Consensus: The Washington Institute for Near East Policy." *Middle East Report*, No. 180, January–February 1993: 10–15.

Bekhait, al-Said (1998). *The Egyptian Press – News Values and False Conscience* (in Arabic). Cairo: Al Arabi Publishing.

Bellah, Robert, Madsen, Richard, Sullivan, William M., Swidler, Ann & Tipton, Steven M. (1985). *Habits of the Heart: Individualism and Commitment in American Life*. Berkeley: University of California Press.

Benhabib, Seyla (1992). "Models of Public Space: Hannah Arendt, the Liberal Tradition, and Jürgen Habermas," in Craig Calhoun (ed.), *Habermas and the Public Sphere*. Cambridge, MA: MIT Press.

Benson, Rodney & Neveu, Erik (eds) (2005) *Bourdieu and the Journalistic Field*. Cambridge: Polity Press.

Benson, Rodney (1998). "Field Theory in Comparative Context: A New Paradigm for Media Studies." *Theory and Society*, Vol. 28: 463–98.

Benson, Rodney (1999). "Field Theory in Comparative Context: A New Paradigm for Media Studies." *Theory and Society*, Vol. 28(3): 463–98.

Benson, Rodney (2000). *Pierre Bourdieu and the Mass Media: New Approaches for Media Sociology*. Paper presented at the Special Session on "Cultural Producers and Politics: The Sociology of Pierre Bourdieu," 95th Annual Meeting of the American Sociological Association, Washington, DC, 15 August 2000.

Benson, Rodney (2006). "News Media as a 'Journalistic Field': What Bourdieu Adds to New Institutionalism, and Vice Versa." *Political Communication*, Vol. 23: 187–202.

Blommaert, Jan (1997) "Intellectuals and Ideological Leadership in Ujamaa Tanzania." *African Languages and Cultures*, Vol. 10(2): 129–44.

Bourdieu, Pierre & Wacquant, Loïc (1992). *An Invitation to Reflexive Sociology*. Cambridge: Polity Press.

Bourdieu, Pierre (1984). *Distinction: A Social Critique of the Judgment of Taste*. Cambridge, MA: Harvard University Press.

Bourdieu, Pierre (1989). "Social Space and Symbolic Power." *Sociological Theory*, Vol. 7 (1): 14–25.

Bourdieu, Pierre (1991). *Language and Symbolic Power*. Translated by Gino Raymond & Matthew Adamson, edited by John B. Thompson. Cambridge: Polity Press.

Bourdieu, Pierre (1998). *On Television*. New York: New Press.

Bourdieu, Pierre (2000). *Pascalian Meditations*. Translated by R. Nice. Cambridge: Polity Press.

Bourdieu, Pierre (2005). "The Political Field, the Social Sciences Field, and the Journalistic Field," in Rodney Benson & Erik Neveu (eds), *Bourdieu and the Journalistic Field*. Cambridge: Polity Press.

Calhoun, Craig (1996). "Social Theory and the Public Sphere," in B. Turner (ed.), *The Blackwell Companion to Social Theory*. Oxford: Blackwell.

Calhoun, Craig (1992) (ed.). *Habermas and the Public Sphere*. Cambridge, MA: MIT Press.

Cappella, Joseph N. & Jamieson, Kathleen Hall (1997). *Spiral of Cynicism: The Press and the Public Good*. New York: Oxford University Press.

Carpentier, Nico (2005). "Identity, Contingency and Rigidity: The (Counter-)Hegemonic Constructions of the Identity of the Media Professional." *Journalism*, Vol. 6 (2): 199–219.

Center for Strategic Studies, University of Jordan (2005). "Revisiting the Arab Street: Research from Within," available at www.css-jordan.org (accessed on 12 June 2006).

Chaker, Mohammed N. (2003). "The Impact of Globalization on Cultural Industries in the UAE." Paper presented at the Hawaii International Conference on Business, June 2003.

Cherribi, Sam (2006). "From Baghdad to Paris: Al-Jazeera and the Veil." *The Harvard International Journal of Press/Politics*, Vol. 11(2): 121–38.

Chouliaraki, Lilie (2006). *The Spectatorship of Suffering*. London: Sage.

Curran, James & Park, Myung-Jin (eds) (1999). *De-Westernizing Media Studies*. London & New York: Routledge.

Dahlgren, Peter (1988). "Crime News: The Fascination of the Mundane." *European Journal of Communication*, Vol. 3: 189–206.

Dahlgren, Peter (1989). "Journalism Research: Tendencies and Perspectives." *The Nordicom review of Nordic mass communication research*, 1989: 3–9.

Dahlgren, Peter (1995). *Television and the Public Sphere*. London: Sage.

Dahlgren, Peter (2002). "In Search of the Talkative Public: Media, Deliberative Democracy and Civic Culture." *The Public*, Vol. 9(3): 5–26.

Dahlgren, Peter (2006). "Doing Citizenship: The Cultural Origins of Civic Agency in the Public Sphere." *European Journal of Cultural Studies*, Vol. 9 (3): 267–86.

Dajani, Nabil H. (1989). *The Vigilant Press: A collection of case studies. An analysis of the press in four Arab countries*. Paris: UNESCO: 75–88.

Dajani, Nabil H. (1992). *Disoriented Media in a Fragmented Society: The Lebanese Experience*. American University of Beirut.

Danaher, Geoff, Shirato, Tony & Webb, Jen (2000). *Understanding Foucault*. London: Sage.

Danermark, B., Ekström, M., Jakobsen, L., & Karlsson, J. (2002). *Explaining Society: Critical Realism in the Social Sciences*. London: Routledge.

Eickelman, Dale F. (1992). "Mass Higher Education and the Religious Imagination in Contemporary Arab Societies." *American Ethnologist*, Vol. 19(4): 643–55.

Eickelman, Dale F. (2002). "The Arab 'Street' and the Middle East's Democracy Deficit." *Naval War College Review*, Autumn 2002, Vol. IV(4): 39–48.

Eliasoph, Nina (1998). *Avoiding Politics: How Americans Produce Apathy in Everyday Life*. Cambridge: Cambridge University Press.

Eliasoph, Nina (2004). "Can We Theorize the Press Without Theorizing the Public?" *Political Communication*, Vol. 21: 297–303.

El-Gawhary Karim (1995). "Sex Tourism in Cairo." *Middle East Reports*, No. 196: 26–7.

El-Khoury, Nasim (2005). *The Arab Media and The Collapse of Linguistic Authorities* (in Arabic). Beirut: Center for Arab Unity Studies.

Ellis, John (2000). *Seeing Things: Television in the Age of Uncertainty*. London: I. B. Tauris.

Ezzi, Abdel Rahman (2004). *Arabs and the Satellite Media*. Al Mostaqbal Al Arabi Series (34) (in Arabic). Beirut: Center for Arab Union Studies.

Fairclough, Norman (1992). *Discourse and Social Change*. Cambridge: Polity Press.

Fairclough, Norman (2002). "Critical Analysis of Media Discourse," in P. Marris & S. Thornham (eds), *Media Studies: A Reader*, 2nd edition. Edinburgh: Edinburgh University Press.

Fandy, Mamoun (2000). "Information Technology, Trust, and Social Change in the Arab World." *The Middle East Journal*, 54, 3: 379–98.

Fandy, Mamoun (2003). "Information Technology, Trust, and Social Change in the Arab World." *The Middle East Journal*, Vol. 54 (3): 379–96.

Faqir, Fadia (1997). "Engendering Democracy and Islam in the Arab world." *Third World Quarterly*, Vol. 18(1): 165–74.

Fargues, Philippe (2003). "Women in Arab Counties: Challenging the Patriarchal System?" *Reproductive Health Matters*, Vol. 13(25): 43–8.

Fay, Brian (1996). *Contemporary Philosophy of Social Science: A Multicultural Approach*. Oxford: Blackwell.

Fedler, Fred, Bender, John R., Davenport, Lucinda & Kostyu, Paul E. (1996). *Reporting for the Media*. Fort Worth, TX: Harcourt Brace College Publishers.

Filmer, P., Jenks, C., Seale, C. & Walsh, D. (2000). "Developments in Social Theory," in Clive Seale (ed.), *Researching Society and Culture*. London: Sage.

Flyvbjerg, Bent (2001). *Making Social Science Matter*. Cambridge: Cambridge University Press.

Fraser, Nancy (1990). "Rethinking the Public Sphere: A Contribution to the Critique of Actually Existing Democracy." *Social Text*, No. 25/26: 56–80.

Fraser, Nancy (1992). "Rethinking the Public Sphere," in Craig Calhoun (ed.), *Habermas and the Public Sphere*, Cambridge, MA: MIT Press.

Furedi, Frank (2003). *Therapy Culture: Cultivating Vulnerability in an Uncertain Age*. London: Routledge.

Galal, Injy (2004). "Online Dating in Egypt." *Global Media Journal*, Vol. 3(4), Spring 2004, available at http://lass.calumet.purdue.edu/cca/gmj/OldSiteBackup/SubmittedDocuments/archivedpapers/spring2004/grad_research/non_refereed/galal.htm

Gamson, William A. (1989). "News as Framing: Comments on Graber," *American Behavioral Scientist*, 33(2): 157–61.

Ghannam, Farha (2002). *Remaking the Modern: Space, Relocation, and the Politics of Identity in a Global Cairo*. Berkeley: University of California Press.

Ghareeb, Edmund (2000). "New Media and the Information Revolution in the Arab World: An assessment." *The Middle East Journal*, Vol. 54, Issue 3.

Giddens, Anthony (1979). *Central Problems in Social Theory: Action, Structure and Contradiction in Social Analysis*. London: Macmillan.

Giddens, Anthony (1984). *The Constitution of Society*. Berkeley: University of California Press.

Giddens, Anthony (1991). *Modernity and Self-Identity: Self and Society in the Late Modern Age*. Cambridge: Polity Press.

Gigilcim, Gönül (1992). "Turkish Immigrants Watching Norwegian Television News: On Identity Management In A Norwegian Context," in Jostein Gripsrud (ed.), *Cultural Identity and the Media*. Bergen: University of Bergen.

Gordon, Joel (2003). "Singing the Pulse of the Egyptian-Arab Street: Shaaban Abd al-Rahim and the Geo-pop-politics of Fast Food." *Popular Music*, Vol. 22(1): 73–88.

Gunter, Helen (2002). "Purposes and Positions in the Field of Education Management. Putting Bourdieu to Work." *Educational Management & Administration*, Vol. 30(1): 7–26.

Habermas, Jürgen (1981/1984-7). *The Theory of Communicative Action*, 2 vols. Cambridge: Polity Press.

Habermas, Jürgen. (1962/1989). *The Structural Transformation of the Public Sphere*. Cambridge, MA: MIT Press.

Habermas, Jürgen (1992). "Further Reflections on the Public Sphere," in Craig Calhoun (ed.), *Habermas and the Public Sphere*. Cambridge, MA: MIT Press.

Haas, Tanni & Steiner, Linda (2001). "Public Journalism as a Journalism of Publics: Implications of the Habermas–Fraser Debate for Public Journalism." *Journalism*, Vol. 2 (2): 123–47.

Habib, Rakan A. (1985). *The Role of the Saudi Broadcasting System in the Utilization of the Classical Form of the Arabic Language in Preserving Culture*. Unpublished PhD thesis. Wayne State University.

Haddad, George M. (1977). "The Present State of Middle East Studies." *Military Affairs*, Vol. 41(2): 83–7.

Hadj-Moussa, Ratiba (2003). "New Media, Community and Politics in Algeria." *Media, Culture & Society*, Vol. 25: 451–68.

Haeri, Niloofar (2003). *Sacred Language, Ordinary People: Dilemmas of Culture and Politics in Egypt*. Basingstoke: Palgrave.

Hafez, Kaj (2002). "Journalism Ethics Revisited: A Comparison of Ethics Codes in Europe, North African, the Middle East, and Muslim Asia." *Political Communication*, Vol. 19, No.2: 225–50.

Hall, Stuart (1992). "The Question of Cultural Identity," in Stuart Hall, David Held & Tony McGrew (eds), *Modernity and Its Futures*. Cambridge: Polity Press.

Hallin, Daniel C. (1986). *The "Uncensored War": The Media and Vietnam*. Berkley & Los Angeles: University of California Press.

Hamdy, Naila N. (2004). "Internet and Egypt's National Development." *Global Media Journal*, Vol. 2(4), Fall 2004, available at http://lass.calumet. purdue.edu/cca/gmj/oldsitebackup/submitteddocuments/archivedpapers/fall2004/refereed/hamdy.htm (accessed on 22 June 2006).

Hamidi, Asef (2004) (ed.). *The Radio and TV Journalism: Keys to Success and Creativity* (in Arabic). Abu Dhabi.

Hannerz, Ulf (1997). *Transnational Connection*. London: Sage.

Hannerz, Ulf (2004). *Foreign News: Exploring the World of Foreign Correspondents*. Chicago: University of Chicago Press.

Hartley, John (1996). *Popular Reality: Journalism, Modernity, Popular Culture*. London: Edward Arnold.

Havrilesky, Heather (2003). "Besieged by 'Friends'. "*Salon*. 14 July 2003, available at http://wwwl.globalpolicy.org/globaliz/cultural/2003/0715 friends.htm

Hassan, Rana S. (2005). "The Impact of *Extreme Makeover* on Egyptian Women." *Global Media Journal*, Vol. 1(2): Autumn 2005 (in Arabic), available at http://www.aucegypt.edu/academic/gmj/05F/05F_Rana.html (accessed on 16 June 2006).

Henry, Ian P., Amaran Mahfoud & Al-Tauqi Mansour (2003). "Sport, Arab Nationalism and the Pan-Arab Games." *International Review for the Sociology of Sport*, Vol. 38(3): 295–310.

Hindkær, Thomas (2001). *Arab discussions and opinions about the cultural dimension of globalization*. Unpublished Masters thesis. University of Southern Denmark (in Arabic).

Hjarvard, Stig (2001) (ed.). *News in a Globalized Society*. Gothenburg: Nordicom.

Höijer, Birgitta (2004). "The Discourse of Global Compassion: The Audience and Media Reporting of Human Suffering." *Media, Culture & Society*, Vol. 26(4): 513–31.

Hourani, Albert (1991). *A History of the Arab Peoples*. London: Faber & Faber.

Hovden, Jan F. (2001). "The Norwegian Journalistic Field: Issues and Problems in an Ongoing Research Project." A Paper submitted at the 15th Nordic Conference on Media and Communication Research. Reykjavik, Iceland, 11–13 August 2001.

Ibrahim, Saad Eddin (1997). "Cross-Eyed Sociology in Egypt and the Arab World." *Contemporary Sociology*, Vol. 26(5): 547–51.

Ibrahim, Saad Eddin (2000). "Arab Social-Scene Research in the 1990s and Beyond: Issues, Trends, and Priorities," in Eglal Rached & Dina Craissati (eds), *Research for Development in the Middle East and North Africa*. International Development Research Center, Canada, available at http://network.idrc.ca/ev.php?ID=32206_201&ID2=DO_TOPIC

Jawad, Rana (2002). "A Profile of Social Welfare in Lebanon." *Global Social Policy*, Vol. 2(3): 319–42.

Jenkins, Richard (2004). *Social Identity*. London: Routledge.

Jenkins, Richard (2000). "Categorization: Identity, Social Process and Epistemology." *Current Sociology*, Vol. 48(3): 7–25.

Jensen, Klaus Bruhn (1998) (ed.). *News of the World: World Cultures Look at Television News*. London & New York: Routledge.

Jensen, Klaus Bruhn (2002) (ed.). *A Handbook of Media and Communication Research: Qualitative and Quantitative Methodologies*. London & New York: Routledge.

Joseph, Suad & Stork, Joe (1993). "Gender and Civil Society: An Interview with Suad Joseph." *Middle East Reports*, No. 183: 22–6.

Kamrava, Mehran (1998). "Non-Democratic States and Political Liberalisation in the Middle East: A Structural Analysis." *Third World Quarterly*, Vol. 19(1): 63–85.

Karabel, Jerome (1996). "Towards a Theory of Intellectuals and Politics." *Theory & Society*, Vol. 25(2): 205–33.

Karam, Imad (2007). "Satellite Television: A Breathing Space for Arab Youth?," in Naomi Sakr (ed.), *Arab Media and Political Renewal: Community, Legitimacy and Public Life*. London: I. B. Tauris.

Kazan, Fayad (1993). *Mass Media, Modernity and Development: Arab States of the Gulf*. Westport, CT: Praeger.

Keane, John (1991). *The Media and Democracy*. Cambridge: Polity Press.

Khaffaf, Moayed Kassim (2005). "The Mental Image of America in the Iraqi Society after the Publication of Images of Prisoner Torture in Abu Ghreib," in Bel Qaziz (ed.), *The American Invasion of Iraq: Its Images and Sources* (in Arabic). Beirut: Center for Arab Unity Studies.

Khalaf, Sulayman & al-Kobaisi, Saad (1999). "Migrants' Strategies of Coping and Patterns of Accommodation in the Oil-rich Gulf Societies: Evidence from the UAE." *British Journal of Middle Eastern Studies*, 26(2): 271–98.

Kienle, Eberhard (1995). "Arab Unity Schemes Revisited: Interest, Identity, and Policy in Syria and Egypt." *International Journal of Middle East Studies*, Vol. 27(1): 53–71.

Khalil, Esam N. (2000). *Grounding in English and Arabic News Discourse*. Amsterdam/Philadelphia: John Benjamins Publishing Company.

Khazen, Jihad (1999). "Censorship and State Control of the Press in the Arab World." *The Harvard International Journal of Press Politics*, 4, 3: 87–92.

Kieran, Matthew (1997). *Media Ethics – A Philosophical Approach*. Westport, CT: Praeger.

Kirat, Mohamed (1987). *The Algerian News People: A Study of Their Backgrounds, Professional Orientations and Working Conditions*. Unpublished PhD thesis. Indiana University.

Koeppel, Barabara (1989). *The Press in the Middle East: Constraint, Consensus, Censorship*. Washington, DC: A Special Middle East Research & Information Project Publication.

Kraidy, Marwan (2002). "Hybridity in Cultural Globalization." *Communication Theory*, Vol. 12 (3): 316–39.

Kraidy, Marwan (2003). "Globalization *avant la lettre*? Cultural Hybridity and Media Power in Lebanon," in Marwan Kraidy & Patrick Murphy (eds), *Global Media Studies: Ethnographic Perspectives*. New York: Routledge.

Kraidy, Marwan (2005). "Reality Television and Politics in the Arab World: Preliminary Observations." *Transnational Broadcasting Journal*, Vol. 15, available at www.tbsjournal.com/Kraidy.html (accessed on 2 February 2006).

Laclau, Ernesto & Mouffe, Chantal (1985). *Hegemony and Socialist Strategy: Towards a Radical Democratic Politics*. London: Verso.

Lacy, Stephen, Fico, Frederick and Simon, Todd (1991). "Fairness and Balance in the Prestige Press." *Journalism Quarterly*, Vol. 68, No. 3: 363–70.

Lakoff, George (1991). *Metaphor and War: The Metaphor System Used to Justify War in the Gulf*, available at http://philosophy.uoregon.edu/metaphor/lakoff-l.htm

Lamont, Michele & Lareau, Annette (1988). "Cultural Capital: Allusions Gaps & Glissandos in Recent Theoretical Developments." *Sociological Theory*, Vol. 6(2): 153–68.

Lash, Scott & Urry, John (1994). *Economies of Signs and Space*. London: Sage.

Lauk, Epp (1996). "Estonian Journalists in Search of New Professional Identity." *Javnost/The Public*, Vol. 3(4).

Lesch, Ann M. (1991). "Palestinians in Kuwait." *Journal of Palestine Studies*, Vol. 20 (4): 42–54.

Levinson, Charles (2006). "Plus ca Change: The Role of the Media in Egypt's First Contested Presidential Elections." *Transnational Broadcasting Studies Journal*, Vol. 2, No.15, available at http://www.tbsjournal.com/

Lewis, Justin (1994). "The Absence of Narrative: Boredom and the Residual Power of Television News." *Journal of Narrative and Life History*, Vol. 4(1 & 2): 25–40.

Lloyd, Cathie (2002). "Thinking about the Local and the Global in the Algerian Context." *Oxford Development Studies*, Vol. 30(2): 151–63.

Longva, Anh Nga (1999). "Keeping Migrant Workers in Check: The *Kafala* System in the Gulf." *Middle East Report*, No. 211: 20–2.

Lull, James (1990). *China Turned On: Television, Reform, and Resistance*. London: Routledge.

Lynch, Marc (2006). *Voices of the New Arab Public: Iraq, Al Jazeera, and Middle East Politics Today*. New York: Columbia University Press.

Mahfouz, Essam (1991). *Theatre: The Future of Arabic* (in Arabic). Beirut: Dar el-Farabi.

Matar, Dina (2006). "Diverse Diasporas, One Meta-Narrative: Palestinians in the UK Talking about 11 September 2001." *Journal of Ethnic and Migration Studies*, Vol. 32(6): 1027–40.

Matheson, Donald (2003). "Scowling at their Notebooks: How British Journalists Understand their Writing." *Journalism*, Vol. 4(2): 165–83.

Maton, Karl (2000). "Languages of Legitimation: The Structuring Significance for Intellectual Fields of Strategic Knowledge Claims." *British Journal of Sociology of Education*, Vol. 21 (2): 147–67.

McFadden, Tom J. (1953). *Daily Journalism in the Arab States*. Columbus: Ohio State University Press.

McNair, Brian (2005). "What is Journalism?," in Hugo De Burgh (ed.), *Making Journalists*. London: Routledge.

Meleis, Afa (1982). "Arab Students in Western Universities: Social Proprieties and Dilemmas." *The Journal of Higher Education*, Vol. 53(4): 439–47.

Mellor, Noha (2005a). *The Making of Arab News*. Lanham, MD: Rowman & Littlefield.

Mellor, Noha (2005b). "Girl Power." *Financial Times Magazine*. 12 November, 2005.

Mellor, Noha (2007, in press). "Journalists as Eyewitnesses," in Madawi Al-Rashid (ed.), *Dying for Faith*. London: I. B. Tauris.

Mendelsohn, Harold (1974). "Behaviorism, Functionalism, and Mass Communications Policy." *The Public Opinion Quarterly*, Vol. 38(3): 379–89.

Miladi, Noureddine (2006). "Satellite TV News and the Arab Diaspora in Britain: Comparing Al-Jazeera, the BBC and CNN." *Journal of Ethnic and Migration Studies*, Vol. 32(6): 947–60.

Mindich, David T. Z. (1998). *Just the Facts: How "Objectivity" Came to Defend American Journalism*. New York & London: New York University Press.

Musallam, Sami (1986). *The Image of Arabs in the German Press* (in Arabic). Beirut: Center for Arab Unity Studies.

Nasr, Salim & Hajjar, Lisa (1997). "A View from the Region: Middle East Studies in the Arab World: Interview with Salim Nasr." *Middle East Report*, No. 205, October–December 1997: 16–18.

Nasser, Munir K. (1979). *Press, Politics, and Power: Egypt's Heikal and Al-Ahram*. Ames: Iowa State University Press.

Negus, Keith (2002). "The Work of Cultural Intermediaries and the Enduring Distance between Production and Consumption." *Cultural Studies*, Vol. 16(4): 501–16.

Nisbet, Erik, Nisbet, Matthew C., Schenfele, Dietram A. & Shanahan, James E. (2004). "Public Diplomacy, Television News, and Muslim Opinion." *Press/Politics*, Vol. 9(2): 11–27.

Ouis, Pernilla (2002). "Islamization as a Strategy for Reconciliation between Modernity and Tradition: Examples from Contemporary Arab Gulf States." *Islam and Christian–Muslim Relations*, Vol. 13(3): 315–34.

Pantti, Mervi (2005). "Masculine Tears, Feminine Tears – and Crocodile Tears: Mourning Olof Palme and Anna Lindh in Finnish Newspapers." *Journalism*, 6(3): 357–77.

Patterson, Thomas (1993). *Out of Order*. New York: Alfred A. Knopf.

Phillips, Louise & Jørgensen, Marianne (2002). *Discourse Analysis as Theory and Method*. London: Sage.

Pieterse, Jan Nederveen (2001). "Hybridity, So What?: The Anti-Hybridity Backlash and the Riddles of Recognition." *Theory, Culture & Society*, Vol. 18 (2–3): 219–45.

Potter, Willis N. (1961). "Modern Education in Syria." *Comparative Education Review*, Vol 5(1): 35–8.

Qandil, Bayoumi (1999). *Hadir Atthaqafa fi Misr (the Present Status of Culture in Egypt)* (in Arabic). Alexandria: Dar al-Wafa.

Quinn, Stephen (2001). "Teaching Journalism in a Changing Islamic Nation." *Media Educator*, Issue No. 11, July–December 2001.

Rachty, Gehan (1978). "Foreign News in Nine Arab Countries." *Communications and Development Review*, 2: 23–5.

Rachty, Gehan & Sabat, Khalil (1987). "Importation of Films for Cinema and Television in Egypt." Paris: UNESCO.

Racy, Ali Jihad (1982). "Musical Aesthetics in Present-Day Cairo." *Ethnomusicology*, Vol. 26(3): 391–406.

Ramarprasad, Jyotika & Hamdy, Naila N. (2006). "Functions of Egyptian Journalists: Perceived Importance and Actual Performance." *The International Communication Gazette*, Vol. 68(2): 167–85.

Reid, Donald Malcolm (1987). "Cairo University and the Orientalists." *International Journal of Middle East Studies*, Vol. 19(1): 51–75.

Riggins, James (1985). "Harvard and the CIA." *MERIP Reports*, No. 136/137, October–December 1985: 33–44.

Robertson, Roland (1992). *Globalization*. London: Sage.

Robertson, Roland (2001). "Globalization Theory 2000+: Major Problematic," in G. Ritzer & B. Smart (eds), *Handbook of Social Theory*. London: Sage.

Rugh, William (1987). *The Arab Press: News Media and Political Process in the Arab World*, 2nd edition. Syracuse: Syracuse University Press.

Rugh, William (2004). *Arab Mass Media: Newspapers, Radio, and Television in Arab Politics*. Westport, CT: Praeger.

Rugh, William (2006). "Anti-Americanism on Arab Television: Some Outsider Observations." *TBS Journal*, Issue 15, Winter 2005/06, available at http://www.tbsjournal.com/Archives/Fall05/Rugh.html (accessed on 12 June 2006).

Saad, Reem (1998). "Shame, Reputation and Egypt Lovers: A Controversy over the Nation's Image." *Visual Anthropology*, 10: 401–12.

Sabagh, Georges & Ghazalla, Iman (1986). "Arab Sociology Today: A View From Within." *Annual Review of Sociology*, Vol. 12: 373–99.

Sakr, Naomi (2001a). *Satellite Realms: Transnational Television, Globalization & the Middle East*. London & New York: I. B. Tauris.

Sakr, Naomi (2001b). "Seen and Starting to be Heard: Women and the Arab Media in a Decade of Change." *Social Research*, Vol. 69(3): 821–51.

Sakr, Naomi (2005). "The Changing Dynamics of Arab Journalism," in Hugo de Burgh (ed.), *Making Journalists*. London: Routledge.

Salamandra, Christa (2003). "London's Arab Media and the Construction of Arabness." *TBS Journal*, No. 10, Spring/Summer 2003 available at http://www.tbsjournal.com/Archives/Spring03/salamandra.html (accessed on 26 November 2006).

Scholte, Jan Aart (2002). *What is Globalization? The Definitional Issue – Again*. CSGR Working Paper No. 109/02. The University of Warwick, Department of Politics and International Studies.

Schudson, Michael (1978). *Discovering the News: A Social History of American Newspapers*. New York: Basic Books.

Schudson, Michael (1982). "The Politics of Narrative Form: The Emergence of News Conventions in Print and Television." *Daedalus*, Vol. 111: 97–113.

Schudson, Michael (1992). "Was There Ever a Public Sphere? if So, When? Reflections on the American Case," in Craig Calhoun (ed.), *Habermas and the Public Sphere*. Cambridge, MA: MIT Press.

Schudson, Michael (2003). *The Sociology of News*. New York: W. W. Norton.

Schudson, Michael (2005). "Autonomy from What?," in Rodney Benson & Erik Neveu (eds), *Bourdieu and the Journalistic Field*. Cambridge: Polity Press.

Seaton, Jean (2005). *Carnage and the Media: The Making and Breaking of News about Violence*. London: Allen Lane.

Sensenig-dabbous, Dima (2000). "Media vs. S. Lebanon: Schizophrenia in an age of globalization." *Media Development* (Journal of the World Association for Christian Communication) 3: 14–17.

Sewell, William H. (1992). "A Theory of Structure: Duality, Agency and Transformation." *The American Journal of Sociology*, Vol. 98(1): 1–29.

Shaheen, Jack ( 2003). "Reel Bad Arabs: How Hollywood Vilifies a People." *The ANNALS of the American Academy of Political and Social Science*, Vol. 588 (1): 171–93.

Shami, Seteney (1989). "Socio-cultural Anthropology in Arab Universities." *Current Anthropology*, Vol. 30(5): 649–54.

Shamri, Suleiman (1998). *The Opposite Direction: An Academic Study* (in Arabic). Riyadh: King Saud University.

Shanor, Donald R. (2003). *News from abroad*. New York: Columbia University Press.

Sharkey, Jacqueline E. (2003). "The Television War." *American Journalism Review*, 25, 4: 18.

Sheller, Mimi & Urry, John (2003). "Mobile Transformations of 'Public' and 'Private' Life." *Theory, Culture & Society*, Vol. 20(3): 107–25.

Shiblak, Abbas (1996). "Residency Status and Civil Rights of Palestinian Refugees in Arab Countries." *Journal of Palestinian Studies*, Vol. 25(3): 36–45.

Shoemaker, Pamela (1991). *Gatekeeping*. Thousand Oaks, CA: Sage.

Siebert, Lauren Marie (2002)."All the Things that Portray Us as Individuals and as a Nation: Read Troupe and Egyptian National Identity in the Twentieth Century." *Text, Practice, Performance*, Vol. IV: 51–63.

Silverstone, Roger (1999). *Why Study Media?* London: Sage.

Soloway, Colin (2003). "Free and Reckless: With Saddam out of Power, the Country's 'News' Industry has Exploded." *Newsweek*, International edition, 11 August 2003: 22.

Splichal, Slavko & Sparks, Colin (1994). *Journalists for the 21st Century: Tendencies of Professionalization Among First-Year Students in 22 Countries*. Norwood, NJ: Ablex.

Splichal, Slavko (2006). "In Search of a Strong European Public Sphere: Some Critical Observations on Conceptualizations of Publicness and the (European) Public Sphere." *Media, Culture & Society*, Vol. 28(5): 695–714.

Sreberny-Mohammadi, Annabelle (1998). "The Media and Democratization in the Middle East: The Strange Case of Television." *Democratization and the Media*, Vol. 5, Issue 2: 179–99.

Street, John (2001). *Mass Media, Politics and Democracy*. Basingstoke: Palgrave.

Suleiman, Yasir (2003). *The Arabic Language and National Identity: A Study in Ideology*. Edinburgh: Edinburgh University Press.

Suleiman, Yasir (2004). *A War of Words: Language and Conflict in the Middle East*. Cambridge: Cambridge University Press.

Sullivan, Sarah (2001a). "Dubai Media City Prepares for Next Phase." *TBS Journal*, Fall/Winter 2001, No. 7, available at www.tbsjournal.com

Sullivan, Sarah (2001b). "Private-Sector Media City Launched in Amman." *TBS Journal*, Fall/Winter 2001, No. 7, available at www.tbsjournal.com

Swales, John (1990). *Genre Analysis: English in Academic and Research Settings*. Cambridge: Cambridge University Press.

Tarabishi, Georges (2000). *Arab Intellectuals and the Discontents of Globalization*, available at http://www.boell-meo.org/en/web/203.htm (accessed on 12 June 2006).

Tash, Adbulkader T. M. (1983). *A Profile of Professional Journalists Working in the Saudi Arabian Daily Press*. Unpublished PhD dissertation. Southern Illinois University.

Taylor, Charles (1994). "The Politics of Recognition," in Amy Gutmann (ed.), *Multiculturalism: Examining the Politics of Recognition.* Princeton: Princeton University Press.

Taweela, Waheed (2002). "New Media in the Arab World: The Social and Cultural Impact." Paper presented at the Conference on New Media and Change in the Arab World. Amman, Jordan.

Tester, Keith (2001). *Compassion, Morality and the Media.* Buckingham: Open University Press.

Thompson, John B. (1995). *The Media and Modernity.* Cambridge: Polity Press.

Thompson, John B. (2005). "The New Visibility." *Theory, Culture & Society*, Vol. 22(6): 31–51.

Thussu, Daya (2000). *International Communication: Continuity and Change.* London: Edward Arnold.

Thussu, Daya (2002). "Managing the Media in an Era of Round-the-Clock News: Notes from India"s First Tele-war." *Journalism Studies*, Vol. 3(2): 203–12.

Thussu, Daya (2004). "International News: Global Flows and Linguistic Barriers." A Paper presented at The Language of Global News Conference. 23 April 2004, University of Warwick.

Thussu, Daya (2005). "Adapting to Globalisation: The Changing Contours Of Journalism in India," in Hugo De Burgh (ed.), *Making Journalists.* London: Routledge.

Tibi, Bassam (1997). *Arab Nationalism: Between Islam & the Nation-State.* Basingstoke: Palgrave.

Tomlinson, John (1999). *Globalization and Culture.* Cambridge: Polity.

Topoushian, Mayda (2002). *Interpreting the Constructed Realities of the 1991 Gulf War: A Comparative Textual Analysis of Two Arab and Two North American Newspapers.* Unpublished PhD thesis. Concordia University, Montreal.

Turkistani, Ahmed S. (1989). *News Exchange via Arabsat & News Values of Arab TV News People.* Unpublished PhD thesis. Indiana University.

Van Dijk, Tuen A. (1984). *Structures of International News: A Case Study of the World's Press.* Report for UNESCO. University of Amsterdam.

Van Dijk, Tuen A. (1988). *News Analysis – Case Studies of International and National News in the Press.* Hillsdale, New Jersey, Hove & London: Lawrence Erlbaum Associates, Publishers.

Van Zoonen, Liesbet (1998a). "A Day at the Zoo: Political Communication, Pigs and Popular Culture." *Media, Culture & Society*, Vol. 20: 183–200.

Van Zoonen, Liesbet (1998b). "A Professional, Unreliable, Heroic Marionette (M/F): Structure, Agency and Subjectivity in Contemporary Journalisms." *European Journal of Cultural Studies*, Vol. 1 (1): 123–43.

Volkmer, Ingrid (1999). *News in the Global Sphere: A Study of CNN and its Impact on Global Communication*. Luton: University of Luton Press.

Volkmer, Ingrid (2001). "International Communication Theory in Transition: Parameters of the New Global Sphere of Mediation," in Stig Hjarvard (ed.), *Media in a Globalized Society*. Gothenburg: Nordicom.

Wahbi, Sahar M. (1996). *Communication Research* (in Arabic), Cairo: Fagr Publishing.

Waters, Malcolm (2001). *Globalization*. 2nd edition. London: Routledge.

Weaver, Paul (1994). *News and the Culture of Lying*. New York: The Free Press.

Weimann, Garbriel & Brosius, Hans-Bernd (1991). "The Newsworthiness of International Terrorism." *Communication Research*, Vol. 18, No. 3: 333–54.

Wells, Robert & King, Erika (1994). "Prestige Newspaper Coverage of Foreign Affairs in the 1990 Congressional Campaigns." *Journalism Quarterly*, Vol. 71, No. 3: 652–64.

Wheeler, Deborah L. (2001). "The Internet and Public Culture in Kuwait." *Gazette*, 63, 2–3:187–201.

Whittle, Stephen (2005). "Journalists as Citizens." *British Journalism Review*, Vol. 16(4): 54–7.

Willnat, Lars & Weaver, David (2003). "Through Their Eyes: The Work of Foreign Correspondents in the United States." *Journalism*, Vol. 4(4): 403–22.

Wodak, Ruth, Cillia, Rudolf de, Reisigl, Martin, Liebhart Karin & Hirsch, Angelika (2000) (eds). *The Discursive Construction of National Identity*. Edinburgh: Edinburgh University Press.

Wright, Lawrence (2004). "The Kingdom of Silence: A Reporter at Large." *The New Yorker*, Vol. 79, Issue 41.

Wu, Wei & Weaver, David (1998). "Making Chinese Journalists for the Next Millennium." *Gazette*, Vol. 60(6): 513–29.

Wyatt, Robert O., Katz, Elihu & Kim, Foohan (2000). "Bridging the Spheres: Political and Personal Conversation in Public and Private Spaces." *Journal of Communication*, Vol. 50: 71–92.

Yacobi, Haim & Shechter, Relli (2005). "Rethinking Cities in the Middle East: Political Economy, Planning, and the Lived Space." *The Journal of Architecture*, Vol. 10(5): 499–515.

Yamani, Mai (2000). *Changed Identities: The Challenge of the New Generation in Saudi Arabia*. London: The Royal Institute of International Affairs.

Yaquobi, Mai (2004). "The Impact of Reality IV on Egyptian Youth." *Global Media Journal*, Vol. 1(2), available at http://www.aucegypt.edu/academic/gmj/05F/05F_May.html (in Arabic).

Zayani, Mohamed (2005) (ed.). *The Al Jazeera Phenomenon: Critical Perspectives on New Arab Media*. London: Pluto Press.

Zelizer, Barbie (1993/1997a). "Has Communication Explained Journalism?," in Dan Berkowitz (ed.), *Social Meanings of News: A Text-Reader*. Thousand Oaks, CA: Sage.

Zelizer, Barbie (1993/1997b). "Journalists as Interpretive Communities," in Dan Berkowitz (ed.), *Social Meanings of News: A Text-Reader*. Thousand Oaks, CA: Sage.

Zelizer, Barbie (2004). *Taking Journalism Seriously*. London: Sage.

Zuhur, Sherifa (2003). "Women and Empowerment in the Arab World." *Arab Studies Quarterly*, Vol. 25, No. 4, Fall 2003.

# Index